The Legacy of
Wilfred Cantwell Smith

Wilfred Cantwell Smith (1916–2000). Photo courtesy of Diana Eck.

The Legacy of Wilfred Cantwell Smith

Edited by

ELLEN BRADSHAW AITKEN

and

ARVIND SHARMA

Published by
STATE UNIVERSITY OF NEW YORK PRESS
Albany

© 2017 State University of New York

All rights reserved

Printed in the United States of America

No part of this book may be used or reproduced in any manner whatsoever without written permission. No part of this book may be stored in a retrieval system or transmitted in any form or by any means including electronic, electrostatic, magnetic tape, mechanical, photocopying, recording, or otherwise without the prior permission in writing of the publisher.

For information, contact
State University of New York Press
www.sunypress.edu

Production, Jenn Bennett
Marketing, Michael Campochiaro

Library of Congress Cataloging-in-Publication Data

Names: Aitken, Ellen Bradshaw, editor | Sharma, Arvind, editor
Title: The legacy of Wilfred Cantwell Smith / Ellen Bradshaw Aitken and Arvind Sharma, editors.
Description: Albany : State University of New York Press, [2017] | Includes bibliographical references and index.
Identifiers: ISBN 9781438464695 (hardcover : alk. paper) | ISBN 9781438464688 (pbk : alk. paper) | ISBN 9781438464701 (e-book)
Further information is available at the Library of Congress.

10 9 8 7 6 5 4 3 2 1

Contents

Ellen Bradshaw Aitken and Arvind Sharma
Introduction   1

Diana L. Eck
Religious Studies—The Academic and Moral Challenge:
Personal Reflections on the Legacy of Wilfred Cantwell Smith   21

John B. Carman
Wilfred Cantwell Smith: Academic Architect   37

Purushottama Bilimoria
The Meaningful "End" of God, Faith, and Scripture   47

Thomas B. Coburn
Anticipating the Emergence of "Contemplative Studies":
Reflections on the Work of Wilfred Cantwell Smith   65

Harvey Cox
Faith and Belief Revisited   77

William A. Graham
Wilfred Cantwell Smith and "Orientalism"   85

John Stratton Hawley
Enabling Antinomies: Tensions and Tensile Strength in
Wilfred Cantwell Smith   99

Jonathan R. Herman
Who Cares If the Qur'an Is the Word of God? W. C. Smith's
Charge to the Aspiring Public Intellectual   117

Amir Hussain
Towards a Hermeneutic of Humanity: Wilfred Cantwell Smith
and the Study of Muslims   135

Sheila McDonough
Wilfred Cantwell Smith in Lahore 1940–1951   147

Robert A. Segal
Diagnosis Rather than Dialogue as the Best Way to
Study Religion   173

Peter Slater
Wilfred Smith's Prophetic Sense of History and Proposal
Regarding Verification   183

K. R. Sundararajan
Study of Religion as Study of Religious Persons   205

Donald K. Swearer
The Moral Imagination of Wilfred Cantwell Smith   217

Wilfred Cantwell Smith: A Bibliography   229

Contributors   243

Index   249

Introduction

Ellen Bradshaw Aitken and Arvind Sharma

I

Professor Wilfred Cantwell Smith (1916–2000) left a deep impression on the study of religion, and his influence has only grown with the passage of time. The Faculty of Religious Studies at McGill University, of which he was once a member, held a symposium on November 6, 2009, to honor and assess this legacy. This volume is the precipitate of that symposium.

II

The legacy of Wilfred Cantwell Smith is of course only further proof of his continuing impact on the academic study of religion, an impact that was already obvious during his teaching and writing career. It may not be out of place to reprise the contribution he made while alive, to help pave the way for assessing his legacy.

Smith received a BA (honors) in Oriental Languages from the University of Toronto in 1938 and went on to pursue higher studies at Cambridge University, where he worked under the famous Islamicist, H. A. R. Gibb. Smith at the time was inclined toward Marxism, and was critical of the British and their approach to the "communal problem," as Hindu-Muslim tensions in India were called at the time. His thesis was therefore rejected. He thereafter taught Indian and Islamic history at the Forman Christian College in Lahore from 1941 onward, and was an eyewitness to the Independence and Partition of India in 1947. His days in Lahore are discussed in detail in this book, in the chapter by Sheila McDonough. He then obtained a PhD in Oriental Languages from Princeton University and began teaching at McGill University, where he founded the Institute of Islamic Studies. Subsequently, Smith served as the director at the Center for the Study of World Religions at Harvard University (1964–73), and then founded the Department of Religious Studies at Dalhousie University in Halifax. He returned to Harvard University in 1978, to work with the Harvard Committee on the Study of Religion. After retiring in 1985, he became a senior research associate of the Faculty of Religious Studies at Trinity College, University of Toronto, and was awarded the Order of Canada in 2000, the year he died. John Carman's essay in this volume explores these various dimensions of Smith's legacy.

III

Smith's influence radiated in pedagogical circles through his numerous students (many of whom have contributed to this volume), but it was in his role as a writer that he exerted his influence over larger academia. In this regard, two broad phases can be discerned; in one, his primary focus was Islam, and in the other, it was religion as such. Smith's early career and his work in Cambridge and Lahore concentrated on Islam; the establishment of the Institute of Islamic Studies at McGill University was perhaps the most visible manifestation of this aspect of his work. The emergence of the next phase is represented by the publication, in 1959, of an essay, "Comparative Religion: Whither—and Why?" in a volume entitled *History of Religions: Essays in Methodology*, edited by Mircea Eliade and J. Kitagawa.[1] According to Frank Whaling, this essay "represents a kind of watershed between Smith's greater concentration on Islam, during his work in Lahore in Muslim India from 1941–49 and his leadership of the McGill Institute of Islamic Studies which he founded in 1951, and his global concern for the total religious situation of mankind which became a feature of his later years."[2]

It is worth recalling that Islam as a religion, and Islamic studies as a branch of academia, did not enjoy the profile in Smith's time that it does today. In fact, when Smith was pursuing Islamic studies, one rarely spoke of the Abrahamic tradition, an expression that places Judaism, Christianity, and Islam under the same umbrella. One spoke, rather, of the Judeo-Christian tradition, and stopped at that. Islam was considered an "Eastern" religion for all practical purposes. Smith's commitment to the study of Islam thus precedes, by several decades, the attention being bestowed on it now. It is not often recognized that it was only after the oil crisis of 1973 that Islam earned the dignity of being bracketed, along with Judaism and Christianity, as a member of the Abrahamic tradition.[3] The public profile of Islam became more prominent after the Iranian revolution in 1979, and even acquired a spectral dimension after the events of September 11, 2001. An Islamic presence is now an inescapable feature of the international landscape, but such was not the case when Smith embarked on its study, almost intuiting the role Islam was destined to play in world affairs.

The nature of Smith's contribution to the study of Islam is equally significant, apart from the fact of his having presciently engaged in it, and is best dramatized by the fact that there is not a *single* reference to Professor Wilfred Cantwell Smith in the book that created such a sensation in Islamic studies, Edward Said's *Orientalism*.[4] This book brought about a seismic shift in the meaning of the word *orientalism* itself. Before this book, orientalism meant "scholarship or learning in oriental subjects."[5] It had a neutral connotation. After the publication of the book the word acquired a pejorative connotation, as a result of the book's claim that such a study of the Orient is inescapably tainted by the ruler-ruled relationship that obtained between the Occident and the Orient. It is perhaps not unfair to assume that Said did not, or would not, or could not, refer to Smith, because he did not find his scholarship of the Orient to be tainted in this way. William Graham's essay in this volume bears on this issue.

That Smith could, even when writing during the age of imperialism, escape its intellectual consequences could well be the outcome of the attitude that Smith espoused toward the study of religion itself, which remains to this day a powerful element in his legacy. Smith discusses the evolving attitudes to the study of religion in his seminal essay referred to earlier, which has been summarized by Frank Whaling as follows:

> In this essay, Smith traced the progress in the study of the History of Religions in various stages. The first stage saw the accumulation and analysis of facts. At first there was the impersonal accumulation of facts about "they," the people of a religion, by scholars still personally uninvolved. The next

stage saw the personalization of the work so that scholars as people, as "we" were investigating "they" who were also seen to be people. Not only was it the glory of the scholar to "study not things but qualities of personal living," the investigator's own personal qualities were also seen to be relevant. A further step came when it was seen that personal relationships with people of other traditions were important so that dialogue was no longer a merely conceptual matter conducted from a study at Oxford, Harvard or Edinburgh with "they" but an actual discussing with other people who through this relationship became "you." A final stage involved not merely the inter-dialogue and study of two people or traditions on the basis of "we-both" are doing this together, but that "we-all" should do this together.[6]

Frank Whaling then goes on to say:

The scholar Wilfred Cantwell Smith has argued in his book *The Meaning and End of Religion* that the notion of monolithic world religions is a fiction that should be abandoned. He even argues that, ultimately, the only religion is that of each individual. Other scholars have enlarged his critical approach. Some have pointed out that the religious experience of women within a religious tradition may be quite different from that of men. (In Islam, for example, women's religious experience takes place at shrines and in the home, whereas men's religious experience is more centered on the mosque.) We should also recognize that within a single world religion, the personal religious experience of an individual will be quite different for a child, a teenager, or an adult. And the meaning of being a "Buddhist" or "Christian" or "Hindu" will differ, depending on the culture or historical period that the individual inhabits. (Think of the difference between being a Christian in the Roman Empire of the first century and being a Christian in North America in the twenty-first century.) Lastly, there is the fact that individuals in some societies, such as in China and Japan, practice forms of religion that effortlessly blend elements from several major religions.[7]

One can also see the legacy of Smith's "personalist epistemology" in the way people have begun to think of how the dialogue, which such religious diversity demands, is to be conducted. Leonard Swidler has produced the "Dialogue Decalogue" for the purpose of providing guidelines for engaging in such dialogue. His fifth commandment reads as follows:

> FIFTH COMMANDMENT: *Each participant must define himself.* Only the Jew, for example, can define what it means to be a Jew. The rest can only describe what it looks like from the outside. Moreover, because dialogue is a dynamic medium, as each participant learns, he will change and hence continually deepen, expand, and modify his self-definition as a Jew, being careful to remain in constant dialogue with fellow Jews. Thus it is mandatory that each dialogue partner define what it means to be an authentic member of his own tradition.
>
> *Conversely, the one interpreted must be able to recognize herself in the interpretation.* This is the golden rule of interreligious hermeneutics, as has been often reiterated by the "apostle of interreligious dialogue" Raimundo Panikkar. For the sake of understanding, each dialogue participant will naturally attempt to express for herself what she thinks is the meaning of the partner's statement; the partner must be able to recognize herself in that expression. *The advocate of "a world theology," Wilfred Cantwell Smith, would add that the expression must also be verifiable by critical observers who are not involved.*[8]

The recognition of this point pertaining to dialogue in the oeuvre of Smith is a useful corrective to the popular and somewhat misleading statement of his position that the believer is always right. Smith is totally with Panikkar in insisting that the participant must recognize himself or herself in what is being said, but adds that this should not be taken to mean that what the participant says about himself or herself is always right, a point dealt with later in more detail.

The fact that one may undergo change, or change one's position in certain respects, as a result of participating in any dialogical process, personal or historical, should remind us that Smith emphasized not merely the *diversity* that characterizes a religious tradition, but also the *dynamism* that characterizes it, that is, its ability to change over time. Willard Oxtoby identifies this element of Smith's legacy with remarkable clarity in the context of Christianity when he writes:

> What, then, has modernity meant for the Christian tradition? Modernity has brought new outlooks on the nature

and possibilities of thought and knowledge. It has offered new insights into the nature of the physical universe, living creatures, and the structure of personality. And it has meant new outlooks on the character of human culture, history, and society. It has meant change. *As the Canadian religion scholar Wilfred Cantwell Smith (b. 1916) has said, to be modern is to be self-conscious about the fact of change and to take an active hand in shaping change itself.*[9]

It is the interweaving of diversity and dynamism, in the context of Christianity in the modern world, which lends such force to the following remarks by Alan Segal and Willard Oxtoby:

> Thus Christianity has largely ceased to play a significant official role in the public life of these secular societies. Many Christians remain convinced that the truth of their gospel leaves no room for other beliefs. Nevertheless, Christians have no choice today but to live as one faith group among many. And even if that were not the case, Jesus' commandment to love our neighbours as ourselves would demand full openness to the identities of our fellow human beings. The plural nature of religious life today is a fact that must be accepted. To see that fact as desirable is to embrace what has come to be known as pluralism.

They go on to say:

> Pluralism presumes a human community whose common values may yet override the particularism of traditional Christian theology. An early proponent of pluralism was the Canadian scholar of comparative religion Wilfred Cantwell Smith (1916–2000). Smith suggested that to be modern is to be self-conscious about change and to take an active hand in shaping it. This chapter's overview of the Christian tradition makes it clear that change has been a feature of Christian history in every age. One would be ill advised to rule out the possibility of dramatic and creative change in the future.[10]

Others have utilized Smith's plural legacy to enrich the discourse of religion in a globalizing world. One widely used text on the subject of globalization and religion has this to say:

> Although at first glance, the religious worlds of humankind seem to have grown up largely independent of one another, a closer look will reveal that hidden threads from different religions and cultures have, for centuries, been woven together to form a new tapestry, one that contributes to the sharing of religious insight in an *age of globalization.* In *Toward a World Theology,* Wilfred Cantwell Smith traces the threads of this new tapestry, and the story he tells is quite amazing. Smith notes, for example, that to fully appreciate the influence on Gandhi of Tolstoy's understanding of the Sermon on the Mount, it is important to know that Tolstoy's own conversion to Christianity, which occurred in a period of midlife crisis, was deeply influenced not only by the Sermon on the Mount but also by the life of the Buddha.[11]

The last few lines allude to a series of interlocking facts, some well known and some less so, to which Smith drew pointed attention. These are (1) Gandhi, the Indian, influenced Martin Luther King, Jr., the Christian, as a votary of non-violence. (2) But Gandhi, the Indian, himself became a votary of non-violence under the influence of Tolstoy, a Christian. (3) Tolstoy himself underwent a religious experience toward the end of his life, as a result of which he became a pacifist. His pacifism influenced Gandhi. (4) But Tolstoy's religious conversion experience came about as a result of reading a story on the life of saints. (5) The story is that of Barlaam and Josaphat. The Christian monk, Barlaam, narrates the story to Prince Josaphat, which contains the account of a person helplessly trapped in a well, who is clinging to a vine gnawed at by two mice, one white and one black (representing day and night). He can hope to gain release from his precarious condition not by clinging to life but by surrendering it to God, which is what Tolstoy did. (6) This story, however, has Indian roots, and the word *Josaphat* is ultimately traceable to the word *Bodhisattva.* Thus (7) "Tolstoy's conversion was brought about in large part by the story of the Christian saint, Josaphat, who was, so to speak, really the Buddha in disguise."[12] From these facts

> We can see that the practice of passing over and coming back, of being open to the stories of others, and of coming to understand one's own tradition through these stories is in fact very ancient. Therefore, when Martin Luther King, Jr., embraced the teachings of Gandhi, he embraced not only Gandhi but also Tolstoy, and through Tolstoy two of the

greatest religious leaders of non-violence: Jesus of Nazareth, whose committed follower King already was, and Siddhartha the Buddha.[13]

Another dimension of Smith's legacy, which some view as problematic, has to do with his emphasis on the perspective of the insider. Scott T. Kline, for instance, writes:

> The Canadian scholar of religion Wilfred Cantwell Smith (1916–2000) is widely known for privileging the perspective of the insider in the study of religion. He writes, "no statement about a religion is valid unless it can be acknowledged by that religion's believers." In effect, Smith is proposing a rule that insiders are the final authority in determining whether or not a scholar's statement about their religion is correct. This rule, however, creates problems for researchers who are interested in studying why insiders act and believe differently. Which insider should be the final arbiter? Or what happens if (or more likely, when) the researcher finds that an insider's claims contradict his or her behaviour? Does the researcher then make a judgment based on criteria outside those of the insiders?[14]

Douglas Cowan reinforces this point while discussing the study of new religious movements. He writes:

> Though new religious adherents are quite happy to take advantage of scholarly findings when they serve the needs of the group, this misunderstands the social function of scholarship; many members consider research that challenges their beliefs an egregious breach of trust. How do we balance the well-known concern of Wilfred Cantwell Smith, that religious adherents should be able to recognize themselves in our academic re-description, with the reality that re-description will in many cases significantly challenge the adherents' worldview? The Church of Scientology, for example, advertises itself as the fastest-growing religious movement on earth, yet there is very little empirical evidence for that claim. Pointing this out to Scientologists, though, often leads to charges of misrepresentation and bias.[15]

On this point the legacy of Smith seems to have been misunderstood. Smith says quite clearly that although "Anything I say about Islam as a living faith is valid in so far as Muslims may say 'amen' to it," yet *"The reverse is not true.* Not every statement *about* Islam that is acceptable to Muslims is *ipso facto* true: one can flatter or beguile."[16]

Smith's desire to in some sense privilege the perspective of the insider is perhaps rooted in his deep humanism, as reflected in the following statement he made:

> We have not understood any action or any saying in another century or another culture until we have realized that we ourselves, had we been in that situation, might well have done or said exactly that. Not that we would have done it; that would mean denying human freedom. We must simply appreciate, must feel and make our readers feel, that of the various possibilities open to us at that point, this particular thought or move or comment would have seemed attractive to us, and perceive the reasons why that would be so. (Smith, unpublished paper)[17]

An interesting direction in which Smith's legacy has been developed is to link it positively with the study of folk religion. Thus, John Morreall and Tamara Sonn write regarding folk beliefs and practices:

> Many scholars of religion view such beliefs and practices as part of lived religion. The study of lived religion de-emphasizes organized religion in favor of less formal expressions of people's spiritual concerns. One of the major proponents of the study of lived religion was Wilfred Cantwell Smith (d. 2000). He taught that religion should not be thought of as an abstract set of beliefs and practices but as the lived experience of individuals in their relationship to the transcendent.[18]

Thomas Coburn's essay in this volume discerns the role of Smith's legacy in a new development, the rise of "contemplative studies." This naturally follows from Smith's concept of religions as living traditions and from his critique of the word *religion* itself. Scott Kline notes, for instance, that "Wilfred Cantwell Smith, the Canadian scholar and former director of the Harvard Center for the Study of the World Religions, recommended using the language of 'traditions' to include both religion and secular humanism."[19] Similarly, "Ninian Smart (1927–2001), who helped pioneer secular approaches to the study of religion, suggested using 'worldviews' as the common term for nationalism, socialism, and religion."[20]

The critique of the Western notion of religion, which is such an important element in the thought of Smith, has been pursued by scholars after him with great vigor and constitutes one of his lasting legacies, even though the field is still fumbling for a word with which to replace the word *religion*.[21]

IV

One may suspect, on reviewing the way people have assessed Smith's legacy, that at times, they may be crediting him with more than is justified. For instance, the discussion of primal religions remains largely marginal to Smith's concerns. He focused, despite his commitment to pluralism, not on the world's religions but on *world religions*, when we use the latter term to denote the three religions of the West (Judaism, Christianity, and Islam), the four religions of India (Hinduism, Buddhism, Jainism, and Sikhism), and the two religions of China (Confucianism and Taoism). And all of them have their scriptures, the study of which interested Smith so much. But these *world religions* do not exhaust the religious heritage of humanity, the most obvious omission being that of primal religions, which are oral in character but surely deserve to be included in any roster of the world's religions. Some would consider this a fair criticism of Smith's work, but here again we might wish to recognize that although Smith himself may not have turned his gaze toward the primal religions, the ripple effect of his legacy of recognizing the plurality and vitality of religions seems to be at least partly responsible for the fact that the gaze of the academic study of religion no longer overlooks primal religions. This is dramatically illustrated by comparing two editions of Huston Smith's famous work on world religions. The book, when it first appeared in 1958 under the title *The Religions of Man*, did not include a chapter on primal religions. When a new edition appeared in 1991 under the title *The World's Religions*, it did.[22]

The point nevertheless has some force, when one considers that the *other* great figure in the study of religion in the twentieth century was Mircea Eliade (1907–1986). He mainstreamed the contribution of archaic religions and "primitive" societies in the study of religion. Smith and Eliade represented the two poles in the field, as it were, at Harvard and Chicago respectively, each associated with one primary orientation to the study of religion, Smith representing the historical approach and

Eliade the phenomenological one. From this it does not follow that their positions were necessarily antipodal,[23] but there was a significant difference of emphasis. While Eliade focused on heirophanies, Smith focused on scriptures. And the focus on scriptures continues to be part of Smith's legacy. As Mary Pat Fisher notes:

> The absolute authority of scriptures is being questioned by contemporary scholars who are interpreting them in their historical and cultural context and thus casting some doubt upon their exclusive claims to truth. Some liberal scholars are also proposing that there is an underlying experiential unity among religions. *Wilfred Cantwell Smith, for instance, concluded that the revelations of all religions have come from the same divine source.* Christian theologian John Hick suggests that religions are culturally different responses to one and the same reality. The Muslim scholar Frithjof Schuon feels that there is a common mystical base underlying all religions, but that only the enlightened will experience and understand it, whereas others will see the superficial differences.[24]

Purushottama Bilimoria's essay in this volume examines this point further.

In one respect, however, Smith's legacy may not have quite worked out exactly as he had hoped or predicted. Smith wrote in 1963: "I seriously suggest that terms such as Christianity, Buddhism, and the like must be dropped, as clearly untenable once challenged."[25] He argued

> that the world had Buddhists, but not Buddhism, Christians but not Christianity, and so forth. Smith suggested that the word "religion" be dropped as well, claiming that monolithic terms such as "religion," "Christianity," "Hinduism" obscure the dynamic and personal quality of religious traditions.
>
> "'Hinduism' refers not to an entity; it is a name that the West has given to a prodigiously variegated series of facts. It is a notion in men's minds—and a notion that cannot but be inadequate. To use this term at all is inescapably a gross oversimplification. There is an inherent contradiction between history and this order of idea."
>
> One day W. C. Smith even wrote, "I am bold enough to speculate whether these terms will not in fact have disappeared from serious writing and careful speech within twenty-five years."[26]

Smith wrote this in 1963. However, as Victoria Urubshurow goes on to point out, "Now over forty-five years after W. C. Smith called for an end to the word 'religion' it shows little sign of expiring, and '-isms' are as convenient as ever."[27]

Nevertheless, Smith's challenge has not been in vain. As Victoria Urubshurow herself notes:

> Due to problems with the "-isms" and monolithic terms that sanitize the messiness of culture, the terminology of this book minimizes their use. Thus "Judaic tradition" generally is used in place of "Judaism" and so forth. Here the word "tradition" should carry a *holistic sense* that conveys the fact that traditions are ongoing with multiple strands that intertwine with many aspects of people's lives. A religious tradition may be thought of as a cultural heritage that is both: (1) kept alive through participation (what W. C. Smith calls "faith"), and (2) continually challenged by ongoing cultural circumstances. At this point it is still not practical to dispense with the word "religion." Thus stuck with the word, one is advised to think of particular religions as dynamic cultural complexes, not as static monolithic entities.[28]

V

Already in 1984, Frank Whaling had hinted at eight concepts potentially embodying the legacy of Smith:

1. His stress upon persons

2. His concern to understand the worldview of others

3. His notion that religious truth must encompass the data of faith as well as the data of the ongoing tradition

4. His global awareness of the total human community

5. His perception that the Transcendent Reality (however defined) is part of the subject matter of the study of religion

6. His emphasis on dialogue and more importantly colloquium as involving corporate critical self-consciousness

7. His conviction that the study of religion although crucial is part of the greater whole of humane knowledge, and

8. His insistence that the views of non-Westerners and persons of other religious traditions must be given due seriousness within this greater whole[29]

These concepts continue to constitute important elements in Smith's legacy. In this volume, for instance, Harvey Cox continues the exploration of belief and faith initiated by Smith, and John Stratton Hawley continues this exploration, along with the exploration of other antinomies in Smith's work. Peter Slater focuses on the issue of verification in particular in the thought of Smith, while K. R. Sundararajan probes the study of religion as the study of religious persons and the transformations it might entail. The contribution by Donald K. Swearer on the moral imagination of Smith is particularly valuable, when we consider that he also, like Smith, served as the director of the Center for the Study of World Religions. Finally, Jonathan Herman explores Smith's views on the role of the public intellectual, a role which Smith himself played with such distinction.

VI

One may conclude this introduction by placing the legacy of Smith in a history-of-ideas framework. It is important, for this framework to work, to realize that the academic study of religion is a relatively recent development in the intellectual history of humanity. Many, in fact most, religions of the world possess a long, even hoary, history of the study of their own religion and even of religious phenomena, from what we now identify as a "confessional" point of view. By contrast, the academic study of religion is of recent vintage; some scholars would date it as commencing securely only in the 1860s.[30] It was one of the consequences of the expansion of European political dominance over the rest of the world, an expansion that had the effect of willy-nilly bringing the peoples of the world together by breaking down their relative isolation. This fact of relative isolation of religions and cultures in premodern times can be exaggerated, but it needs to be clearly recognized before Smith's legacy can be assessed in a history-of-ideas framework. As John Hick explains:

> Until comparatively recently each of the different religions of the world had developed in substantial ignorance of the others. There have been, it is true, great movements of expansion which have brought two faiths into contact: above all, the expansion of Buddhism during the last three centuries B.C.E. and the early centuries of the Christian era, carrying

its message throughout India and Southeast Asia and into China, Tibet, and Japan, and then, the resurgence of the Hindu religion at the expense of Buddhism, with the result that today Buddhism is rarely to be found on the Indian subcontinent; next, the first Christian expansion into the Roman Empire; then the expansion of Islam in the seventh and eighth centuries C.E. into the Middle East, Europe, and later India; and finally, the second expansion of Christianity in the missionary movement of the nineteenth century. These interactions, however, in the cases of Christianity and Islam, were conflicts rather than dialogues; they did not engender any deep or sympathetic understanding of one faith by the adherents of another. It is only during the last hundred years or so that the scholarly study of world religions has made possible an accurate appreciation of the faiths of other people.[31]

It was then that the foundations of the academic study of religion were laid, and central to them was a West in relation to the Rest. Thus, from its very inception, the study of religion was cast in an outsider-insider framework, with Europe, the outsider, looking at the rest of the world.

If we accept this insider-outsider dichotomy as a basis for further examining religious studies, which also emerged with the rise of the West, then one may use this dichotomy to identify four directional models of communication between the insider and outsider, as follows: (1) from insider to insider, (2) from outsider to outsider, (3) from outsider to insider, and (4) from insider to outsider.[32]

It is now possible to argue that:

In the study of religion, these four combinations represent not merely logical combinations but chronological phases as well. While "the religion of study," which finds a prominent place in each religious tradition, was basically carried out between insiders and insiders, the initial phase in the study of religion was characterized by the opposite: it was carried out among outsiders. With the educational penetration of the colonies by the West, however, the situation acquired an additional dimension: it came to involve communication from outsiders to insiders about the insider's own religion. Western orientalists, for example, explained at least to Westernized Hindus what Hinduism was. This dominance began to recede with the end of the age of imperialism and the need to engage the perspective of the insider came to be increasingly felt. The mode of communication from the insider to the outsider now came into play.[33]

In such a context, the legacy of Smith can be identified as twofold: (1) although Smith's own age was dominated by the "outsider to outsider" mode of discourse, he clearly saw, or rather foresaw, that the "insider to outsider" phase was about to commence; (2) Smith equipped the field of religious studies conceptually to deal with this situation when it arose.

Smith has foreseen what his Australian colleague Eric Sharpe would later identify as the "response threshold."

> A "response threshold" is crossed when it becomes possible for the believer to advance his or her own interpretation against that of the scholar. In classical comparative religion this was hardly a problem since most of the scholar's time was spent in investigating religions of the past. Interpretations might be challenged, but only by other specialists working according to Western canons and conventions. Today, by contrast, a greater proportion of study is devoted to contemporary, or at least recent, forms of living traditions. . . . The response threshold implies the right of the present-day devotee to advance a distinctive interpretation of his or her own tradition—often at variance with that of Western scholarship—and to be taken seriously in doing so.[34]

We meet Smith already standing on this response threshold long before anyone got there.

Notes

1. Mircea Eliade and Joseph M. Kitagawa, eds., *History of Religions: Essays in Methodology* (Chicago: University of Chicago Press, 1959), pp. 31–58.
2. Frank Whaling, ed., *The World's Religious Traditions: Current Perspectives in Religious Studies: Essays in Honour of Wilfred Cantwell Smith* (Edinburgh: T & T Clark, 1984), pp. 4–5.
3. Personal communication from Professor Alwi Shihab.

4. Edward Said, *Orientalism* (London: Routledge and Kegan Paul, 1978).

5. *Merriam-Webster's Collegiate Dictionary*, 10th ed. (Springfield, MA: Merriam-Webster, 2002), p. 818.

6. Frank Whaling, *World's Religious Traditions*, p. 5.

7. Michael Molloy, *Experiencing the World's Religions: Tradition, Challenge, Change*, 4th ed. (Boston: McGraw-Hill, 2008), pp. 22–23.

8. Leonard Swidler, "Dialogue Decalogue: Ground Rules for Interreligious Dialogue," *Journal of Ecumenical Studies* 20, no. 1 (Winter 1983), pp. 2–3, emphasis added.

9. Willard G. Oxtoby, "The Christian Tradition," in *World Religions: Western Traditions*, ed. Willard G. Oxtoby (Toronto: Oxford University Press, 1996), p. 343, emphasis added.

10. Alan E. Segal and Willard Oxtoby, "The Christian Tradition," in *A Concise Introduction to World Religions*, eds. Alan E. Segal and Willard Oxtoby (Dun Mills, Ontario: Oxford University Press, 2007), p. 192, emphasis added.

11. John L. Esposito, Darrell J. Fasching, and Todd Lewis, *Religion and Globalization: World Religions in Historical Perspective* (New York: Oxford University Press, 2008), p. 547, emphasis added.

12. Ibid., p. 548.

13. Ibid., p. 549.

14. Scott T. Kline, "The Study of Religion," in *World Religions—Canadian Perspectives: Western Traditions*, ed. Doris R. Jakbosh (Toronto: Nelson Education, 2013), p. 10.

15. Douglas E. Cowan, "New Religious Movements," in Doris R. Jakbosh, ed., *World Religions*, p. 248.

16. Wilfred Cantwell Smith, "Comparative Religion: Whither—and Why," in Eliade and Kitagawa, eds., *History of Religions*, p. 43, emphasis supplied.

17. John Morreall and Tamara Sonn, *The Religion Toolkit: A Complete Guide to Religious Studies* (West Sussex, UK: John Wiley & Sons, 2012), p. 13.

18. Ibid., p. 162.

19. Scott T. Kline, "Study of Religion," p. 11

20. Ibid.

21. See S. N. Balagangadhara, *The Heathen in His Blindness: Asia, the West and the Dynamic of Religion* (Leiden: E. J. Brill, 1994); Harjot S. Oberoi, *The Construction of Religious Boundaries: Culture, Identity and Diversity in the Sikh Tradition* (Delhi: Oxford University Press, 1994); W. H. McLeod, *Who Is a Sikh? The Problem of Sikh Identity* (New Delhi: Oxford University Press, 2002); Daniel Dubuisson, *The Western Construction of Religion: Myths, Knowledge, and Ideology*, trans. William Sayers (Baltimore, MD; London: John Hopkins University Press, 2003); Tomoko Masuzawa, *The Invention of World Religions: Or, How European Universalism was Preserved in the Language of Pluralism* (Chicago: University of Chicago Press, 2005); Arvind-Pal S. Mandair, *Religion and the Specter of the West* (New York: Columbia University Press, 2009); Arvind Sharma, *Problematizing Religious Freedom* (Dordrecht: Springer, 2011). Also see Mitch Numark, "Trans-

lating *Dharma*: Scottish Missionary-Orientalists and the Politics of Religious Understanding in Nineteenth-Century Bombay," *Journal of Asian Studies* 70, no. 2 (May 2011), pp. 471–500.

22. Huston Smith, *The World's Religions* (San Francisco: Harper, 1991), chapter IX.

23. See Arvind Sharma, *To the Things Themselves: Essays on the Discourse and Practice of the Phenomenology of Religion* (Berlin: Walter de Gruyter, 2001), p. 5.

24. Mary Pat Fischer, *Living Religions*, 8th ed. (London: Laurence King Publishing, 2011), p. 511, emphasis added.

25. Wilfred C. Smith, *The Meaning and End of Religion* (Minneapolis, MN: Fortress Press, 1991 [1963]), p. 194. Cited by Victoria Kennick Urubshurow, *Introducing World Religions* (New York: Routledge, 2008), p. xix.

26. Ibid. The two citations are from pp. 144 and 195, respectively. 27. Ibid. 28. Ibid.

29. Frank Whaling, ed., op.cit., p. 6, numbering added and sentences rearranged.

30. Eric J. Sharpe, *Comparative Religion: A History* (London: Gerald Duckworth & Company, 1986) pp. 27–28.

31. John Hick, *Philosophy of Religion*, 4th ed. (Englewood Cliffs, NJ: Prentice Hall, 1990), p. 109.

32. Arvind Sharma, *To the Things Themselves*, p. 5.

33. Ibid.

34. Eric J. Sharpe, "Study of Religion: Methodological Issues," in *The Encyclopedia of Religion*, editor-in-chief Mircea Eliade, vol. 14 (New York: Macmillan, 1986), p. 81.

Bibliography

Balagangadhara, S. N. *The Heathen in His Blindness: Asia, the West and the Dynamic of Religion*. Leiden: E. J. Brill, 1994.

Cowan, Douglas E. "New Religious Movements." In *World Religions: Canadian Perspectives—Western Traditions*, edited by Doris R. Jakbosh. Toronto: Nelson Education, 2013.

Dubuisson, Daniel. *The Western Construction of Religion: Myths, Knowledge, and Ideology*. Translated by William Sayers. Baltimore, MD: Johns Hopkins University Press, 2003.

Eliade, Mircea, and Joseph M. Kitagawa, editors. *History of Religions: Essays in Methodology*. Chicago: University of Chicago Press, 1959.

Esposito, John L., Darrell J. Fasching, and Todd Lewis. *Religion and Globalization: World Religions in Historical Perspective*. New York: Oxford University Press, 2008.

Fischer, Mary Pat. *Living Religions*. 8th ed. London: Laurence King Publishing, 2011.

Kline, Scott T. "The Study of Religion." *World Religions: Canadian Perspectives—Western Traditions*. Edited Doris R. Jakbosh. Toronto: Nelson Education, 2013.

Hick, John. *Philosophy of Religion*. 4th ed. Englewood Cliffs, NJ: Prentice Hall, 1990.

Mandair, Arvind-Pal, S. *Religion and the Specter of the West*. New York: Columbia University Press, 2009.

Masuzawa, Tomoko. *The Invention of World Religions: Or, How European Universalism Was Preserved in the Language of Pluralism*. Chicago: University of Chicago Press, 2005.

McLeod, W. H. *Who Is a Sikh? The Problem of Sikh Identity*. New Delhi: Oxford University Press, 2002.

Merriam-Webster's Collegiate Dictionary. 10th ed. Springfield, MA: Merriam-Webster, 2002.

Morreall, John, and Tamara Sonn. *The Religion Toolkit: A Complete Guide to Religious Studies*. West Sussex, UK: John Wiley & Sons, 2012.

Molloy, Michael. *Experiencing the World's Religions: Tradition, Challenge, Change*. 4th ed. Boston: McGraw-Hill, 2008.

Numark, Mitch. "Translating *Dharma*: Scottish Missionary-Orientalists and the Politics of Religious Understanding in Nineteenth-Century Bombay." *Journal of Asian Studies* 70, no. 2 (May 2011), pp. 471–500.

Oberoi, Harjot, S. *The Construction of Religious Boundaries: Culture, Identity and Diversity in the Sikh Tradition*. Delhi: Oxford University Press, 1994.

Oxtoby, Willard G. "The Christian Tradition." In *World Religions: Western Traditions*, edited by Willard G. Oxtoby. Toronto: Oxford University Press, 1996.

Said, Edward. *Orientalism*. London: Routledge and Kegan Paul, 1978.

Segal, Alan E., and Willard Oxtoby. "The Christian Tradition." In *A Concise Introduction to World Religions*, edited by Alan Segal and Willard Oxtoby. Dun Mills, Ontario: Oxford University Press, 2007.

Sharma, Arvind. *To the Things Themselves: Essays on the Discourse and Practice of the Phenomenology of Religion*. Berlin: Walter de Gruyter, 2001.

———. *Problematizing Religious Freedom*. Dordrecht: Springer, 2011.

Sharpe, Eric J. *Comparative Religion: A History*. London: Gerald Duckworth & Company, 1986.

———. "Study of Religion: Methodological Issues." In *The Encyclopedia of Religion*, vol. 14, edited by Mircea Eliade. New York: Macmillan, 1986.

Smith, Huston. *The World's Religions*. San Francisco: Harper, 1991.

Smith, Wilfred Cantwell. "Comparative Religion: Whither—and Why?" In *History of Religions: Essays in Methodology*, edited by Mircea Eliade and Joseph M. Kitagawa. Chicago: Chicago University Press, 1959.

———. *The Meaning and End of Religion*. Minneapolis, MN: Fortress Press, 1991.

Swidler, Leonard. "Dialogue Decalogue: Ground Rules for Interreligious Dialogue." *Journal of Ecumenical Studies* 20, no. 1 (Winter 1983).

Whaling, Frank, ed. *The World's Religious Traditions: Current Perspectives in Religious Studies: Essays in Honour of Wilfred Cantwell Smith.* Edinburgh: T & T Clark, 1984.

Urubshurow, Victoria Kennick. *Introducing World Religions.* New York: Routledge, 2008.

Religious Studies—The Academic and Moral Challenge

Personal Reflections on the Legacy of Wilfred Cantwell Smith

Diana L. Eck

When Wilfred Cantwell Smith delivered his inaugural lecture at Harvard Divinity School in 1964, he told his audience in Memorial Church in the heart of Harvard Yard, "It is the business of a university to discern and clarify what is going on, inside a galaxy or a neuron, or indeed, in a religious community. Part of the excitement of academic inquiry is the constant discovery that more is going on than one might have supposed: that what seemed simple is complex; that what seemed static is in motion; that what seemed a disarray of brute facts is a sophisticated system of subtle interrelationships."[1] Wilfred placed the challenge of the modern study of religion before a university community fifty years ago: the challenge to scholars in both the humanities and the social sciences of discerning just what is "going on" inside a religious community and in the minds and hearts of those whose lives are shaped by these communities.

Studying religion with Wilfred Cantwell Smith entailed the constant discovery that more is going on than we supposed and that the study of religion is as exciting and demanding as any academic undertaking could be. Today, decades later, as fields such as cognitive neuroscience attract the very best undergraduate minds, we need more than ever to refresh the vision of just how challenging the intellectual and moral work of the study of religion really is in a world of religious turbulence and religious vision. In the fifty years since W. C. Smith's inaugural address at Harvard, well-funded academic research has discerned and clarified galaxies and neurons, stem cells and the human genome. It is not clear, however, that we have made enough progress in discerning and clarifying the energies of religious communities. We too often stand in almost mute astonishment before the lineages of the Muslim Brotherhood, the thousands of religiously based NGOs, the liberation theologies of South America, the wayside healing shrines of the Balkans, or the fifty million Hindus who converge in pilgrimage to bathe in the River Ganges during the Kumbh Mela. Our understanding of the worlds of our fellow human beings as they gather in communities, live their lives, and die their deaths must keep pace with the velocity of global change. As Wilfred put it succinctly, "Our vision and our loyalties, as well as our aircraft, must circle the globe."[2] He conveyed to colleagues and students alike the global reach, the excitement, and the urgency of the study of religion.

I was among the graduate students who worked with Wilfred Cantwell Smith at Harvard in the late 1960s and early 1970s. These were formative years for me, having come to the study of religion from an academic background in South Asian studies and with a wide grounding in my own faith, having grown up in a liberal and socially active Methodist church in Montana. I came to Harvard to study the religious traditions of India, primarily those we refer to as Hindu. However, in the intense weekly colloquia with Wilfred in the Common Room of the Center for the Study of World Religions it became clear that my life experience as a Christian was also relevant to the study I was undertaking. That was a surprise to me. I was well aware of the critical and linguistic skills and the painstaking work that would be involved in studying and trying to understand the religious life of a community not my own. But that the critical self-consciousness of one's own presuppositions, one's own tradition, one's own faith, would be part of the intellectual bargain was new and intriguing to me. That the study of another tradition requires the excavation of one's own presuppositions and worldview—whether Christian or Jewish, secular or humanist—was to me a bold and somewhat unsettling proposition.

In the course of those years of study, I found, with Wilfred's help, the most valuable thing one can find in doctoral studies: my own life's work. It would involve the study of India's religious traditions whose histories were braided with one another through centuries of interaction. It would involve the global study of religion in all its diversity, depth, and dynamism. It would involve the continual rethinking of the very categories and approaches of the academic study of religion. And it would also involve the continual rethinking and critical reappropriation of my own religious faith. I emerged a hybrid of sorts—a scholar of India, a scholar of religion more broadly, and a theologian involved in the excavation of my own faith.

The study of religious life of South Asia was itself a challenging undertaking, as Wilfred well knew. In prepartition India, he had studied Islam in South Asia and had taught at Forman College in Lahore. Forman was and is a Christian college, founded in 1864, and there Wilfred lived with colleagues, staff members, and students who were mostly Hindus, Muslims, and Sikhs. Within a few years, this beautiful, cosmopolitan city that had long been the cultural heart of Pakistan would be seared with the violence and agony of the partition of India and Pakistan. It was there that Smith developed an intellectual perspective able to see clearly the ways in which the religious communities of humankind are not separate chapters bound together in a "world religions" book, but are deeply involved in one another's history, bound together as neighbors in the villages and cities of the world. Years later, his provocative article, "The Crystallization of Religious Communities in Mughal India," became for me and many of his students a template for asking questions about how it is that the "religions" so named have come into being in the dynamic process of what we call history. From a cosmopolitan culture with the universalist visions of Guru Nanak and Akbar in the sixteenth century, what happened to create the boundaries, the formalism of what became the Sikh *khalsa* of Gobind Singh and the Islamic formalism of Sirhindi and Aurangzeb in the seventeenth century? How do the entities that we call "religions" become reified? Rather than presuppose their existence, we must investigate this process.

What we call "religion" is in a constant process of historical change. As I worked in seminars with Wilfred, I began to realize that when he spoke of the "history" of religion, it was this quality to which he referred: the fact that our religious traditions are dynamic. They are not systems with all the stasis that the word "religion" implies, but more like rivers, rolling, thundering at times, meandering, and sometimes petering out. He used the term "religious tradition" to suggest this cumulative movement. To study the history of religion is not to dig for origins, but to follow the rivers as they move, flow, water new lands, and nourish extraordinary creations. Of course, when it comes to religious traditions, Smith noted that for some in religious communities "to admit fluidity is to undermine, to call attention to it is unfriendly, to proclaim it is suicidal."[3] They have a deep commitment to a view in which some "essential" core persists, and only the transient peripheral matters change. By this reckoning, however, Smith as historian tells us "everything was in process of becoming peripheral, that the 'essential' was dwindling to insignificance."

And of course the study of religion is not only inherently historical in this sense, but also inherently comparative. And this term, too, Wilfred used in a distinctive way. By comparative study, Wilfred did not mean what Eliade called "morphology," the study of this or that form, symbolic structure, or element across religious communities. He meant, rather, the comparative perspective in which our study is constantly undertaken. In India, for example, it is clear that nothing can be adequately understood if one insists on pulling a particular thread—Buddhist, Jain, Hindu, Sikh, Muslim—from the skein of the whole and studying it in isolation. They have participated in one another's histories and have long been part of a common context. In his seminar "Historical Interrelations," Smith invited us to consider sixth-century BCE India with what we now call *shramana*, Buddhist, Jain, Upanishadic developments; the first-century Mediterranean with the interrelations of a multitude of old and new communities; third-century China where Buddhist monks encountered those whose views have come to be called Confucian or Taoist; and medieval Spain with its legendary *convivencia* of Jewish, Muslim, and Christian thought. In the late twentieth century, he argued, our awareness of the variegated religious history of humankind has made it impossible to study religious traditions in isolation. Because the scope of our awareness has broadened, comparative study is a necessity, investigating the historical interrelations of religious communities we have come to think of as separate.

The global interrelations of today's world perhaps make it easier to recognize the fact that nowhere on earth is "religious life" simple or singular. Religious people and communities dwell in increasingly complex contexts with global communications bringing impressions of people we do not know to our homes and schools in Madras and in Montreal. The migration of peoples—both as desperate refugees and ambitious immigrants—sharpens the day-to-day awareness of one another. Understanding the religious life of any city, region, or community inevitably involves us in the study of religious life in its multiplicity and interrelations.

But there is yet another sense of the comparative dimension of Wilfred's work: that the very process of thinking, translating, and understanding is rigorously relational. The word I would use, though Wilfred used it more guardedly, is *dialogical*. He preferred the term *colloquy* to *dialogue*, recognizing the multisidedness of the engagement of a scholar with his or her interlocutors. As a humanist, Wilfred insisted that there are people on both sides, indeed all sides, of the process of intellectual investigation and understanding in both the humanities and social sciences. In the study of human life and society there are no "outsiders," but only variously situated insiders, including we ourselves. In this context, all knowledge is fundamentally self-knowledge, knowledge of a human community of which we are inevitably a part. The deliberative process of learning is inherently dialogical, and must increasingly be self-consciously so. That inaugural address at Harvard was titled "Mankind's Religiously Divided History Approaches Self-Consciousness." Though perhaps clumsy as a title, its message is essentially a methodology.

For those of us in the study of religion, our subject is not so much a set of texts, philosophies, and practices, but the people and communities who have lived their lives and died their deaths in the various worlds of meaning we have come to call "religions." Not only are the religious lives, texts, icons, and rituals we study situated in particular and inevitably complex historical, intellectual, and cultural contexts, so are we who attempt to understand them. Wilfred was a post-Orientalist decades before Edward Said wrote, challenging the very idea that one could produce knowledge of the other without the voice, the challenge, the disputation, the participation of the other. He recognized that speaking "about" needed to be replaced by speaking or conversing "with." And without putting it quite this way, he saw that moving beyond an objectifying Orientalist perspective meant moving into the methodological terrain of dialogue, a way of working in which both the voices of those we study and the voices of the scholars situated in the contexts we study become integral to the process of understanding.

We ourselves come to our studies with a voice and with a particular historical, intellectual, religious context. That is a problem only if we are not scrupulously self-conscious about it. Gaining increasing clarity about our own situatedness, our own form of questioning, our own position—whether methodological, religious, secular, even antireligious—is critical, lest our own subjectivities, our own languages, our own categories of thought be unwittingly universalized in our work. "Even the secular rationalist is coming to be seen as a person like another: not a god, not a superior impersonal intellect, monarch of all it surveys, but a man with a particular point of view."[4] Secular rationalism is, of course, a point of view particularly prized in the academy, but in the ongoing attempt to understand what is going on in a religious community it is a view that must enter into exchange and dialogue with others.

"[T]he secular intellectual, like the religious believer, takes his place as a member of one group of men, one of the world's communities, looking out upon the others."⁵

For those of us in the West who study the traditions of Asia, there is no move beyond the authorial presumption of an Orientalist mode of thinking than a radically dialogical move, recognizing that the community of conversation and disputation in which we participate is worldwide, that the people about whom we write also respond to us and we in turn to them, that critique and mutual critique is part of our discourse. There are people on all sides of the postcolonial conversation—subaltern, secular, and pluralist; Hindu, Christian, and Muslim; European, South Asian, and North American. A dialogical approach requires one important thing: our presence, our critically self-conscious presence in our work, lest we become merely polemical or political.

Wilfred's Workshop

Wilfred created communities of scholarship that embodied this view—namely, the Islamic Institute at McGill, where Muslims and non-Muslims studied Islam together, and the Center for the Study of World Religions at Harvard, where students and scholars from around the world both lived and studied together. It was a colloquy carried on in many languages, continually challenging and reworking the presumed normativities of an English-speaking Western university setting. Every seminar—such as the graduate seminars in which the draft chapters of *Faith and Belief* were presented and discussed—included those of us who worked primarily in Chinese, Sanskrit, Pali, or Arabic. Every seminar discussion challenged an old vocabulary that had been taken for granted. There is virtually no word we now use to do our intellectual work in the study of religion that has not been studied, investigated historically and comparatively, and considered in the semantic range of a global community of scholars in Wilfred's intensive collaborative seminars. We had to contend with "religion" itself, with "tradition," "faith," "scripture," and "transcendence." We thought about the vocabulary of *dharma, shraddha, sampradaya, shruti,* and *veda*. The Hindu philosopher J. L. Mehta recalled that working in this way with Wilfred in the company of his colleagues and students was like participating in the emergence of "a new mode of thought," learning, as he put it, from "a great craftsman at work in his own workshop."⁶

The excavation and interrogation of our vocabulary, the way of thinking that relentlessly queried our category-formation, became second nature to those of us who worked with Wilfred. By the time he came to Harvard, Wilfred had already taken on the most foundational word of our study, "religion," making us think hard about the ways in which that rather stubborn noun had come to be used in the course of its Western history, as if it were a sphere of life that could be circumscribed. Wilfred invited us to think afresh through the conceptual vocabulary that our various viewpoints presented, through traditions that had been religious in many describable ways, but had no word at all corresponding to this noun *religion*. *Dharma* in some ways covered the semantic range of *religion*, but it also connoted law, ethics, and social order. Not only was the utility of the term *religion* questioned, so were the particular terms that had come into common discourse as names of various "religions"—the "isms" of Hinduism, Buddhism, Taoism, and Shintoism.

In his classic study, *The Meaning and End of Religion*, Wilfred proposed the term *religious tradition* as more adequate, for it is a cumulative, dynamic, and historical term connoting movements, not systems. Perhaps it better conveys the reality of religious movements that are more like rivers than monuments—rushing then slowing, converging and splitting, always in motion. To adequately study any religious tradition means looking at its texts and authoritative sources, its interpreters and theologians, its poets and prophets, its activists and reformers, its lovers, artists, and musicians, its institution builders and subverters, and all that they have built and subverted. And of course, each religious tradition has given us thinkers who have looked at the world of religious and cultural difference and developed interpretations of the religious "other." All this and much more is part of the cumulative religious tradition we have come to call "Christianity" or "Hinduism."

And our cumulative traditions, he insisted, include those that go under the name of "secular," like the energetic tradition of investigation and learning the West inherits from Greece and Rome—*philosophia*. In his 1983 presidential address at the American Academy of Religion annual meeting, "The Modern West in the History of Religion," he elaborated the point that the secular perspective is not a position affording one a unique position from which to view more adequately the whole of human religiousness. Rather, it can more adequately be understood as a worldview alongside others, interpreting others, sometimes distorting them by interpreting them within the frame of its own normativities, in ways not so unlike the ways in which people grounded in one religious world or another might be prone to distort the image of the other. Through the efforts of W. C. Smith the secular and religiously complex

"Modern West" took its place alongside South Asia, East Asia, and the Greek, Hellenistic, and Roman worlds as a multireligious context of doctoral study that could be explored within Harvard's program in the Study of Religion, foregrounding the ways in which it defies the analysis of any particular worldview or perspective.

In the course of these years, in what Mehta called the "workshop" of his seminars and colloquia, Wilfred challenged an old vocabulary and brought forth a new one. He tackled the word *faith*, for example. We probed overlapping but distinctive vocabularies that pointed not to a set of things to be intellectually affirmed, but to an orientation of the heart: *Credo* in Latin, *Shraddha* in Sanskrit, *Sadda* in Pali, *Iman* in Arabic. One may study much about the texts, interpreters, and rites and reformations, icons and iconoclasts of the Christian tradition, for example, but there is something else that is more elusive: that quality of heart, that turning of the mind, that setting of the foot on the path, that engagement that Wilfred calls *faith*. The term is straightforward in its early Christian sense: *credo*, I give my heart to this. Painstakingly, he documented the gradual shift in the word's meaning, from faith as a verb to faith as a noun. To believe, in old English, was to be-love, to hold dear. It had little to do with propositions to be affirmed, as in "I believe in one God," but with an orientation of the whole person. Wilfred's careful work on the history and divergence of faith and belief has been influential far beyond our own field, in, for example, Byron Good's work on the problem of belief in medical anthropology.[7] And beyond its intellectual influence in the academy, his work has had relevance to many people, including many of my own students, who struggle with "belief" in their own lives. In asking, "How did the meanings of faith shift from a quality of heart and an act of engagement to an opinion held?" Wilfred gave new life to the faith of many who have found the test of "believing" certain things had sent them straight to what Bishop Spong called the "church alumni association."

Faith and Belief and *Belief and History* are both landmark books in the history of the study of religion. So, too, is his final such book, *What Is Scripture?* It is a collaborative study that emerged from Harvard colloquia, NEH seminars, and years of his own research. What is the meaning of this term *scripture*, a term appropriated so often unreflectively in a wide range of fields and traditions? Looking at the texts described as scripture—Torah, Bible, Qur'an, Shruti, Veda—he proposes that the category of "scripture" describes not a book or text alone, but the relation of a community to that text, in some cases to a whole library of texts.

Scripture, as he argues, is not a book, but a way of holding a book. It is the dynamic involvement of a community that makes its scripture. It is a relational concept, not an a priori attribute of any particular text. It is, like many terms within our purview, a verb, not a noun.

Theological Thinking

Going back to that opening convocation address, we see Smith's vision for the most rigorous of academic enterprises—the deep-drilling investigation of religious communities and the human engagement, the faith, that gives them vital power. Students who study neurons and galaxies could find no greater challenge than this.

But there was another message in that same convocation address: the theological and moral challenge of religious studies in the world in which we live and the specific role of Harvard Divinity School in the enterprise of theological thinking. Understanding our human religious diversity—both the ways in which we are different and the ways in which we are deeply alike—was and is a great intellectual challenge. But Wilfred made clear that this is also a great moral challenge. Indeed, it is the greatest challenge we face: "Today (our religious traditions and civilizations) not only meet, but interpenetrate; they meet not only each other, but jointly meet joint problems, and must jointly try to solve them. They must collaborate. Perhaps the single most important challenge that humankind faces in our day is the need to turn our nascent world society into a world community."[8]

He challenged those of us who, like himself, are Christians, to recognize not only the intellectual difficulties, but also the moral consequences of exclusivist and arrogant theological ideas, and to participate in shaping the ongoing history of Christianity in ways that explicitly recognize the theological brilliance of, for instance, an Al-Ghazzali or a Ramanuja. "From now on," he said, "theological discussion must be explicitly of that kind of God who over the centuries has been in relation to the lives of individual persons religiously involved in the varying particular ways our modern knowledge reveals. I do not know how theologians will deal with the questions that our new awareness of mankind's religious diversity poses. I do know, however, that these questions will now be among those with which in one way or another they must deal."[9] Now, some fifty years later, there has been a virtual avalanche of writing and thinking on Christian theological thinking in relation to other worlds of faith, thought, and practice. And we know today that

Jewish, Muslim, Hindu, Sikh, and Buddhist thinkers are also engaged in constructive thinking that takes seriously the global context, the insight, and the vision distinctive to each religious tradition. Thinkers in the realm of philosophy and ethics, such as the Dalai Lama in the Buddhist tradition, Tariq Ramadan in Islam, and Rabbi Jonathan Sacks in the Jewish tradition are taking up the challenge of foundational thinking on their own tradition in the light of others.

Wilfred Cantwell Smith was something of a pioneer in this work, as a Christian who took the global context seriously. Theologian Langdon Gilkey wrote an overview of Smith's theological voyage and described it this way: "He sails his own sort of course into the unknown. As a result, he is disputed and even scorned by those who prefer to ply the more familiar shores, namely not a few theologians and especially the more cautious students of religion who, hovering over their safe but limited secular charts, stay well within our still undisturbed coastal waters."[10]

In and Out of Harvard

Wilfred was invited to Harvard twice and left Harvard twice. He came to Harvard Divinity School as a professor in 1964 and as director of the Center for the Study of World Religions. Wilfred and Muriel lived in the director's apartment, and the Wednesday-evening colloquia in the Common Room were attended, I should say "religiously," by graduate students and faculty affiliated with the comparative study of religion. He was one of the few historians of religion on the Harvard faculty, and his signature course, Humanities 11, was a year-long offering taken by over a hundred students, both from Harvard College and Harvard Divinity School.

In 1973, he left the Center in the capable hands of John B. Carman and returned to Canada, to Dalhousie University in Halifax, to undertake the writing that had long been postponed—*Faith and Belief*, *Belief and History*. There was a fine festival in the Center courtyard in the spring of 1973 to see him off. In 1978, however, Wilfred and Muriel returned to Cambridge, when Wilfred became chair of the newly formed Committee on the Study of Religion, located now in the Faculty of Arts and Sciences. His academic appointment was in Near Eastern Languages and Civilizations, and by this time the Study of Religion had a Faculty of Arts and Sciences home on Massachusetts Avenue near the law school. Under the new academic unit, the Study of Religion for the first time included both an undergraduate and doctoral component. For the next six years, I had the great privilege of serving with Wilfred as a junior colleague and participating in the creation of the new undergraduate concentration in the Comparative Study of Religion.

After he retired for the second time, Wilfred and Muriel moved back to their native Toronto. There, he remained true to his understanding that our own religious history is dynamic, always changing, and that our faith is new each morning. Both he and Muriel took a keen interest in bringing a new vision of justice to the church in general and the United Church of Canada specifically. By this time, they were fully aware that Dorothy and I had long been a committed couple and that families everywhere included gays and lesbians. In their eighties, they became articulate advocates for the full inclusion of gays and lesbians in the whole life of the church, including the ministry. And one more thing: Wilfred, who had long contended that "mankind" meant all of us, began to recognize that the term "man" meant men and women—except, of course, when it did not. He enrolled the help of his granddaughter Ursula in rewriting his book, *The Faith of Other Men*, in inclusive and, now, more accurate language. When I last spoke with him several weeks before his death, I told him what a wonderful job she had done, that the new book, now titled *Patterns of Faith Around the World*, was superb, that I was using it in the introductory week of my course on religious diversity. He was pleased and wondered if more of his writings should be reworked in this way.

On March 10, 1988, Wilfred returned to Harvard for the Ingersoll Lecture, which he gave on the subject of transcendence. It was his last major lecture here. Wilfred said, "I am not at all afraid of dying, which I shall be doing one of these days—as will all of you, just as surely although perhaps not so soon as I. Moreover, I never have been afraid of death—my own death—since the age of seven-and-a-half; though it was a decade or so after that before I moved well beyond the *idea* of life-after-death."[11]

Far more interesting than life after death, he said, was the notion of eternal life. "I am rather fond of it," he said, but not so much as "a continuation in linear sequence" of the life we now know, but rather "eternal life is with us every moment, at right angles to life on earth." He went on, "I find that illuminating, recognizing that eternity intersects our immediate existence and we live from day to day in an added dimension." This is the notion of transcendence that he explored in that Ingersoll lecture: a dimension of experience "not to be comprehended though it is to be apprehended."[12]

At Work on the Page

Working with Wilfred as a student was not only the intense colloquy of scholars and the visioning of a new world society. There were scholarly disciplines to be learned, every one of which he undertook with care. Every footnote—and there were many of them—had to be precise. The first seminar paper I wrote for him was on the uses of the term *shraddha* in the Bhagavad-Gita. When he returned it, I discovered that he had taken the time to check each of my footnotes to be certain that the citations were correct. I was both astonished at this level of mentorship, and felt honored by his care. In Wilfred's own writing, he nuanced words, phrases, and ideas in long, often too long, sentences, punctuated with precision. For example, in writing about the "humane sciences" and objecting to the very divisions of subjects into the humanities, social sciences, and life sciences, he offered the following paragraph-long sentence: "The phrasing 'humane sciences' is apt insofar as it may suggest a superseding of that dichotomizing within the study of human affairs, and may suggest also a certain continuity (but emphatically not sameness) between our study of the objective world of nature, in the 'sciences' and the study of those human affairs; between, that is, our study of the external world of things, and our study of ourselves."[13] In all this, he somehow found time to write a multitude of memos. Tucked inside my well-worn copy of *Webster's New World Dictionary* is a paper from 1972, a purple mimeographed memo entitled "That and Which." It begins, "English reads more smoothly, and more forcefully, if one observes the classical discrimination between the uses of 'that' and 'which' as relative pronouns. My standard illustration is the following pair of sentences, which communicate (or should communicate) quite different meanings:

> Enter the house, turn left, and open the first door that is red.
>
> Enter the house, turn left, and open the first door, which is red."

As his junior colleague in the new Study of Religion program at Harvard, I again had a chance to witness his scrupulous attention to detail. Then, in the days before Post-its, he would type little two-by-four-inch chits to his office assistants and to me, chits that displayed, in minute form, the character of a man whose mind and heart were as wide as world, and whose attention was as careful as the punctuation mark. I collected them all, and perhaps embarrassed him too much at his retirement dinner, his second farewell party, by reading a few. This pink one to Mr. Anastasi, his assistant:

The envelope that I took to-day to Prof. Stendahl was addressed, I notice, "K. Stendahl." I did nothing to modify this, but it does move me to remark that it is a form that participates in a phrase of cultural development more recent than is representative of me. For my generation, the use of titles of one sort or another (Mr., Mrs., Miss, Dr., Professor, the Rev. Mr., or whatever) was standard, and the omission of any discourteous. That is no longer true for most (younger) people, but the discourtesy persists for older ones. If you think of it, which you may not manage all the time, I realize, I should feel that anything going out over my name including some title would be more sincere. Is this ridiculous, do you feel? Perhaps it is becoming so. WCS Feb. 10, 1983.

And he typed out this green chit to me after his farewell in 1984:

Diana: Wishing to re-iterate, and with renewed emphasis, my gratitude and delight and appreciation and emotion and all for last night, I have decided that rather than speaking to you, as first I thought, I clearly must rather send you a chit! The physical size of it precludes anything remotely like the fullness that ought to be evinced; but that is minor compared to my incapacity to do that anyway. So: why not admit inadequacy and say a simple, "thanks." WCS May 23, 1984.

Let me close with a Vedic hymn Jaravalal Mehta cast in his own words as part of his contribution to a festschrift for Wilfred Cantwell Smith: "Let the sacred threads that bind us to divinity not be broken. Let the sacred threads by which we weave the colored web of our song remain intact. May we not lose track of the paths that run between the gods and men, nor fail in our hospitality to the Immortal that has come as a guest in the mortal's house. May we not lose sight of the trace left by the bird in flight."

Notes

1. Wilfred Cantwell Smith, "Mankind's Religiously Divided History Approaches Self-Consciousness," first published in the *Harvard Divinity Bulletin*, October 1964, p. 1. Subsequently abridged and included in Willard B. Oxtoby, ed., *Religious Diversity: Essays by Wilfred Cantwell Smith* (New York: Crossroads Publishing Company, 1976).

2. Wilfred Cantwell Smith, *The Faith of Other Men* (New York: New American Library, 1965), p. 92. Republished as *Patterns of Faith Around the World* (Oxford, UK: One World Publications, 1998).

3. Smith, "Mankind's Religiously Divided History," p. 3.

4. Wilfred Cantwell Smith, "Comparative Religion: Whither—and Why?" in *Religious Diversity* (New York: Crossroads Publishing Company, 1976), p. 149.

5. Ibid.

6. J. L. Mehta, "My Years at the Center," in *Philosophy and Religion: Essays in Interpretation* (New Delhi: Munshiram Manoharlal, 1990), p. 73.

7. Byron Good, "Medical Anthropology and the Problem of Belief," in *Medicine, Rationality, and Experience: An Anthropological Perspective* (Cambridge, UK: Cambridge University Press, 1994), pp. 1–24.

8. Wilfred Cantwell Smith, "The Christian in a Religiously Plural World," in *Christianity and Other Religions*, eds. John Hick and B. Hebblethwaite (Philadelphia: Fortress Press, 1980), pp. 94–95.

9. Wilfred Cantwell Smith, "Mankind's Religiously Divided History," pp. 14–15.

10. Langdon Gilkey, "A Theological Voyage with Wilfred Cantwell Smith," *Religious Studies Review* 7/4 (1981), pp. 298–310.

11. Wilfred Cantwell Smith, "Transcendence: The Ingersoll Lecture," *Harvard Divinity Bulletin* (Fall 1988), p. 10.

12. Ibid.

13. Wilfred Cantwell Smith, "Objectivity and the Humane Sciences: A New Proposal," in *Modern Culture from a Comparative Perspective*, eds. Wilfred Cantwell Smith and John W. Burbridge (Albany: State University of New York Press, 1997), p. 121.

Bibliography

Gilkey, Langdon. "A Theological Voyage with Wilfred Cantwell Smith." *Religious Studies Review* 7/4 (1981): pp. 298–310.

Good, Byron. *Medicine, Rationality, and Experience: An Anthropological Perspective*. Cambridge, UK: Cambridge University Press, 1994.

Mehta, J. L. *Philosophy and Religion: Essays in Interpretation*. New Delhi: Munshiram Manoharlal, 1990.

Smith, Wilfred Cantwell. "Mankind's Religiously Divided History Approaches Self-Consciousness." In *Religious Diversity: Essays by Wilfred Cantwell Smith*, edited by Willard B. Oxtoby: 96–114. New York: Crossroads Publishing Company, 1976. Originally published in *Harvard Divinity Bulletin*, October 1964.

———. *The Faith of Other Men*. New York: New American Library, 1965. Republished as *Patterns of Faith Around the World*. Oxford UK: One World Publications, 1998.

———. "Comparative Religion: Whither—and Why?" In *Religious Diversity Essays by Wilfred Cantwell Smith*, edited by Willard B. Oxtoby: 138–57. New York: Crossroads Publishing Company, 1976.

———. "The Christian in a Religiously Plural World." In *Christianity and Other Religions*. eds. John Hick and B. Hebblethwaite: 87–107. Philadelphia: Fortress Press, 1980.

———. "Transcendence: The Ingersoll Lecture." *Harvard Divinity Bulletin* (Fall 1988): pp. 10–15.

———. "Objectivity and the Humane Sciences: A New Proposal." In *Modern Culture from a Comparative Perspective*, edited by Wilfred Cantwell Smith and John W. Burbridge: 121–46. Albany: State University of New York Press, 1997.

Wilfred Cantwell Smith

Academic Architect

John B. Carman

We meet to honor Wilfred Cantwell Smith, our teacher, colleague, and friend, ten years after his death, in a symposium at which we have been asked to reflect on his legacy. I want to speak about three legacies that teacher-scholars may bequeath, both to those of their own generation and to those of many generations thereafter. Wilfred Smith has left us all three of these legacies.

First, there is the legacy inherited by one's students. Some of them may be the teacher's personal disciples. Often they are those who feel themselves shaped by a teacher who remains their example of good teaching and sound scholarship. The personal experiences that some here have already shared are only a few of many examples of Wilfred Smith's distinctive legacy to his students at McGill, Dalhousie, and Harvard, and perhaps even earlier at Forman Christian College. These students are now scattered across North America and, indeed, around the world.

Second, there is the legacy passed on to all those influenced by a scholar's writings, especially writings informed by perceptive description and rigorous analysis, and inspired by a vision of the field as a whole. Wilfred Smith was that kind of scholar. He has had many disciples among those who were not his direct students and who never met him. Even those who disagree with some of his views have to reckon with him as a formidable intellect and certainly one of the great scholars in the comparative study of religion.

Bequeathing the first legacy is rare enough. Reaching readers with the second legacy is even more difficult. Wilfred Smith did both. He also, moreover, left us with a third legacy. It is on this that I want to focus, especially since most of the contributors will be concentrating on one of the first two legacies. This third legacy is the creation, revision, and maintenance of academic institutions. Only a few teacher-scholars in any generation have started or changed even one academic program. Wilfred Smith established the Institute of Islamic Studies here at McGill and started a Department of Religious Studies at Dalhousie. During his first nine years at Harvard (1964–1973), he greatly expanded the doctoral program in world religions initiated by Robert Slater. A year before leaving Cambridge for Halifax, he persuaded the dean of the Harvard Faculty of Arts and Sciences to take to the Faculty a plan that would involve rescinding a twenty-year ban on religion courses for undergraduates in Harvard College. (His *Introduction to the History of Religion* was already an exception.) This was a plan for an undergraduate concentration in the comparative study of religion. When he returned to Harvard in 1978 as chair of the Committee on the Study of Religion, he led a revision of the doctoral programs that introduced a comparative ("generic") foundation for all the PhD fields in the study of religion.

These three legacies are related, but they are not identical. Many who know Wilfred Smith only from his writings have no idea as to what courses he taught or on what committees he served, and they certainly do not know the requirements of the programs he supervised. On the other hand, many students enrolled in programs he started or revised never had the opportunity to take a course with him, and some may never have read even one of his books. Even so, their education has been influenced and perhaps decisively shaped by his innovations.

"Architect" is my metaphor for such an institution-builder. My choice may have been influenced by his son Julian being a professional architect. Wilfred Smith's predecessor as director of the Harvard Center for the Study of World Religions, Robert Slater, was closer to being a "builder" in the literal sense, for it was his idea to house the new program in a building that would be residential as well as academic. The name "Center" was first applied to the building, and he was much involved in the planning.[1] In any case, I like the metaphor for Wilfred Smith's efforts as an academic administrator because he, like an architect, played a variety of roles. At times he had to lay out the grand design. At other times he was like a hands-on supervisor of construction. He also was a consultant for those engaged in other academic building projects, both near at hand and far away. Not only did he fashion a detailed argument to convince an initially skeptical Harvard dean and faculty, but he also spent much time during the year before he left for Dalhousie in planning with the colleagues who had to turn his "blueprint" into the functioning reality of a new religion major. When he returned to Harvard five years later, he became responsible for this new program, but he gave much of his time and attention to introducing a comparative perspective into the doctoral programs. He spent endless hours over the next two years with the whole committee and its subcommittees on this revision, working with colleagues in a variety of departments in Arts and Sciences and the Divinity School.

Architects must often adapt their plans to fit the site and the materials available, are certainly limited by the budget, and often must follow the wishes of their patrons. Wilfred Smith was able and willing to negotiate, to make compromises on his ideal plan to accomplish as much as possible. While firmly convinced of his own vision, he expected his colleagues to agree only on what he considered the essentials, and even here he did not always succeed.

Robert Slater, a former colleague at McGill, urged Wilfred Smith to accept Harvard's invitation to become the second director of the Center. Wilfred and Muriel Smith, along with their five children, came from Montreal and made the Center their home, living there with doctoral students, visiting scholars, and visiting professors. The Smiths presided over an international academic community that gradually increased in numbers beyond the available apartments, because so many students wanted to study under Wilfred Smith's leadership. His vision for the Center was expressed in various talks he gave, in many letters responding to inquiries, and in his distinctive memoranda. Two years after coming to Harvard, he spelled out his vision at some length in a memorandum from which I take the following:

> [O]ne of the new intellectual ventures of our day . . . is the aspiration to understand human religiousness. . . . In the past, religious understanding . . . was for long sought only for one's own tradition, normatively. More recently, particular instances of other men's beliefs and practices . . . have been studied, descriptively, though often separately. . . . The new task currently being taken up within the academic enterprise is that of endeavouring to find the relationships among the various particulars . . . and of striving towards an intellectual

> understanding of human religiousness as a whole. As one contribution to the pursuit of such a goal, the Harvard Center for the Study of World Religions has recently been established. This university has long contributed strikingly . . . to illuminating this or that part of the total complex. . . . The task is . . . long-range. It will be the collaborative work of many universities. . . . As the name suggests, the Center gives attention to the chief traditions of Asia—Hindu, Buddhist, Muslim, etc. and to the Christian and Jewish in relation to these.[2]

Here we see the new intellectual challenges both related to and distinguished from past and present methods of studying religion, but also pointing to university resources that could be coordinated in new ways. A subsequent paragraph treats teaching as a departmental responsibility, while a center for study encourages and coordinates the teaching its students need in various departments, but he also notes postdoctoral seminars that will eventually lead to undergraduate courses. Nothing is said about the informal dialogue among neighbors living together in a center that is also a residence. Social science approaches to religious studies are recognized but not emphasized, perhaps because they do not fit into an inquiry into all ways of being religious that claims to privilege the multiple norms of the participants above an objective study from outside. In any case, many of the brief statements in this memorandum anticipate developments at Harvard and elsewhere in the years after it was written.

While there was an administrative dimension to each new development, the more important fact was the start of new patterns of cooperation among faculty and students who formerly thought of ourselves as working in quite distinct fields and now are finding new ways of thinking about what we were already doing. The Center's residential community, while not mentioned explicitly in this memorandum, perhaps provided a model for new forms of interdepartmental cooperation. It is also possible that earlier changes in academic and personal relations at the Islamic Institute anticipated both the theoretical and practical steps taken by Wilfred Smith at Harvard, some of them many years after he left McGill. In a memorandum like this one, and indeed in much of his writing, the theoretical statements seem quite abstract, but he insisted that the study of religion is the study of persons. For him it was also a study *by* persons, and these persons accomplish a great deal more if they work together across all kinds of imagined divides. He wanted to build the institutional bridges to make such cooperation possible, indeed, more than possible, mutually desirable.

Sometimes an architect submits a design for a project far away, as did the many architects who competed for the opportunity to design the Sydney Opera House. Wilfred Smith was asked for advice on new academic projects in many universities around the world, and in many cases he had no control over how his advice was carried out. The one project in which I, too, was involved started with a letter from India. He was invited to present his views to a high-level commission appointed by the Indian government, under the leadership of Dr. Kothari, to propose revisions for the entire educational system of India, at all levels. In August 1965, Wilfred Smith went to India and met with the commission. Instead of multiplying the number of departments of religion by appointing one professor at each university, he proposed establishing strong departments of comparative religion at a few universities, in which different staff members would specialize in different religious traditions and would also collaborate on seminars comparing different aspects of these traditions and the faith of their adherents. He also proposed that Indian universities should recognize the process of secularization in modern India as itself a subject worthy of study.

Somewhat to his surprise, the Education Commission and the University Grants Commission said that they were accepting his recommendations in principle and would try to implement them. A few months later Wilfred Smith arranged for me to go to India for three years to see what was happening and to give whatever assistance I could. He arranged for me to meet Dr. Kothari as soon as my family and I reached New Delhi. Within a few months I learned that while there were many new departments named "Comparative Religion," at only one place, the Punjabi University in Patiala, was much of the full proposal being put into effect. The Danforth Foundation was prepared to help fund a new program there and at two other universities in India, but the government never approved the transfer of funds.

However, through its representative J. Edward Dirks, the Danforth Foundation did finance a consultation in Bangalore in September 1967, the "Study of Religion in Indian Universities." Most of the scholars invited did come, and they presented a number of informative papers on the present state of scholarship on the various Indian religious traditions. Some sharp differences came to light, especially as to the main purpose of religious studies in Indian universities. Many Hindu philosophers wanted to emphasize the unity of Indian religions, while scholars studying the minority religious traditions wanted the distinctiveness of each religious community to be recognized. Would any approach that was not dominated by a single point of view (usually some version of modern Vedantic philosophy) be able to accomplish the commission's aim of inculcating "moral and spiritual values" in millions of Indian students? By the time that he came to India for this meeting, two years after making his proposal, Wilfred Smith was very doubtful that the essential ingredients in his plan for strong and multifaceted departments of comparative religion would actually be present in the new departments, except perhaps in two or three universities. He was quite forthright about this in his concluding address at the Bangalore consultation, from which I quote the following excerpts:

> One of the reasons why religion . . . departments are springing up with such power in Western . . . universities at the present time is . . . that at a very deep level indeed the Western world is today asking itself a question as to what religion really is. . . . And it is not only asking itself the question, but is in a sense beginning to be haunted by it. . . . Now it is my impression that India is asking itself no such question. Hindu society is on the whole sure that it knows what religion is (am I wrong on this?). Muslim society here is on the whole too frightened to be interested in other men's faith; and too bewildered to ask systematic questions about its own. . . . A society that is not asking itself such a question does not have the urge to institute departments of religion. My guess is that a desire to perpetuate traditional values is not in itself an adequate basis for such study. A University is not that kind of a place. One might get a true inquiry if there were an honest questioning as to what has gone wrong with values in society; but again it is my impression that those who wish to perpetuate values have not deeply realized that we do not really know how to do it.[3]

Along with the trenchant analysis you may sense in these remarks more than a little disappointment. What if half a dozen Indian universities had not only appointed scholars in the many religious traditions of Asia but had also succeeded in conducting truly comparative seminars? We had assembled at that Bangalore meeting a range of able scholars who could have staffed a few such departments, but Indian society, acting through the scholarly advisory committees of the Indian government, did not have the will to carry out this foreign architect's design.

At the personal level, Wilfred Smith's disappointment was mitigated by many valuable acquaintanceships he renewed or made for the first time. He was most impressed by the paper presented by Dr. J. L. Mehta, a professor of philosophy at Banaras Hindu University, who, with the help of the philosophies of Gadamer and Heidegger, analyzed both appreciatively and critically the very different Indian and Western assumptions about "understanding" itself.[4] Dr. Mehta soon after that came to the Harvard Center as a visiting professor and then during the 1970s returned for five years for a postretirement appointment.

From this whole series of events I learned much about Wilfred Smith's daring vision in planning large-scale projects, but also about his patience in dealing with disappointment. Certainly academic departments and programs are subject to frequent changes, and that may be hard to accept if one has invested much thought and energy in starting, revising, or renewing an academic institution.

The actual architect of the Harvard Center building was Jose Luis Sert, dean of the Harvard School of Design, who lived in the neighboring house behind the Center. He was so possessive about his creation that he did not want even the cushion covers in the student apartments or the color of their front doors changed without his consent. Wilfred Smith and I had to experience far greater changes both in the Center building and in its academic programs after we were no longer directing its affairs. He was a realist about the impermanence of academic institutions, but he also could dream great dreams.

There is a personal reason why I have focused on Wilfred Smith's third legacy. It was in his role as an academic architect that I observed him from close by, and it was in this dimension of his academic presence that we worked very happily together. Our first meeting was in New Haven in the spring of 1963, perhaps for only half an hour. I had just returned from India and was about to join the Harvard Center and the Divinity School for three years as an assistant professor. He had just left McGill and was about to leave for a sabbatical year in India, before coming back to become the Center's second director. I knew of his reputation as an innovative scholar, and I had recently read his new book, *The Meaning and End of Religion*, with whose argument I found myself in disagreement.[5] The book didn't come up in this first conversation. Instead, I listened to his vision for the Center he was soon to head.

(I wish I could now remember just what he said.) I listened and was quickly convinced that he was a leader I could follow. He articulated a vision of comparative studies that I shared, and I sensed his remarkable combination of conviction, compassion, and humility. Later Wilfred and Muriel, and my wife Ineke and I became good friends, as well as joint participants in an effort, only partially successful, to build and maintain an international academic community involving personal dialogue.

I should mention the strong sense of moral responsibility with which Wilfred Smith lived out all the dimensions of his vocation. He felt responsible to his students and colleagues, to the world community that he envisaged, and to God. There was, finally, his gift of friendship. One of the Indian Muslim scholars to whom he introduced me was Dr. Hasan Askari, who was then at Osmania University in Hyderabad. I was telling him of my surprise that Wilfred Smith could be so openly critical about Islamic society in India and Pakistan, much more critical than I could be in writing about Hindu society. I shall never forget Dr. Askari's response: "Ah, but you see—Professor Smith, we love him!"

Notes

1. Peter Slater has aptly contrasted his father's view with that of Wilfred Smith: "To Slater the Anglican, the Center was a building enabling people to meet informally. As such, it was intrinsic to the program. . . . To Smith, the Presbyterian/United Churchman, 'centers' were people in colloquy, not bricks and mortar. But without the building, there would have been much less opportunity for the kinds of encounters sought for by the original benefactors and valued by those who lived there." This is quoted from the manuscript draft, "Dialogical Imagination and the Study of Religion," chapter 2, p. 9, in John B. Carman and Kathryn Dodgson, *Community and Colloquy: The Center for the Study of World Religions 1958–2003* (Cambridge, MA: Center for the Study of World Religions, Harvard Divinity School), p. 31.

2. Excerpt from "Memorandum on the Center for the Study of World Religions, September 1966," quoted in Carman and Dodgson, *Community and Colloquy*, p. 41. The understanding of the scope of "World Religions" in the last sentence quoted evoked protests from African American and African students at Harvard Divinity School. I have described the controversy over "leaving out Africa" in *Community and Colloquy*, pp. 32 and 39.

3. Wilfred Cantwell Smith, "University Studies of Religion in a Global Context," published in *Study of Religion in Indian Universities: A Report of the Consultation held in Bangalore in September, 1967* (Bangalore Press, n.d.), pp. 81–82.

4. J. L. Mehta, "Problems of Inter-Cultural Understanding in University Studies of Religion," published in the same *Report*, pp. 33–48.

5. Wilfred Smith's interpretation of how the concepts of "religion" and "faith" developed in Western culture forced me to clarify my own views. I presented my response many years later at a conference in which we both took part at Washington and Lee University, "Religion as a Problem for Christian Theology," in *Christian Faith in a Religiously Plural World*, eds. Donald G. Dawe and John B. Carman (Maryknoll: Orbis Books, 1978), pp. 83–103.

Bibliography

Carman, John. "Memorandum on the Center for the Study of World Religions, September 1966." In *Community and Colloquy: The Center for the Study of World Religions 1958–2003*, edited by John Carman and Kathryn Dodgson. Cambridge, MA: Center for the Study of World Religions, Harvard Divinity School, 2006.

———. "Religion as a Problem for Christian Theology." In *Christian Faith in a Religiously Plural World*, edited by Donald G. Dawe and John B. Carman. Maryknoll: Orbis Books, 1978.

Mehta, J. L. "Problems of Inter-Cultural Understanding in University Studies of Religion." In *Study of Religion in Indian Universities: A Report of the Consultation held in Bangalore in September, 1967*. Bangalore Press, n.d.

Smith, Wilfred Cantwell. "University Studies of Religion in a Global Context." In *Study of Religion in Indian Universities: A Report of the Consultation Held in Bangalore in September, 1967*. Bangalore Press, n.d.

The Meaningful "End" of God, Faith, and Scripture

Purushottama Bilimoria

In this short tribute I shall take up four aporias and the ensuing attempted reformulations that the late and much-celebrated Professor Wilfred Cantwell Smith had to offer not only to the discipline of the study of religions, but more specifically to the history and philosophy of religion, in the cross-cultural context. From my experience as an editor-in-chief of *Sophia*,[1] I have learned a lot more than I did from my own narrower training about the sorts of issues Professor Smith was tackling, and how the legacy he bequeathed to the intellectual (albeit academically circumscribed) world has made a marked difference to the study of world cultures and *lebenswelt*. The episthematics or aporias that I focus on are:

1. The problem of God and transcendence
2. Faith over belief
3. Scripture and meaning
4. Ritual and text

The Problem of God and Transcendence

Smith was challenged—as were a whole host of scholars coming out of the history of religions movement, whether in Europe or Chicago or Sydney—by the view that all religions across the world do not share even a remote conception of divinity that veers toward a monotheistic concept of God, such as we see doctrinally entrenched in the Abrahamic traditions with their roots in the Semitic episteme (or perhaps in the earlier Zoroastrian challenge to pagan polytheism of the ancient era). In the 1983 presidential address to the American Academy of Religion (and if only I could recall the hand gestures accompanying the fiery words that I inscribed in my notebook as I audited the lecture!), Smith was almost suggesting that it was blasphemous to limit the *transcendence* experienced by peoples of other cultures to the narrower belief in the monolithic arithmetic of God (*Gott*) or even Deity (in the theistic and deistic or fideist senses).

This is what he had to say: "That transcendence, if it is even recognised as a reality people live in, is reduced to beliefs within their minds. The notion that religions are things that certain people believe, that believing has been what religious people primarily do, is a vastly devastating one, serving secularist coherence and self-confidence. To believe in God—to believe that God exists—is a somewhat blasphemous attitude to the Deity, although it has taken me a long time to see this, an arduous wrestling with Asian data to recognise what was happening to us here."[2]

Even the intellectual grasping of that anomie of transcendence is not sufficiently robust for Smith, because the hermeneutic of the passage misses some of the simple intricacies and paradoxes about what Smith still liked to call the Deity, by which he meant transcendental reality, the Mystery. Consider, for instance, the so-called "primitive races"—mired in what Zaehner dubbed as "praeternatural religions"—who were not yet, at least in the fashion of the Kantian-Hegelian prejudice of the "raw man," sufficiently "cooked" or "stewed" to exude certain "rational capacities." Under the Enlightenment theory, these people would barely merit the honor of being "belief-holders" of any description, for they have barely gone beyond their quaint conception of nature as anything other than an awe-filled plenum suffused with spirits, ancestors, ghosts, monsters, crawly creatures in the nether regions, etc. We know that the aboriginal people in many nations were largely classified by early anthropologists of religion as fitting this category, and their strong spiritual identity with the land reinforced this categorization. But today these very people have refused to be inducted into the theocentric doxastic paradigms of theology in the name of the exported Queen, Country, and God of the Church. Then there are the people connected to but severed from the Indo-Aryan Ur-volk (ancestors of present-day Europeans in large measure), the Indo-Iranians who may be perceived by the same paradigm to have moved a little closer in their monistic (All-is-One) universalism, but still fall short of the pristine, pure, and wholly sanctimonious Other, that did not fray into the voluptuous vulgarities, libidinally erotic, perversely perfidious, and at the same time stoically monastic profundities of the Brāhmanic Tāntra-Vedānta traditions.[3]

Now such considerations inexorably weighed heavily on the thinking of Smith, and so he was—though by no means alone in this pursuit—prepared to dispense with the fanciful language that had for so long and almost unself-consciously come to dominate the discourses in theology, natural philosophy, and incipiently also the study of religions even as it struggled to gain recognition as a legitimate discipline within the academic realm of arts and social sciences. Philosophy of religion continues to be obsessed with the question of the existence of God—alongside the apologetic strains of the problem of evil and theodicy. The many conceptions of *transcendence* that abound in the academic study of cultures and their spiritual pathways surreptitiously hide their primary reference, if not preference, toward a monotheistic conception of divinity, even when there are noble gestures toward an inclusiveness that one nowadays notices with some deeper appreciation in the nondualistic and particularistic conceptions (think of Mādhyamika, Daoism, not to mention postmodernist and feminist critiques of theology).[4] Smith, as I read him, is not entirely clear on his own agenda—if he had one, other than remaining committed in his personal life to a much modified Christian theology, without perhaps a definite ontology or grand metaphysics informing his faith—as was characteristic of scholars of *religionswissenschaft* only a generation or two earlier. The latter ameliorating factor aside, the point is that he appeared to be willing to completely eschew, that is, to rescind, what he saw as the intellectual virtues of a monotheistic conception, which for him incorporated a hankering for truth, justice, love, beauty, and freedom. In his argumentation, however, Smith did not notice how such virtues were also anchored—for the question is, where is the anchor here?—in the numerally (not numerically) diverse deities, the gods, goddesses, benign and wrathful beings, ghosts and spirit hosts, in, say, the Vedic or for that matter the animistic traditions (consider Bangladeshi Bauls, Indonesian Sufism, or Balinese Hinduism). This is how a tradition finds sustainable meaning in the face of the challenges of existence (and the coextensive threat of nonexistence within the womb as it were of existence itself, the *sat/asat* dialetheism) and brings order and coherence to the disharmony, disease, and entropic chaos all around.

Faith over Belief

Through an etymological study of "religion" (*religio*, in Latin), Smith contends that the term, which at first and during most centuries denoted an attitude toward a relationship between God and "man,"[5] has through conceptual slippage come to mean a "system of observances or beliefs,"[6] a historical tradition that has been institutionalized through a process of reification. Whereas *religio* denoted personal piety, "religion" refers to an abstract entity (or transcendental signifier) that Smith claims does not exist. Smith argues that the term, as *vera religio* found in Lucretius and Cicero, was internalized by the Catholic Church through Lactantius and Augustine to mean "true religion," not "the true religion," and as such equated with piety and justice or the personal moral-spiritual journey over and above abstract, doctrinal pursuits. During the Middle Ages, *religio* or *vera religio* were superseded by the term "faith," which by contrast Smith favors. In the Renaissance, via the Christian Platonist Marsilio Ficino, "*religio*" becomes popular again, retaining its original emphasis on personal practice even in John Calvin's *Christianae Religionis Institutio* (1536).[7]

In his comprehensive study of Smith's theological patterning, Grunschloss avers that Smith does not offer a convincing philological or historical proof for his thesis that "faith" is the common core of all religions, and that Smith cannot "prove" the fundamental difference between faith and belief.[8] Nevertheless, Smith finds the term "faith" to be often more useful than the reified term "religion" and the naturalistically biased trope of "belief," because for Smith faith, which is a key episteme of theology (perhaps after Calvin and Luther) describes more accurately a person's objective as well as subjective poles of spirituality; for example, a Chinese person might venerate his dead ancestors, or a Buddhist might be more concerned about karma as fate than the wrath of the deities who are consequently used as symbols and imageries within meditative visualization practices but are not accountably objects of any such belief descriptive of the contents of the response. A "belief," with its naturalistic bias, has a certain propositional structure and lends itself to cognitive and rational affirmation or disaffirmation, and is open to semantic and syntactical scrutiny as well as doubt; or it may remain neutral as to its correctness.[9] Faith has none of these properties, or those requiring its "work" or function to be judged by the same parameters and naturalistic criteria that apply to belief.[10] Consider Gettier's strict requirement of epistemological and logical strictures of justified true belief: a belief is nothing if it cannot be justified with empirical observations and collaborative evidence; even then, it might fail because the supposed conclusion—the belief—might be derived equally naturally from two counterfactually conflicting premises;[11] it doesn't matter in analytical dissection whether the whole holds together against the grain of the dissipating and fragmentary parts (and the fragmentation under the ruse of deconstruction or "tearing" is taken to its logical conclusion in postmodernism[12]). Such an outcome would have the inwardly felt truths of religion subjected to the rigors and limitations of logic that might never allow the subjective, phenomenological dimension of religion to emerge and survive. The outcome at best would be an unrequited scepticism, a provisional or probationary acceptance of the truth of a belief-state that might in the very next moment stand falsified. Is it worth taking such a risk? A way out of this principle of uncertainty-rendering is to switch the epistemology and paradigm references that do not grind down such "heavy-duty" epistemological requirements; Smith has argued that while objective empirical evidence and corroboration are necessary for meaningfulness of a religious statement, it is not sufficient unless there is confirmation also by the subjective testimony of the insider or member of the respective faith.[13] An integral part of faith, Smith asserts, is a personal response to that proposition or experience. Faith implies engagement, interaction, while belief involves only an intellectual assertion that something may be true and correct.[14]

A true intellectual in Smith's *weltanschauung* is one for whom the intellect is that by which everything is unified, whereby the parts are made coherently to fit together into a whole, as in a jigsaw puzzle. Here is the passage where Smith says that a true intellectual is more likely to be an honest henotheist veering toward monotheism than to be a part-time pseudotheistic wanderer, much less a polyglotytheist:

> Such persons [i.e., intellectuals] at their best are monotheist: for them truth, justice, beauty, and love—including, if they are also Christians, the redemptive love of a man on a cross—are ultimately one; these do not constitute a congeries of disconnected values. Also, human integrity itself is finally one also with these other virtues, which appear separate only from a distance. Such persons are not henotheist: not the kind of intellectual who worships truth alone among the several virtues, and thinks of the intellect as one aspect only of life, coordinate[d] somehow with (or disparate from) various

others. Rather, for the true intellectual the intellect is that by which the personality is unified, the parts are made coherent. Nor are they polytheist, pursuing truth during the week, but God on Sunday; or pursuing the intellect and its tasks from 9 to 5, but pursuing love and community at home, and joy on the week-ends.[15]

But in more realistic terms, this would mean, for example, that a Hindu intellectual of the older Vedic-Brahmanical persuasion with the concomitant polytheistic and ritual overload would be deemed to be a fragmented believer. In such a scenario, faith would not jell into a coherent whole given the lure of the different, competing gods, for each of whom he is forced to engage in different performatives and enchantments. Indeed, this disposition would not warrant the name of "faith" in Smith's ontotheology. However, as Michael Myers points out, the Vedic intellectual need not be viewed as a compartmentalized polytheist in Smith's sense. Although the differentiated rituals do mark out and occupy diverse sacred spaces (visualize the Vedic yāgaśāla, the geometric template for planetary rituals to the dismembered body-parts of the cosmic Puruṣa), it is nevertheless the case that the entire cosmos is infused with a sense of divinity—almost in the panentheistic fashion. Myers touches on Smith's reservations on this score and correctly notes that the Vedic gods represent in discrete forms all that any civilization worth its salt would value: namely truth, justice, beauty, love, compassion, good health, progeny, ecological balance, food, karmic balancing, eros and its fulfilment: there is a minister-in-charge for each department of life and the elements in the vast expansive (ever-expanding) cosmos. The sharp polarity in the dualism of the natural and supernatural, sacred and profane, existence (*sat*) and non-existence (*asat*) is not recognized in the Vedas. "In the beginning there was neither being nor non-being," as the Nāsadīya sūkta in the Ṛgveda's tenth mandala puts it rhetorically.

If "faith" for Smith is the "integration of a coherent personal life with the universe around us, a universe seen as endowed with coherence and order" and a personal praxis at that, then even at the risk of a mild apologia the Vedic religious orientation ought to go through as a specimen of faith. One could go further, following G. C. Pande,[16] and defend a reading of henotheism in the Vedas that is markedly different to Smith's construct of the ideal henotheist; even so, nothing would be detracted from the foregoing argument. The deitary separatism implied in both the polytheistic and henotheistic conceptions is overridden in the

Mīmāṃsā orthopraxis wherein the deity invoked in the mantra accompanying the ritual performative is considered in fact to be effervescent māntric-effects; that is, the particular *devatā* or deity is only the name for a contingent place-marker of the intended potency to be generated in and through the sacrificial and supplicative procedure. The deity or deities that are invitingly stamped in the sacrifice with names such as Agni, Vayu, Aditi, Indra, and others, are granted pseudoexistence, a momentary *prāṇa*, breath, *Es-pirit*, in the wider imaginary of what might pick out the divinities of light—literally, *div-*, *divya*, *deva*, *devatā*, *deity*, *dues*, *dei*, *divine*—had the Mīmāṃsā any inkling toward theism of any variety and persuasion that was to grip the post-Purāṇic Hindu worldview. But they were decidedly not interested in the project of theocentric divine-jacketing of their ephemeral gods, or better stated, the māntric-effects.[17] In yet other Indic discourses the Vedic deities, uncovered in the passing, dressed and undressed, and sent onward with the smoke of the sacrificial fire, have no necessary or lasting existence beyond that critical moment; for they are already empty thrones filled with ritually produced energetics signifying—and this is most important—transpersonal truths of order, virtue, valor, compassion, forgiveness, justice, beauty, and love.

Scripture and Meaning

In his other seminal work, *What Is Scripture?*,[18] Smith called for a radically different conception of scripture—*scriptura écriture*—one that is fully grounded in the historical and comparative pathways, and one that anchors religious meaning in personal acts of relating to the divine rather than to the texts as such. He also proposed thinking of scripture as a primary mode of human language alongside prose and poetry.

The function of scripture is a bit like that of the principles in an enlightened constitution, which does not have rigid or enforceable authoritative power, but rather offers guidance to the citizens when they wish to see enhancement of a code of conduct or relationship with the community.

To that end one also marks changes in nuances in the definition of the term "scripture" or "the Heavenly Book," the presumed authoritative canons within religious traditions, to the point of rendering the use of the trope "scripture" otiose or obsolete.

Thus, for example, what would Judaism, Christianity, or Islam be if they ceased to be conceived of primarily as "Religions of the Book" (*kutub*, "Book of Books")?[19] As William Graham points out in "The

Idea of a Heavenly Book," central to these quintessential "scriptural religions" or, better, "book religions," is the idea of a celestial writ revealing to the selected, a certain divine knowledge or set of decrees, as an expression of divine omniscience, subsequently fixed as "holy writ." And the "written book" is considered a physical attribute of the divine as opposed to human knowledge.[20] Smith wishes to turn the "thick" doctrinal and dispensatory understanding of scripture as something fundamentally given—the "holy writ" that is revealed by a founder or at least foundational figureheads sanctioned and authorized to do so—into a "thin" hermeneutic of seeing scriptures essentially as a "how to . . ." set of prescriptive or injunctive and prudential (what in Sanskrit would be called *bhāvanas*) incentives, inducements, even allurements toward a particularly desirable or commended goal.

Scripture, then, is a product purely of a human activity, perhaps even a nonessential, though valuable byproduct, much like poetry written in a state of love, divine *jouissance*, or eros, according to Smith, and its meaning is given to it by the community and its seers who brought it into being and live by it. So Smith could pronounce this telling and in some ways devastating verdict: *"There is no ontology of scripture"*[21]; whether "scripture" is "a viable category is therefore a matter finally of no great moment. The concept has no metaphysical, nor logical, reference; there is nothing that scripture finally 'is' . . . at issue is not the texts of scripture that are to be understood and about which a theory is to be sought, but the dynamic human involvement with them." It is more an *adverb* than a noun pointing to "a mode of our relating to the world" (emphasis added).

We are informed that "we are heir to a shift in meaning of the term 'scripture' from its specifying something originally celestial to its characterizing various matters on this earth," and that "people make a scripture." What he means is that scripture is the depository of the cumulative tradition whose self-understanding it self-referentially and reflexively is. These and many other descriptions cannot be gainsaid. However, in time, the objective and subjective data, the past religious life of the community, their temple inscriptions, their music and dances created in celebratory moments, are transformed into theological statements, into propositional doctrines, dogmatic decrees, and doxastic beliefs, and a teleology far exceeding the letter in which they are or were initially, in their originary intentionalities, heard, inscribed or embossed. Their transmissive purpose for the next generation as the ground of transcendence is somehow lost sight of. So for Smith, scriptures come to be regarded as unique and transcendental by certain representatives of the communities, when in reality they are purely human re-constructs. He turned increasingly to the genealogy and role of scripture in the Asian traditions to deconstruct the supernaturalist underpinnings in Western (Abrahamic) conceptions of scripture, and by historicizing its actuality to reverse the established Western doctrine. Concluding the application of his personalist humanist thesis to "The Hindu Instance," Smith notes: "It is the human awareness of transcendence that makes scripture intelligible—to those involved, certainly, but also to observers attempting to understand."[22]

The upshot of the argument here is that no religion can claim uniqueness for its scripture (at least not in the externalist sense, for a "private language" inside one's head, as Wittgenstein ingeniously pointed out, is indeed solipsistically unique to that specific head and no one else has the right to challenge that pride and sense of privacy or secret rapport between the mind and its own coded messaging system, musings, poetry, and expressions of longing, desire, failure, regret, loss, and so on).[23] This kind of insight was a long time coming. Indeed, as William Graham also notes, it is the Western awareness of the Islamic idea of *kutub'al-kitab*, and the eighteenth-century popularity of the Indian Veda in particular, and the Chinese "classics" to some degree also, "that led in the Enlightenment and post-Enlightenment period to wider currency of the idea of other scriptures and books of wisdom that could claim great antiquity as well as importance in their cultures comparable to that of the Bible in the West."[24] The process however has been a slow one, and it is something Smith spent much of his life attending to.

Anecdotally, when I came to Montreal, maybe a decade ago, to pay homage to the great professor, amid the floorboards in his home that were being ripped up for possible replacement, Smith beamed with palpable animated excitement as I narrated to him my theory of authorless revelation that gave primacy to the preeminence of language—that is, "the Veda as word" over and above any personal author, *auctor*, divine or human, much less a seminal founder, that I found in the classical Mīmāṃsā doctrine of revelation-without-a-revealer (*apauruṣya-śruti*). "Signatures" are added later, and even to render it in the concrete form as "text" qua written scripture is more a supplement than an integral part of the testimonial transmission of the self-subsistent transcendental signifiers.

We talked for quite some time, and I explained that even though Sanskritic scholars, Indologists, and historians have aired doubts about the Mīmāṃsā attempts at the blank ahistoricization of the Vedas this implies—almost an amnesiac reaction, holding its sacredness and revelatory status as somehow timeless, eternal, nonnegotiable in temporal terms that served other ideological ends (power as the defined outcome)—it still warrants closer scholarly attention in the context of a comparative study of scriptures.

I went on to explain that my own heuristic reading is that much is still salvageable in the idea of "*śruti*" (Shruti) as the "heard word," the "primeval sound," "the originary meaning" that is based on a philosophical doctrine of an intimate relation between word, meaning, and knowledge. With a mischievous pun on the title of my host's most famous book, I cited an adage I have attributed to an authorless revelation in my own textual-scholarly forays and with which I began my AAR paper on Mīmāṃsā exego-hermeneutics: "In the beginning was the Word, the Word was with Meaning, the Word was Meaning."[25] He responded with the broad chuckle of a seasoned sympathetico-scholar. I continued that in my book on *śabdapramāṇna* and *śruti-prāmānya* (reissued in 2008), I have argued that there is a particular way in which Testimony (*śruti* as *śabda*: what has come to be known as "verbal testimony") is considered to be authoritative if the truth conditions satisfy the structures of warrantability and when certain standards are met, ranging from linguistic causal processes to epistemological determinacies and conformity to principles of coherence, testability for defects, and possible falsification, as well as assertability in all possible worlds.

Smith listened with great interest and responded that his own thinking had been gradually moving in that direction and that while he made some cautious and positive remarks about the approach to scripture in Hinduism (in the chapter cited), he was rather more sympathetic to what he was beginning to understand as "transpersonal revelatory texts" (from conversations that he had with the late T. R. V. Murthy and Shivaraman, both formerly based at McMaster).

Of course, I had to protest that the Mīmāṃsā position could not be collapsed with that of the Vedānta or Purāṇic and Śaiva approaches, and that there was something even more radically connected with the Mīmāṃsā scepticism if not outright denial of an unconstellated or unpopulated conception of singularity in respect to divinity (or *transcendence* even in the milder Smithian sense, as the forces that make up the universe and its order), and that the Mīmāṃsā actually argue against the existence of God (as believed elsewhere in the tradition, both philosophical or theological and popular).[26]

Yet the staunchest defenders of orthodoxy regarding the inviolability of scriptural authenticity could commit the blasphemy and heresy of rejecting what in other traditions was taken for granted: that is, the conjunction of God and scripture is an even greater blasphemy. Smith once suggested that Christians could come to believe that the Qur'an is (also?) the Word of God; well, that to a Mīmāṃsāka would seem an apologetic and rather overdetermined move: why not regard the pristine scriptures of each tradition as their version of what Heidegger in the context of language called "the House of Being," as language speaking truths, rather than truths having to depend on a speaker, even a cognitive agent or rechronicler of truth? In other words, the relation to be properly explored is that between the cumulative truth-claims and sacred-making experiences (what Smith might understand by "faith") as reflected and transmitted in the speech of the community (their *vācanas*), rather than with the ecclesiastical straightjacket of a divine founder or revealer and the word dispensed to the community. Alas, our conversation ended as the domestic noise distracted the professor's attention and I was due at my next appointment . . . But when I returned to scan the chapter on Hindu scriptures Smith referenced in our talk, I felt remiss that I had missed some of the subtler nuances in Smith's own *écriture* and his overall project of subverting the erstwhile adage "Scripture is the Word of God."[27]

Smith was clear in these passages that Hindus in India "lived in a significantly scriptural relation to their fellows and the world around them, and to their personal destiny."[28] More significantly, it is not the thesis that the "Ṛg Veda is sounding eternally and self-subsistently" that captures the truth (though he did not dismiss the philosophical merits of this imagery), but that in the thesis of the primacy of the Vedas is the recognition that the *ṛṣis*, sages, had penetrated to considerable depths certain mysteries and spiritual verities, and this "transcendental knowledge" was then placed through verbal testimony within reach of some at least, in particular forms of words. "It is an error of perception to think that a 'belief' that 'the Vedas' were (are?) of spiritual worth has been something added on to the texts."[29] And here he comes close to echoing the Heideggerian mantra of "Language as the House of Being," viz.: "Spiritual truth has been made, has made itself, audible, learnable, appropriable. It is not for traditional Hindus words—certain words—are veda, so much as that veda, lo and behold, is words. Indeed, one should write, '. . . is words!' The exclamation mark should not be left out, so spectacular has this miracle been seen to be, so venerable, so precious."[30] And we might add, "So precise."

Ritual and Text

I move to the final issue: ritual and text (which also threads the discussions so far into a singular *écriture*). In Smith's work, even though he eschews all nondehistoricized and comparative conceptions of divinity as the Transcendence common across all religions, and that too is anchored in personal relations with the universe and the order around, as a matter of praxis rather than assertion of beliefs or propositional tropes, rituals do not get as much prominence or priority. There are some, such as Robertson Smith, inspired by James Frazer, and Mary Douglas, who would argue that the origins of religions recede back to rituals as part of the inclusiveness of filial relations and family resemblances—the deities and spirits on a par with other family members—worked out in extended kinship systems.

One certainly can argue that rituals more than texts and dogmas made the Vedic tradition what it was; that the model human and religious activity in the Veda is sacrifice, enacted in ritual form: deity, material offerings, mantra, everything that is given up, in the sacrificial act. Even the gods had to be sacrificed, and *sacrifice sacrificing sacrifice* was the very first act, without which nothing would have been possible. The gods sacrificed one of the ascended gods (who would have otherwise qualified as the One God of monotheism, certainly so within the henotheistic-panentheistic framework) as Puruṣa with a thousand arms and many heads; his ritualized death assured the life of the worshipful people; most mythologies know of this self-relinquishment on the part of the community that either has very little or too much material and spiritual booty. It was their way of clinching a pact with the gods—their distant ancestors and the overseeing cosmic superintendents—to help preserve the social order homologous with the universal order (ṛta), and keep away all threats and perturbations to their quiet peace and desires of life. The much-cited adage of William Robertson Smith comes to mind here: "Religion did not exist for the saving of souls but for the preservation and welfare of society, and in all that was necessary to this end every man had to take his part, or break with the domestic and political community to which he belonged."[31]

In the Mīmāṃsā school, as I have already discussed at some length above, the gods are simply the many—what I have called *effervescent māntric-effects*—that arise with the smoke in the act of sacrifice and the offering of the oblations (when done according to exact prescriptions or injunctions) accompanied with mantras, chanting, even sincere bhakti (devotional worship) as a supplement; they vanish the moment their function has been called upon and the (desired) End/end(ing) reached. This is, in fact, for the ancient Hindus and their motley survivors, the most meaningful act possible.

Likewise for the One Supreme Transcendent Almighty, All-powerful, Omniscient Being, whether conceived within the portals of the triangular geometry of the Trinity, or as the One of Which Neither Greater Nor (for that matter) Smaller can be Conceived (as the Upaniṣads would put it). Alternatively, the God of the scriptures is to be believed in, for who else could grant such splendorous texts, and also the texts point amply to such an almighty as existing—the circularity of the logic notwithstanding). But this All-splendorous Deity himself arises and disappears as just another god or divinity or supernal energy from within the texture of the Word; for He too is the function in the work—the *event*—of the intricate co-unioning of text and ritual (as Francis X Clooney SJ has so convincingly shown us elsewhere through a close reading of the Mīmāṃsā tracts).[32] At the end/End of the sacrifice, the Transcendental Signified that is reached, or, better, achieved, through the meaning-rendering and sacred-making ritual is in fact crossed out (like so: ~~Transcendental Signified~~). It is put under the erasure (as the postmodernist would say), and is left utterly deconstructed, or negated (*dvaṃsā/abhāva bhavati*), even as the bricks of the altar and all alterity are destroyed by the community. The participants at the ritual partake of the remains of all the elements in the sacrifice—including the *apūrva*, the "hitherto unseen potencies/effects" generated—and distribute them throughout the community; even the animals on the ground and vultures above come out to stake their share. The final remains amount to that of which no less could be conceived (or as the Upaniṣads put it: the one-thousandth strand of the miniscule end of the hair that you no longer have on your skull-top!) This is what I mean by the meaningful End of "God," Scripture, and Ritual into a completely new hermeneutical *écriture* of the Traces of a faithless transcendental signified, self-revelatory authorless Word, and ritually enacted *mantric effects*. It is something, as Smith would have appreciated, that we learn not just about other cultures, but *from* other cultures (in which the learner is at once the other but also an insider—as Smith speaks of his own sojourn within Islam).

Last but not least, and linking the analysis here to the earlier discussion of God-talk, if historians of religions have been busily engaged in dehistoricizing all elements of religion—including the term "religion" and names we have come to give to specifically diverse faiths—such as "Hinduism" or "aboriginal religion"; remember that Smith is a realist about history, or the past—then we should not complain if maverick spokesmen for science and philosophers of that ilk too make such loud noises against any and all God-talk (e.g., in *The God Delusion*[33]). For to be sure, having done the groundwork ourselves, hedged our bets on the Pascalian wager each way, and not taken care to iron out the ripples and incoherencies inherent even in the vestigial notions of "Transcendence" (the Transcendental with all its universalistic and essentialist overcasts), it remained for the floor-sweeping philosophers and popularists such as the Hitchens, Harris, Dennett, and Dawkins horsemen (the four constituting a quantum-trinity), to clean out the dusty pew and rid the temples of all that had remained—a rather nebulous, nonfunctionalist, somewhat shaky, demythologized, dehistoricized, deconstructed "faith in transcendence" against the weight of their own studies (let us say social-scientifically informed) of "lesser" religions or religions of minority communities, indigenous traditions, and so on.

And what need would there be to make "A Case for God" as with the repentant Karen Armstrong—influenced, she admits, by Smith—when she herself produced one of the finest studies on the history of God: perhaps *History* as God but no longer *God/the Geist* as history? The more persistently we hold on to the idea of God in the monotheistic strain—and notice that that is the title of the first chapter in Dawkins, as clearly this is his target of attack—the more ammunition we scholars provide to the so-called "New Atheist" camp.

If there is no conception of theism that secularism and modernity since the Enlightenment have stood up against, then there would be no argument against such a "God" either. We are working with an obsolete trope, a belief indeed whose "use-by-date" may have passed, and we are obliged therefore to report to the self-professed atheistic trinity and their global cohorts that their darts aim at the wrong moving target, and that theirs is a lot of empty noise plus a celebrity accolade heaved in; they would be better off directing their arguments elsewhere. This attack by the atheists still remains a challenge for the theologians, but hardly, we have to say, for the scholar of religious traditions or the philosopher of religion.

Following Smith and moving his spirit into the twenty-first century, I'd like to turn Heidegger's sage adage on its head: *We are indeed too late for God and too early for the gods.*

Notes

1. See http://www.springer.com/social+sciences/religious+studies4journal/11841.

2. Wilfred Cantwell Smith, "The Modern West in the History of Religion," American Academy of Religion, presidential address, annual meeting, 1983, *Journal of the American Academy of Religion* 52, no. 1 (March 1984), pp. 3–18.

3. Vide G. W. F. Hegel, *Phenomenology of Spirit*, trans. A. V. Miller (Oxford, UK: Oxford University Press, 1977).

4. See Mary Catherine Hilkert, "Feminist Theology: A Review of Literature," *Theological Studies* 56, no. 2 (June 1995): 327–52; Susan Frank Parsons, *The Cambridge Companion to Feminist Theology* (Cambridge, UK: Cambridge University Press, 2003).

5. Wilfred Cantwell Smith, *Meaning and End of Religion* (New York: Macmillan, 1963), pp. 25–26.

6. Ibid., p. 29, elucidated on p. 213, note 45.

7. For some reservations and possible neglect here of the backward reading via orientalist discourse, see Talal Asad, "Reading a Modern Classic: W. C. Smith's *The Meaning and End of Religion*," *History of Religions* 40, no. 3 (Feb. 2001), pp. 205–22.

8. Klaus K. Klostermaier, "Religionswissenschaft als Welt-Theologie: Wilfred Cantwell Smith's interreligiose Hermeneutik," *Journal of Ecumenical Studies* 34 (Winter 1997), pp. 133–34.

9. See W. C. Smith, *Faith and Belief: The Difference between Them* (Princeton, NJ: Princeton University Press, 1987), p. 35.

10. Ibid.

11. "Unless, of course were the principle of non-contradiction to be set aside and the conflict would likely dissolve. Some modern logicians indeed have argued that perhaps it should be the case in the realistic recognition of the diversity in procedural thinking and cultural diversity that we have become more aware of in today's world than might have been so at the dawn of the Enlightenment." Graham Priest, "What Is So Bad About Contradictions?" *Journal of Philosophy* 95, no. 8 (August 1998); *In Contradiction: A Study of the Transconsistent*, 2nd ed. (Oxford, UK: Oxford University Press, 2006).

12. See Mark C. Taylor, *After God* (Chicago: University of Chicago Press, 2007).

13. W. C. Smith, *Towards a World Theology: Faith and the Comparative History of Religion* (London: Macmillan, 1981), pp. 60–61.

14. Smith, *Faith and Belief*, pp. 4–5, 50.

15. Michael Warren Myers, *Brahman: A Comparative Theology* (Richmond, Surrey, UK: Curzon Press, 2001), pp. 64 and 34.

16. G. C. Pande, "Two Dimensions of Religion," in *Culture and Modernity: East-West Philosophic Perspectives*, ed. Eliot Deutsch (Honolulu: University of Hawaii Press, 1991), pp. 430–51.

17. P. Bilimoria, "Māntric Effect, Noetics of Supplication, and the Apūrva in the Mīmāṃsā," in *Sanskrit Studies*, Vol. III, ed. Shashi Prabha Kumar (New Delhi: Special Centre for Sanskrit Studies, Jawaharlal Nehru University, with DKPrintworld (P) Ltd., 2014), pp. 224–49.

18. W. C. Smith, *What Is Scripture? A Comparative Approach* (Minneapolis: Fortress Press, 1993).

19. To someone from the Sanskritic textual tradition, who heard the Vedas recited every morning next door with the finesse of the biblical and hymnal Christian chanting that I would hear hours later in the Catholic church next door to the mission school I was attending, the implied suggestion that the Indian religions, at least Hinduism and remnants of Zoroastrianism among its Parsi forebears, were not religions of the Book struck me as anathema.

20. William A Graham, *Beyond the Written Word: Oral Aspects of Scripture in the History of Religion*, part II: "Of Written and Spoken Scripture" (Cambridge, UK: Cambridge University Press, 1987, 1993), pp. 50–51, 60.

21. Ibid., p. 237 (Smith's emphasis, as if the sentence were an adage).

22. Smith, *What Is Scripture?*, p. 145.

23. Ludwig Wittgenstein, *Philosophical Investigations* (Oxford, UK: Blackwell Publishing, 2001 [1953]), pp. 243, 244–71. Of course Wittgenstein argues against this position.

24. Smith, *What Is Scripture?*, p. 57.

25. See my "Dialogic Fecundation of Western Hermeneutics and Hindu Mimamsa in the Critical Era," in *Hermeneutics and Hindu Thought: Toward a Fusion of Horizons*, eds. Arvind Sharma and Rita Sherma (Dordrecht: Springer-Verlag, 2008), pp. 43–76.

26. P. Bilimoria, "Hindu Doubts About God: Towards a Mīmāṃsā Deconstruction," in *Indian Philosophy: A Collection of Readings*, ed. R. W. Perrett (New York: Garland, 2001), pp. 87–106.

27. Smith, *What Is Scripture?*, p. 143.

28. Ibid.

29. Ibid., p. 135.

30. p. 135; see also pp. 142–45.

31. See Catherine Bell, *Ritual Perspectives and Dimension* (Oxford, UK: Oxford University Press, 1997), p. 4.

32. Francis X. Clooney, *Thinking Ritually: Rediscovering the Pūrva Mīmāṃsā of Jaimini* (Vienna: Sarnmhing de Nobili, 1990).

33. Richard Dawkins, *The God Delusion* (Boston: Houghton Mifflin, 2006). A woefully badly argued book.

Bibliography

Asad, Tasal. "Reading a Modern Classic: W. C. Smith's *The Meaning and End of Religion*." *History of Religions* 40, no. 3 (Feb. 2001), pp. 205–22.

Bell, Catherine. *Ritual Perspectives and Dimension*. Oxford, UK: Oxford University Press, 1997.

Bilimoria, P. "Māntric Effect, Noetics of Supplication, and the Apūrva in the Mīmāṃsā." In *Sanskrit Studies*, Vol. III. edited by Shashi Prabha Kumar, pp. 224–49. (New Delhi: Special Centre for Sanskrit Studies, Jawaharlal Nehru University, with DKPrintworld (P) Ltd., 2014).

———. "Hindu Doubts About God: Towards a Mīmāṃsā Deconstruction." In *Indian Philosophy: A Collection of Readings*, edited by R. W. Perrett, pp. 87–106. New York: Garland, 2001.

———. "Dialogic fecundation of Western Hermeneutics and Hindu Mīmāṃsā in the Critical Era." In *Hermeneutics and Hindu Thought: Toward a Fusion of Horizons*, edited by Arvind Sharma and Rita Sherma, pp. 43–76. Dordrecht: Springer-Verlag, 2008.

Clooney, Francis X. *Thinking Ritually: Rediscovering the Pūrva Mīmāṃsā of Jaimini*. Vienna: Sarnmhing de Nobili, 1990.

Dawkins, Richard. *The God Delusion*. Boston: Houghton Mifflin, 2006.

Graham, William A. *Beyond the Written Word: Oral Aspects of Scripture in the History of Religion*. Cambridge, UK: Cambridge University Press, 1987.

Hegel, Vide G. W. F. *Phenomenology of Spirit*. Translated by A. V. Miller. Oxford, UK: Oxford University Press, 1977.

Hilkert, Mary Catherine. "Feminist Theology: A Review of Literature." *Theological Studies* (June 1995), pp. 327–52.

Klostermaier, Klaus K. "Religionswissenschaft als Welt-Theologie: Wilfred Cantwell Smith's interreligiose Hermeneutik." *Journal of Ecumenical Studies* 34 (Winter 1997), pp. 133–34.

Myers, Michael Warren. *Brahman: A Comparative Theology*. Richmond, Surrey, UK: Curzon Press, 2001.

Pande, G. C. "Two Dimensions of Religion." In *Culture and Modernity: East-West Philosophic Perspectives*, edited by Eliot Deutsch, pp. 430–51. Honolulu: University of Hawaii Press, 1991.

Parsons, Susan Frank. *The Cambridge Companion to Feminist Theology*. Cambridge, UK: Cambridge University Press, 2003.

Priest, Graham. "What Is So Bad About Contradictions?" *Journal of Philosophy* 95, no. 8 (August 1998), pp. 410–26.

———. *In Contradiction: A Study of the Transconsistent*, 2nd ed. Oxford, UK: Oxford University Press, 2006.

Smith, Wilfred Cantwell. "The Modern West in the History of Religion." *Journal of the American Academy of Religion* 52, no. 1 (March 1984), pp. 3–18.

———. *The Meaning and End of Religion*. New York: Macmillan, 1963.

———. *Faith and Belief: The Difference between Them*. Princeton, NJ: Princeton University Press, 1987.

———. *Towards a World Theology: Faith and the Comparative History of Religion*. London: Macmillan, 1981.

———. *What Is Scripture? A Comparative Approach*. Minneapolis: Fortress Press, 1993.

Taylor, Mark C. *After God*. Chicago: University of Chicago Press, 2007.

Wittgenstein, Ludwig. *Philosophical Investigations*. Oxford, UK: Blackwell Publishing, 2001.

Anticipating the Emergence of "Contemplative Studies"

Reflections on the Work of Wilfred Cantwell Smith

Thomas B. Coburn

> The faculty of voluntarily bringing back a wandering attention, over and over again, is the very root of judgment, character and will. . . . An education which should improve this faculty would be *the* education *par excellence*. But it is easier to define this ideal than to give practical directions for bringing it about.[1]

Introduction

One of the concepts that Wilfred Smith employed throughout his career without much explication was *transcendence*. Pressed by his colleagues, he finally took up this topic late in his career, in the 1988 Ingersoll Lecture, in ways that are fertile for thinking about contemplative life. With characteristic nuance, he writes:

> The relation between what I am calling mundane and what I am calling the transcendent has been variously conceived. Whether the two are continuous, or overlapping, or radically disparate; two sides of the same coin or in irresolvable conflict; whether what seems the higher is in fact the same as the lower but differently perceived, or more penetratingly perceived, and so on—these are questions to which diverse answers, to put it mildly, have been given. What exactly is the nature of the transcendent transcends our conceptual

grasp. . . . That it is there, and is important, cannot reasonably be gainsaid. . . .

The key word [here is] "reasonably." This much, at least, I submit, must be conceded by any reasonable person: that, as an hypothesis, it makes more coherent and illuminating sense of a far wider range of the observable facts of human life today, than does its negation, that we human beings—each of us individually and all of us corporately—live in what I am calling the double context of mundane and transcendent: a mundane that is shot through with transcendence, a transcendent that we apprehend, although in always mundane—and often distorted, sometimes even demonic; yet always improvable—ways. The human problem is to cope with this double-context situation. The intellectual problem is to understand it.[2]

Meeting Professor Smith

I was introduced to Wilfred Cantwell Smith in the fall of 1967. I had enrolled in the Divinity School at Harvard after two years of teaching secondary school, one of them in the Arab world, having loved the interaction with adolescents and hoping to sort out whether I was a teacher, a preacher, or something else. One of the early pieces of advice I received was to enroll in a required survey course on world religions in the School of Arts and Sciences: "It's a very difficult course. Take it now and get it out of the way." So I showed up in Sanders Theater and over the course of the fall was introduced to the mind—and heart—of W. C. Smith. By November I knew I had found my life's work. I have been pursing that work as an historian of religion ever since, leavening regular teaching and scholarship with forays into administration. More than any other individual, it was Smith and his vision of religious life that launched me on this trajectory.

Those were heady days in the late 1960s and early '70s—and tumultuous. Part of the allure of working with Smith, for me and I think for my fellow students, was the way it affirmed that, underneath all the roiling social and political turmoil of the day, there were important, complicated issues that were buried deep in history, with long-term, including contemporary, ramifications. *The Meaning and End of Religion*, of course, was testimony to this vision, providing both invitation and challenge to join in the inquiry into what it is that we humans have been up to in the religious dimension of our lives. It was a compelling vision, embodying a profoundly intellectual kind of charisma, and it drew me and others into serious intellectual work far beyond what I had ever imagined, and I loved it.

With forty years of hindsight, what I find most striking about Smith's work is its prophetic quality, his striking ability to anticipate intellectual and cultural issues before they had come over the horizon into common awareness. In this essay I want to explore one example of how Smith's work ramifies for a growing movement in higher education. This movement has emerged in recent decades under the name, in different universities, of "contemplative education," "contemplative studies," "creativity and consciousness studies," or "integrative education." One of the institutions embodying this movement is the one I led from the summer of 2003 until July of 2009—Naropa University in Boulder, CO. But the movement is far broader than a single institution, and it extends into every corner of the university, from the humanities and arts to the natural sciences. When I accepted Naropa's presidency, I did so because I believed that that university's efforts to craft a synthesis of the contemplative traditions of Asia with the liberal arts tradition of the West had the potential to fill a void in the educational experience of many of today's undergraduates, a void I had seen attested to by some of the best students at some of the best institutions. I continue to believe this is the case, and contemplative studies are increasingly robust nationwide, with new horizons opening regularly, thanks in part to recent developments in neuroscience, exemplified by the Dalai Lama's ongoing collaboration with such scientists.[3] I have come to believe that, along with the intellectual rigor, excitement, and timeliness of Smith's vision of religious life to which I responded in my youth, I was also responding to its implications for what we now call "contemplative education." There was, I believe, a contemplative strand in his understanding of religious life that called out to me, and I think to others, along with his stunningly articulate and brilliant intellectual work. In the ongoing evolution of higher education, that strand is now calling out to others, particularly to those who put teaching at the center of their professional and personal identities. That is what I will explore here. Let me begin by sketching some of the central issues in contemplative education and then suggest some of the ways Smith's work appears to have anticipated these developments.

Contemplative Education

What, then, is contemplative education? Rather than drawing exclusively on the institution I know best, Naropa University, with its emphasis on the integration of contemplative *practice* with academic study—an emphasis that reflects the Kagyu and Nyingma lineages of the founder, Chogyam Trungpa Rinpoche—let me also focus on the work that is unfolding elsewhere, particularly at Brown University under the leadership of Professor Harold Roth. At Brown, there has been a concerted effort to develop the *theory* of contemplative studies, along with contemplative practice. While there is considerable variety in this nascent field—as attested in the September 2006 issue of the *Teachers College Record* devoted to "Contemplative Practices and Education"—there is reasonable agreement on six important points.

First, a caveat: contemplative education does not signal the reappearance of the spiritual excesses of the 1960s, nor an encroachment of the New Age on the academy. It carries an appreciation, as well as an awareness of the limitations, of conventional liberal education, which it seeks not to displace, but to supplement—to make more whole, drawing not just on cognition, but on affect, cultivating the full range of human capabilities. It is complementary to the view of education that prevails in most colleges and universities, which it sees as necessary but not sufficient for producing truly liberally educated graduates. Like Smith himself, contemplative studies is deeply committed to intellectual inquiry, even as it sees the shortcomings in the contemporary academy of much that passes for genuine, humane investigation. Contemplative studies is at least as demanding as anything in traditional academic disciplines. An indication of this rigor is found in the extraordinary challenges experienced by some of the great contemplatives as their spiritual paths unfolded—St. John of the Cross, Ramakrishna, Milarepa, and others. The discipline and rigors of the most challenging conventional learning often pale in comparison to the discipline and rigors of contemplative learning, because the contemplative challenge is not just a matter of the intellect. This is why the faculty at Naropa University is keenly aware that the first semester of the BA curriculum, which intentionally guides students through the deconstruction of their conventional egos, must be accompanied and followed by compassionate guidance in reconstructing a wiser, deeper, more mature identity. Such a deepening and reconstruction is a goal across the contemplative education movement.

Second, while contemplative education draws deeply on the subject matter of religious studies, it is not fundamentally about religious life. The program developed by Ed Sarath at the University of Michigan is a program in jazz and contemplative studies.[4] Rather, contemplative education is about paying the kind of attention that William James describes in the epigraph at the head of this essay: "The faculty of voluntarily bringing back a wandering attention, over and over again, is the very root of judgment, character and will. . . . An education which should improve this faculty would be *the* education *par excellence*. But it is easier to define this ideal than to give practical directions for bringing it about." Diana Chapman Walsh, president emerita of Wellesley College and a leader in this emerging field, puts the matter this way: "I've found that the contemplative disciplines . . . help me stabilize my mind, engage in deeper reflection, quiet my heart, manage my stress, see my blind spots, and ground in a truth I can trust. . . . I . . . have come to rely on contemplative practice not for religious or spiritual guidance but as a vehicle for *learning*—learning another way of being in the world, of cultivating a mindful and ethical integrity and of coming to see more clearly the force fields I inhabit, and the tricks my mind can play."[5] Higher education has been a latecomer in recognizing the promise of contemplative practices for learning, and meanwhile at the K–12 level there is mounting evidence that simple mindfulness practice produces student gains both in the ability to focus and master subject matter and in the social skills required to relate constructively to one's peers.[6] In a world where the complexity of multitasking rears its head at every turn, this kind of attentiveness provides a fresh clarity that is often experienced as revolutionary.

Third, contemplative studies is breaking new ground in epistemology. Harold Roth, chair of the Brown University initiative, writes:

> Our scientific knowledge of how the world works has never been stronger, but our ability to use it to transform our lives to create greater personal and social harmony remains relatively weak. We can use our technology of the outer world to treat previously incurable diseases, but our mastery of the "technology" of the inner world is so rudimentary that we can barely contain the passions that lead us to destroy the very human life that we, paradoxically, struggle so hard to preserve. We have become the masters of *third-person* scientific investigation, but we are mere novices in the arts of *critical first-person* scientific investigation.[7]

What contemplative studies does is to ground students "in the philosophy, psychology, and neuroscience of contemplative practice as a third-person study," and to "emphasize the critical first-person study that is often found in the musical, dramatic, and visual arts and in laboratory science courses. By *critical*, we mean that students would be encouraged to engage directly with these techniques without prior commitment to their efficacy. They would then step back and appraise their experiences to gain a deeper appreciation of their meaning and significance."[8]

> [In other words] students will learn to identify contemplative states of consciousness both as objects and subjects of study. They will be able to discuss and explore the nature of such contemplative experiences as mindfulness, concentration, intuition, tranquility, and "flow" as they occur throughout a wide range of human endeavors. . . . It is through studying and experiencing the contemplative aspects found in these various disciplines [that range across the humanities, creative arts, and natural sciences], through critically examining their relevance and significance, and through applying them to their lives that students . . . discover fundamental dimensions of their nature as human beings. It is through this dual approach that students . . . learn how to cultivate the awareness of the present moment that is the heart of contemplative experience and the basis of compassionate action, and they will be able to understand its scientific basis and philosophical significance.[9]

What this points toward is a kind of "lab work," where that phrase has two complementary meanings. On the one hand, it indicates that in addition to the cognitive mastery of almost any subject matter, students are asked to engage it, not just with the implicit, often casual reflexivity that is prized in conventional liberal education, but systematically, using the tools of introspection that have been cultivated in the world's contemplative traditions. On the other, it refers to the groundbreaking work taking place at the intersection between neuroscience and contemplative studies under the inspiration of the Dalai Lama in the Mind and Life project. Reporting on work in the lab of Richard Davidson at the University of Wisconsin that examines changes in the brain structure of experienced meditators, His Holiness writes, "Mindfulness meditation [turns out to] strengthen . . . the neurological circuits that calm a part of the brain that acts as a trigger for fear and anger. [This is true for non-Buddhists who have been taught mindfulness practice and] raises the possibility that we have a way to create a kind of buffer between the brain's violent impulses and our actions. . . . We would do well to remember that the war against hatred and terror can be waged on this, the internal front, too."[10] Ultimately, contemplative education aspires to nothing less than creating a new kind of human being—intellectually discerning, emotionally stable, religiously and spiritually inclusive, wise, compassionate.

Fourth, although I have sometimes described Naropa University's work on contemplative education as situated at the confluence of the contemplative traditions of Asia and the liberal arts tradition of the West, and while Buddhist meditation practices are employed more commonly than others in advancing contemplative education—for instance, in the work of the Center for Contemplative Mind in Society[11]—this is chiefly because Buddhism's nontheistic nature makes it more readily accessible to those without a religious or spiritual heritage or, in Smith's terms, without a "cumulative tradition." The movement, however, is broader than any particular contemplative or religious tradition, and Father Thomas Keating and Rabbi Zalman Schachter-Shalomi have played important roles, Christian and Jewish, respectively, in the movement's development. Naropa's Buddhist founder did not intend to establish an exclusively Buddhist institution.

Fifth, all colleges in the country aspire to cultivate in their students the fundamental liberal arts skills of reading, writing, and speaking. But very few systematically address the reverse side of speaking, that is, listening—listening to heart as well as head, and listening to the other individual or group quietly, patiently, letting them have their own voice uninterrupted, without trying to straighten them out. Contemplative education adds to the familiar list of liberal arts skills the skill of *listening*, and this entails real discipline, directed inwardly toward oneself and outwardly toward others. In a world where the facts of diversity and difference are so often contentious, the deep, intentional, nonjudgmental, active listening that is part of contemplative education offers a glimmer of what it might mean *actually to celebrate the differences* that so often divide us, individually and in our various groupings, rather than seeing them as sources of conflict.

Finally, contemplative education is about the rehabilitation of the concept and the reality of what it means to be "contemplative." For complex historical reasons I cannot explore here, the modern Western resonance of the concept "contemplation" is that it is primarily the property of anchorites, hermits, and recluses: the image of the yogi meditating in a Himalayan cave captures this stereotype. But the historical record shows that, in virtually all traditions and throughout history, contemplatives have lived their lives along a spectrum. At one end, there are indeed solitary individuals who have withdrawn from the world. But at the other end there are the social activists, those engaged in the struggle for peace, justice, and social equity, actively embodying the quality of compassion that flows from contemplation. One thinks of Martin Luther King, Thich Nhat Hanh, Mahatma Gandhi, Dorothy Day, and countless others, all deeply contemplative and all deeply engaged in transforming the world. Once one gets beyond the stereotype, one sees contemplative activists everywhere. Contemplative education introduces students to this broad range of possibility, so they can decide for themselves if and how they would like to bring their contemplative lives to bear on the world.

Smith's Anticipation of Contemplative Education

Let me now suggest four points where Smith's work anticipates what we now call "contemplative education." He, of course, was wonderfully fastidious in his use of language, and I do not wish to suggest that he would have chosen the phrase "contemplative education" to describe what is happening in the academy and in religious life. But clearly *something is happening here* and I believe that, as an historian, he would be interested in these developments in academic and religious life, particularly since they grow out of some of the same issues that he himself engaged with so deeply.

First, running through Smith's work is a deep affection for the mystics and contemplatives of the world's religious traditions. He commonly invokes Sufi perspectives, and I suspect that, if one were to do a source analysis of Smith's references, the Taoist Zhuangzi (Chuang Tzu), whom Smith calls "one of my best friends," would be among the most commonly cited.[12] Smith was intrigued by Dag Hammarskjöld, whose "private meditation language . . . [was] continuous with certain strands in the overt religious tradition of his society, particularly those of the mystics," but whose religiousness was almost without overt observable phenomena.[13] Forty years ago Smith noted that Hammarskjöld had kindred spirits in Muslim and Hindu circles. That number has surely increased exponentially in the interim.

Second, and in a similar vein, Smith's understanding of the inner life of faith appears to be strikingly similar to the cultivation of inner life that is central to contemplative education. Consider the following:

> Faith is not a factor in a man's life, alongside others. . . . It is not one element in the total pattern of that person's life; rather, it is the pattern that the other elements form. . . . To understand a man's faith is to ascertain how he sees the world (and feels it)—all of the world, from economics to art, from failure in an examination to the crying of a neighbour's child. If a man loses his faith, it may be that no one of the factors in his life has changed; the difference is simply that they no longer cohere into an integrated pattern.[14]

Along with the nurturance provided by "cumulative tradition," it is deep interiority—the pattern that constitutes faith—that, for Smith and for his contemplative kin, is the pith of religious life.

And then there is the matter of objectivity. Smith repeatedly affirms that objectivity is the proper epistemological posture for understanding objects, and that it is part of intellectual rigor, but not the whole. The alternative to objectivity for Smith is not subjectivity, but what he called a "personalist" perspective, which recognizes the distinctively human and interpersonal qualities of our lives.[15] In 1967 he wrote: "One of the most exciting adventures of our day is the emergence of critical and disciplined participant observation, whereby [a scholar] studies not just other [human beings], 'objectively,' but [one's] own group—ideally, [hu]mankind—in a critical, disciplined, intellectually rigorous, empirical, academic way."[16] This kind of reflexivity has subsequently been richly developed by scholarship in gender and multicultural studies into what postmodernists now call "intersubjectivity"—a way of knowing that acknowledges the centrality of relationship and dialogue, between groups and between individuals, in the shared construction and discovery of knowledge. That Smith anticipated these developments is evidenced in one of his earliest and most challenging formulations of the goal of the comparative study of religion: "*[I]t is the business of comparative religion to construct statements about religion that are intelligible within at least two traditions simultaneously.*"[17]

Finally, one of the acknowledged universals in contemplative life, and in contemplative education, is emphasis on attending to the present moment, cutting through the linear sense of time, releasing a concern with past and future, and living with undivided attention to what is right here in front of us. What strikes me now, decades after working with Smith, is how very contemplative, how very mystical, is his understanding of "faith," the common core of religious life, about which he wrote so much. Consider these words: "For any man whose faith is vivid, even whose faith is at all alive, there are two qualities of that faith . . . that stand out, so far as questions of temporality are concerned: first, that it is timeless; second, that it is present. If religion is anything at all, it is something that links the present moment to eternity. Not to understand that is to have no feel for the religious life at all."[18] Juxtapose this statement with Wittgenstein's claim that is so broadly affirmed in contemplative and mystical life: "Death is not an event in life: we do not live to experience death. If we take eternity to mean not infinite temporal duration but timelessness, then eternal life belongs to those who live in the present."[19]

Throughout his work, Wilfred Smith had an extraordinarily profound understanding of religious life. It is now clear to me that, in addition to this being a result of his enormous erudition, it is also a function of his feel for the contemplative life. Correspondingly I have come to think of him as a twentieth-century al-Ghazali: rigorously and stupendously intellectual, and simultaneously deeply and profoundly mystical. As this new field of contemplative studies continues to unfold, it would appear that here, as on so many other fronts, Wilfred Smith was there first, if not thinking our thoughts before us, then at least planting and beginning to nurture their seeds.

Notes

1. William James, *The Principles of Psychology* (New York: Henry Holt, 1890), vol. 1, p. 424.

2. Wilfred Cantwell Smith, "Transcendence: The Ingersoll Lecture," Harvard Divinity School, March 10, 1988, *Harvard Divinity Bulletin* (Fall 1988), pp. 10–15.

3. See Rick Hanson with Richard Mendius, *Buddha's Brain: The Practical Neuroscience of Happiness, Love, & Wisdom* (Oakland, CA: New Harbinger Publications, 2009); Daniel Siegel, *Mindsight: The New Science of Transformation* (New York: Random House, 2010); and Harold Roth, "Against Cognitive Imperialism: A Call for a Non-Ethnocentric Approach to Cognitive Science and Religious Studies," *Religion East and West* no. 108 (October 2008), pp. 1–26. An excellent introduction to a range of initiatives in integrative and contemplative education, and a powerful rationale for their expansion, is Parker J. Palmer and Arthur Zajonc, with Megan Scribner, *The Heart of Higher Education: A Call to Renewal—Transforming the Academy through Collegial Conversations* (San Francisco: Jossey-Bass, 2010).

4. Ed Sarath, "Meditation in Higher Education: The Next Wave?" *Innovative Higher Education* 27, no. 4 (Summer 2003), pp. 215–233; Ed Sarath, "Med-

itation, Creativity, and Consciousness: Charting Future Terrain within Higher Education," *Teachers College Record*, "Special Issue: Contemplative Practices and Education" 108, no. 9 (September 2006), pp. 1816–41.

    5. Diana Chapman Walsh, "Higher Education in a Time of Stress: 'The Kingdom is Now or Never,'" paper presented at the Association for Contemplative Mind in Higher Education Annual Conference: "The Contemplative Heart of Higher Education" (April 24–26, 2009, Amherst College, Amherst, MA).

    6. See http://www.garrisoninstitute.org/index.php?option=com_content&view=article&id=75&Itemid=77 (accessed January 11, 2011).

    7. Harold D. Roth, "Contemplative Studies: Prospects for a New Field," *Teachers College Record*, "Special Issue: Contemplative Practices and Education" 108, no. 9 (September 2006), p. 1,787.

    8. Roth, "Contemplative Studies," p. 1789–90.

    9. Ibid.

    10. Tenzin Gyatso [The Dalai Lama], "The Monk in the Lab," *New York Times*, April 26, 2003, A29.

    11. http://www.contemplativemind.org/ (accessed January 11, 2011).

    12. Wilfred Cantwell Smith, "Methodology and the Study of Religion: Some Misgivings," in *Methodological Issues in Religious Studies*, ed. Robert D. Baird (Chico, CA: New Horizons Press, 1975), p. 1.

    13. Wilfred Cantwell Smith, "Traditional Religions and Modern Culture," in *Religious Diversity*, ed. Willard G. Oxtoby (New York: Crossroad, 1982), pp. 71, 76.

    14. Smith, "Traditional Religions," p. 72.

    15. Wilfred Cantwell Smith, "The Teaching of Religion: Academic Rigour, and Personal Involvement," address to the Canadian Society for the Study of Religion, Carlton University, Ottawa, June 12, 1967.

    16. Smith, "Teaching of Religion," p. 19.

    17. Wilfred Cantwell Smith, "Comparative Religion: Whither—and Why?" Originally published in *The History of Religions: Essays in Methodology*, eds. Mircea Eliade and Joseph M. Kitagawa (Chicago: University of Chicago Press, 1959), pp. 31–58. Reprinted in Oxtoby (ed.), *Religious Diversity* (138–57), p. 152. The emphasis is original with Smith, an indication of the issue's importance to him.

    18. Smith, "Traditional Religions," p. 67.

    19. Ludwig Wittgenstein, *Tractatus Logico-Philosophicus*, trans. D. F. Pears and B. F. McGuinness (London: Routledge and Kegan Paul, 1961), p. 6.4311.

Bibliography

Barbezat, Daniel P., and Mirabai Bush. *Contemplative Practices in Higher Education*. San Francisco: Jossey-Bass, 2014.

Gyatso, Tenzin, [The Dalai Lama]. "The Monk in the Lab." *New York Times*, April 26, 2003), p. A29.

Hanson, Rick, with Richard Mendius. *Buddha's Brain: The Practical Neuroscience of Happiness, Love, & Wisdom*. Oakland, CA: New Harbinger Publications, 2009.

James, William. *The Principles of Psychology*, vol. I. New York: Henry Holt, 1890.

Palmer, Parker J., and Arthur Zajonc, with Megan Scribner. *The Heart of Higher Education: A Call to Renewal—Transforming the Academy through Collegial Conversations*. San Francisco: Jossey-Bass, 2010.

Roth, Harold. "Against Cognitive Imperialism: A Call for a Non-Ethnocentric Approach to Cognitive Science and Religious Studies." *Religion East and West* no. 108 (October 2008), pp. 1–26.

———. "Contemplative Studies: Prospects for a New Field." *Teachers College Record*, "Special Issue: Contemplative Practices and Education" 108, no. 9 (September 2006), pp. 1787–1815.

Sarath, Ed. "Meditation in Higher Education: The Next Wave?" *Innovative Higher Education* 27, no. 4 (Summer 2003), pp. 215–33.

———. "Meditation, Creativity, and Consciousness: Charting Future Terrain within Higher Education." *Teachers College Record*, "Special Issue: Contemplative Practices and Education." 108, no. 9 (September 2006), pp. 1816–41.

Siegel, Daniel. *Mindsight: The New Science of Transformation*. New York: Random House, 2010.

Simmer-Brown, Judith, and Fran Grace. *Meditation and the Classroom: Contemplative Pedagogy for Religious Studies*. Albany: SUNY Press, 2011.

Smith, Wilfred Cantwell. "Transcendence: The Ingersoll Lecture," *Harvard Divinity Bulletin* (Fall 1988), pp. 10–15.

———. "Methodology and the Study of Religion: Some Misgivings." In *Methodological Issues in Religious Studies*, edited by Robert D. Baird, 1–30. Chico, CA: New Horizons Press, 1975.

———. "Traditional Religions and Modern Culture." In *Religious Diversity*, edited by Willard G. Oxtoby. New York: Crossroad, 1982.

———. "The Teaching of Religion: Academic Rigour, and Personal Involvement." Address to the Canadian Society for the Study of Religion, Carlton University, Ottawa, June 12, 1967, unpublished address.

———. "Comparative Religion: Whither—and Why?" In *The History of Religions: Essays in Methodology*, edited by Mircea Eliade and Joseph M. Kitagawa. Chicago: University of Chicago Press, 1959. Republished in *Religious Diversity*, edited by Willard G. Oxtoby. New York: Crossroad, 1982.

Walsh, Diana Chapman. "Higher Education in a Time of Stress: 'The Kingdom Is Now or Never.'" Paper presented at the Association for Contemplative Mind in Higher Education Annual Conference, "The Contemplative Heart of Higher Education." Amherst College, Amherst, MA, April 24–26, 2009, unpublished essay.

Wittgenstein, Ludwig. *Tractatus Logico-Philosophicus*. Translated by D. F. Pears and B. F. McGuinness. London: Routledge and Kegan Paul, 1961.

Faith and Belief Revisited

Harvey Cox

I have a dream. Or maybe it is a fantasy. Years from now when I am happily settled in the heavenly realms, I hope to open a salon and introduce to each other several people who never met on earth. It will be quite a gathering, and I intend to listen for a few millennia before I jump in. The theme will be the difference between faith and belief viewed from multiple perspectives.

In addition to Wilfred, once my colleague at Harvard, the first person I want at the symposium is Julia Kristeva, the Romanian-French feminist, writer, psychoanalyst, and feminist philosopher. An odd couple indeed, but they will soon be joined by many others.

Wilfred spent much of his career persuading people that faith and belief should never be confused with each other. He drew on his vast knowledge of history of religions and comparative cultural history to make his point. And he certainly convinced me. Kristeva, in her recent book *This Incredible Need to Believe* (New York: Columbia University Press, 2009) makes a similar case, drawing on her practice as an analyst and her knowledge of literature and philosophy.

It should be said immediately that the title of Kristeva's book is misleading. She uses the word "believe" with the same meaning Smith attaches to "faith." Kristeva calls it "pre-religious belief," and insists that it must not be confused with the specific contents of the various historical religions, which we must continue to interrogate critically, asking all the "big questions," such as, are they true or false, absolute or constructed, damaging or beneficial?—questions scholars of religion and theology never tire of. But at the same time we must recognize the psychic nexus from which this "pre-religious belief" arises, which both Smith and myself would call "faith" (*pistis*). It suggests "confidence in," not subscribing to one or another religious idea. More on this later.

Kristeva is deeply influenced by Jacques Lacan (in turn influenced by Freud), but her work is anything but psychologically reductionist. Her decision not to delve into the metaphysics of whether that in which the psyche places confidence is "really there" stems from a genuine sense of humility. She wants to talk about what she knows something about.

So what is the psychic source of this Kristevian "pre-religious belief" or faith? In answering this she steps beyond or before Freud's focus on the Oedipal struggle of the infant to overcome his or her immersion in the mother and to come to terms with the "other," the father figure. Freud famously saw this as a battle, indeed a battle unto death (*Moses and Monotheism*), the need to slay the father figure. But Kristeva, drawing on her own experience as an analyst, describes a "pre-Oedipal" relationship. The infant needs to feel some passionate sense of confidence (mixed with both love and hate) toward this powerful "other." But it is precisely this relationship that permits the infant to differentiate itself from the mother and thus properly *to exist*, to come into individual being. For Kristeva, this enabler, this creator of my being as a person, is not just the actual father, but a kind of ideal Other, and coming to terms with this Other is an inescapable determinate of being a human being. She also argues that, although the historic religions have often misdirected this need, modern secularism has made the worse mistake of ignoring it or denying it. The result is nihilism and ennui.

She might have added (but did not) that the result could also be idolatry, the projection of the need-to-believe onto inappropriate objects. We have witnessed the awful results of this idolatry in recent history as nation, race, class and even "my religion" have become the objects of such misdirected faith or belief.

It seems that Henry Adams sensed this aberration. When he visited the Great Hall of Dynamos at the Paris Exhibition in 1900, he wrote that he felt the mighty machinery "as a moral force, much as the early Christians felt the cross." He went on to say that even the earth itself, with its annual or daily revolutions, seemed somehow less impressive "than this huge wheel, revolving within arms-length at some vertiginous speed and barely murmuring—scarcely humming an audible warning to stand a hair's breadth further for respect of power—while it would not wake the baby lying against its frame. Before the end, one began to pray to it; inherited instinct taught the natural expression of man before silent and infinite force."[1]

Henry Adams was not a conventionally "religious" man, but he could admit to a desire to pray to the giant dynamo. This may not sound as odd today as it might have to his first readers. The sense of awe many feel toward titanic rockets or even the ghastly power of nuclear weapons makes Adams's sentiment entirely plausible. Kristeva's analysis adds a note of intensity. She observes a mixture of love and hate in the infant's attitude, later projected onto the divine father. But Adams's statement also reminds us of how various and sometimes dangerous the objects of awe can be. It also tells us that prayer, or something akin to it, is a "natural instinct," perhaps something like George Santayana's "animal faith" (another guest at the confab we will meet in a moment). Awe and prayer, and also faith, precede any particular beliefs or ideas. But recognizing this still leaves us with the very large question of what then *is* the appropriate "object" of faith?

Clearly, if faith is as primal and as comprehensive as it is, and if it involves an orientation of the whole self, then its object must be no less comprehensive. If not, then faith itself becomes distorted. The "object" of faith cannot be an "object" in the usual sense. Faith, rightly understood, might best be described by the poetic biblical phrase, "Deep cries out unto deep." It opens me, often in fear and trembling to all that (to extrapolate from Kristeva) is "not me," which is never reducible to me, and which is always *there* in its sheer otherness. Many different words have been used to characterize this "other," but they all turn out to be inadequate. Still, since we are language-using creatures we have to try, realizing that any word will fall short. This is the luxuriant field in which the student of religious history prowls.

Anyone can understand why many people remain so confused about the relationship between faith and belief. These words have endured a tortuous history, one that Wilfred explores in several of his books. For example, the Latin word *credo*, which we translate as "I believe," derives from a combination of the word *cordia*, meaning "heart," and *do*, which means to put or place or give. In classical Latin, *credo* meant to trust, rely on, or place one's confidence in someone or something. But when we translate *credo* as "I believe," everything that follows becomes distorted, because "believe," for most people, means assenting to something without sufficient evidence. It has even come to mean subscribing to an idea or proposition. Historians of language point out that the English word "believe" derives from the same root as the current German word *belieben*, which is closely related to *Liebe* and means "to hold dear." Thus, both "faith" and "belief" have suffered distortions from the buffeting of linguistic history. But today "faith" still retains at least some of its overtones of confidence and fidelity. But "believe" has often become shorthand for, "Well, maybe so, but I have my doubts." (*Je crois que oui.*) This means that the transposition from faith to belief in Christian history literally moved its locus from the heart to the head. Wilfred argues that this was largely a modern development, in part a byproduct of the technicalization of culture. I would argue that it set in much earlier, with the period of frenzied creed making introduced by Constantine in an effort to shore up his crumbling empire with a unifying ideology.[2]

In any case, the convoluted careers of these words makes clear that when faith is subsumed under belief, and belief is then equated with assent to certain ideas *about* God, Jesus, or anything else, it is time to retrieve the early Christian usage of faith as comprehensive trust, and Christianity as a way of life not a system of beliefs. At root (Kristeva would agree), faith is a relationship, not an opinion. But what words can we turn to when such central ones have been so badly twisted? In his book *Stages of Faith*, the psychologist of religion James Fowler (whom I have already invited) makes a persuasive suggestion. The question of faith today, he writes, is the question of "On what or on whom do you set your heart? To what vision of right-relatedness between humans, nature and the transcendent are you loyal? What hope and what ground of hope animate you and give shape to the force field of your life and how you move into it?"[3]

Fowler makes the useful observation that in English, as well as in some other languages, we do not have a verb that corresponds to the noun, "faith." We can talk about "believing" but we cannot talk about "faith-ing." Fowler points out that the absence of such a verb has had at least two dire effects. First, it means we cannot translate either the Hebrew or Greek terms for faith adequately, since they both have both noun and verb forms. This makes faith a static rather than a dynamic concept. But just as importantly, our lack of a verb like "to faith" has caused endless confusion. It forces us always to use "faith" as a thing, as something I "have" or do not "have," some *thing* that I am searching for or have lost or couldn't care less about. This trivializes faith by pushing it from the most fundamental level of life—our basic orientation toward the reality we both confront and are a part of—to the much less significant level of an idea or opinion we can hold or not hold, or as the current phrase has it, "whatever."

There is an old debate in theology that pits *fides quaerens intellectus* (faith seeking understanding) against *intellectus quaerens fides* (understanding seeking faith). But the argument is misleading. Every intellectual quest is already grounded in some kind of elemental posture. That life stance always precedes any thinking about it. True, thinking about it can cause us to confirm or modify our basic orientation, or even to change it. But what makes us think about it is often some personal upheaval, the kind of thing that happens when we collide with events that shake us to our foundations. Even then, however, we inevitably begin, continue, and conclude our quests from some more deep-seated perspective.

When I first started teaching at Harvard, and enjoyed a warm friendship with Wilfred Cantwell Smith, I kept hearing delightful stories about a charming, brilliant, but eccentric philosopher named George Santayana, who had taught philosophy in the Yard nearly a century ago. He is another person I would like to introduce to Wilfred. More than just a thinker, Santayana was a poet, an essayist, a literary critic, and a novelist, which would make him an even more fascinating guest. In a book entitled *Skepticism and Animal Faith*, published in 1923, Santayana moves the emergence of faith a bit beyond Kristeva's infantile stage. He claims in this book that "faith" is an indispensable feature of all human beings, necessitated by our being organic creatures who live in an environment. To survive in this situation, he argues, we must both explain the things around us to ourselves (which is how science develops) and also find out what meaning and value they have for us (which is where history and philosophy come in.) What we discover in these two endeavors is constantly confirmed or disconfirmed as we continue to interact as persons with our world. However, to carry out these essential activities—explanation and evaluation—says Santayana, we need something more primary than either of them. We need a "basic confidence" that what we encounter in the world is really there, and not the product of our imagination or wishful thinking. This basic confidence Santayana called "animal faith," and insisted that it is *prior* to any kind of proof or disproof.

"Animal faith" may not have been the best choice of terms. Santayana used the term to suggest that in this sense "faith" is instinctive, inherent, and intuitive. It is interesting that thirty years later, Ludwig Wittgenstein, who must also be part of this conversation, and is thought by some to be the most influential philosopher of the twentieth century, used the phrase "something animal" when he was describing the convictions we need to survive, although they can neither be proven nor disproven.

For Kristeva, Fowler, and Santayana, to be a human being is of necessity to be a "faith-*er*," to engage throughout life in what, if we had such a verb, we would call "faith-*ing*." It means that from infancy until our dying day we place our confidence and trust, even our hope, in *something*. That something may be myself or it may be my money or my government or my fame. This is why I want to add one of my own teachers, H. Richard Niebuhr, to our growing entourage. He once slyly wrote that this something might be "God, or country or Yale." But it is always something. Even the absolute nihilist, if there is such a creature, lives with a certain strange confidence that the Nihil will not suddenly turn out to be something else, thus upsetting his fundamental world view. As human beings we have in common that we are all "faith-ing" animals. But this brings us back to Henry Adams and the dynamo, and the ontological question: toward what or in what do we direct our faith-ing?

Let's make sure Martin Luther is included in our carousing. If there is enough beer, he will surely come, even though he obviously never read anything by George Santayana. And I doubt that Santayana, a Spaniard who was described by his friends as a "Catholic agnostic," ever read much, if any, of the great reformer's many treatises. But if he had ever looked into Luther's commentary on the Ten Commandments, he would have discovered a genuine forerunner of his idea of "animal faith." When Luther comes to the commandment: "Thou shalt have no other gods before me," his explanation is a stroke of sheer genius. He does not discuss what the word "God" may or not mean. Rather he asks, "What does it mean to *have* a god?" Interestingly, like Kristeva, he brackets the "God out there" question, and focuses on the existential one. His answer is that "trust and faith of the heart alone make both God and idol . . . for the two, faith and God hold closely together. Whatever then thy heart clings to . . . and relies upon, that properly is thy god."[4] Luther then goes on to claim that if money or power or fame is what we "cling to and rely on," then they are our gods. Thus Luther links faith with God (or gods) in such a way that they can never be easily separated. Recent theologians have sometimes rephrased Luther's insight in the more contemporary idiom of "values." In his *The Meaning of Revelation*, Richard Niebuhr writes: "As long as a man lives he must believe in something for the sake of which he lives; without belief in something that makes life worth living man cannot exist. . . . Man, as a practical, living being never exists without a god or gods, some things there are to which he must cling as the sources and goals of his activity, the centers of value."[5]

It is true that in this passage Niebuhr uses the word "belief," but in the full context of his book and his other works, it is clear that he means "faith" as Luther talked about it, not "belief" as we ordinarily use the word today. In any case, here we can see the languages of philosophy and theology overlap. To talk about "faith" is to talk about the instinctual and intuitive confidence we need to survive in the world. If Luther and Santayana, the blustery German peasant and the refined Castilian gentleman, are now already in heaven—and since one was a heretic and the other an agnostic I am sure they are—they will have been enjoying each other's company when the rest of us arrive. But only up to a point. Unless one or the other has undergone a radical conversion, they will eventually disagree about the big underlying question: on exactly what should you and I have faith or place our confidence?

But this conversation will require another, enlarged celestial conversation, with quite a few more guests. Still, might we open the subject in the heavenly city of Montreal?

Notes

1. Quoted by Peter Hellman in "Man of the Century," *Smithsonian* 37, no. 9 (Dec. 2005), p. 94, from Adams's "The Virgin and the Dynamo."
2. For a full discussion of the etymologies of these terms, see Wilfred C. Smith, *Faith and Belief* (Princeton, NJ: Princeton University Press, 1979), p. 76.
3. James Fowler, *Stages of Faith: The Psychology of Human Development and the Quest for Meaning* (San Francisco: Harper and Row, 1976), p. 14.
4. Quoted in H. Richard Niebuhr, *Radical Monotheism and Western Culture: With Supplementary Essays* (New York: Harper, 1960), p. 119.
5. H. Richard Niebuhr, *The Meaning of Revelation* (New York: Macmillan, 1960), p. 77.

Bibliography

Fowler, James. *Stages of Faith: The Psychology of Human Development and the Quest for Meaning.* San Francisco: Harper and Row, 1976.
Hellman, Peter. "Man of the Century." *Smithsonian* 37, no. 9 (Dec. 2006), p. 94.
Niebuhr, Richard H. *The Meaning of Revelation.* New York: Macmillan, 1960.
———. *Radical Monotheism and Western Culture: With Supplementary Essays.* New York: Harper, 1960.
Smith, Wilfred Cantwell. *Faith and Belief.* Princeton, NJ: Princeton University Press, 1979.

Wilfred Cantwell Smith and "Orientalism"

William A. Graham

Edward Said's groundbreaking book, *Orientalism* (1978), moved well beyond previous studies of Occidental engagement with "the Orient"—for example, the classic work of Raymond Schwab, *La renaissance orientale* (1950). In his work, Said (1935–2003) undertook a wholesale analysis and critique of Western hegemonic domination of "the Orient" since the eighteenth century, not only politically and economically but culturally and intellectually. He did so through a Foucaultian and Gramscian analysis of the sociopolitical context of basic power imbalance in which European-American treatment, both in public media and in academic scholarship, of the non-Western world, especially the Near Eastern part of it, is seen as the handmaiden of Western imperialism, colonialism, and domination of the rest of the world—preeminently in the nineteenth and twentieth centuries, although it began much earlier.[1]

His book is arguably the most important interpretive work of the late twentieth century regarding modern scholarly approaches to the non-Western world in general, and the Islamic and Arab Middle Eastern world specifically. As such it has become a standard point of reference in postcolonial and subaltern studies as well as in Middle Eastern, Indian, and other Asian studies fields, and it has had a major influence in all these areas. It has made "orientalism" into a commonly used, negative shorthand designation for varied kinds of Western bias, chauvinism, and hegemonic motivation in conceiving and describing non-Western cultures and peoples, both within and beyond the academy. While Said's subsequent writing on orientalism did not convey the same polemical tone or blanket condemnation as his critiques in *Orientalism*,[2] the book's all-but-blanket indictment of Western treatment of "the Orient," whether political or intellectual, has remained the primary touchstone for subsequent scholarly efforts to move beyond any imbrication with imperialist and colonialist attitudes and agendas in trying to interpret and understand any sector of the non-Western world.

This being said, despite the brilliance of many of Said's insights, his book is highly polemical in tone and correspondingly uneven and selective in its data and argumentation.[3] Said rather indiscriminately threw together the accounts of Western travelers to the Orient and Western scholars of the Islamic world. He was often selectively unfair to individual Islamicists (from Sylvain Levi or Louis Massignon to Gustav von Grunebaum or H. A. R. Gibb). In his selection of European-American orientalist scholars to attack, he ignored (or was ignorant of) orientalists who did not fit his purposes. His apodictic, blanket censure of Western scholarly study of non-Western, especially Islamic, cultures was based almost solely on selected citations from a small, selected group of English and French Islamicists and Arabists.

In what follows, we focus on some of the work of Wilfred Cantwell Smith (1916–2000), one of those twentieth-century, anglophone "Western" scholars of "the Orient" whose scholarly critique of reductionist and chauvinistic orientalist scholarship in fact presaged Said's arguments, but whose work Said either ignored or was unaware of. Not unlike Marshall G. S. Hodgson, perhaps the other most obvious American Islamic-studies scholar whom Said never mentions, Smith was arguably an "orientalist" who was delineating and practicing, long before Said's book, an approach to the Islamic and other Afro-Asian worlds of the classic "Orient" that was different from, and highly critical of, the kind of "orientalism" that Said's blanket criticism would later stigmatize for all subsequent students of non-Western studies.

It seems odd at first that Said would not have made some effort to mention orientalists who did not fit his paradigm, perhaps chief among them Smith, a Canadian who had had founded and directed McGill University's Institute of Islamic Studies in the 1950s. Smith had spent six years during World War II teaching in a Christian missionary college in Lahore, in British-colonial northwest India (during which time he was working also on a doctorate in oriental studies at Cambridge University). His older brother Arnold, a Canadian career foreign service diplomat, capped his diplomatic career by becoming the first secretary general of the British Commonwealth in 1965. On the face of it, especially since

Smith was by the 1970s a particularly prominent senior North American orientalist, what better counterexample or exception to Said's "orientalist" establishment might he have found—a Western "orientalist" who was part of the Anglo-American Islamic-studies establishment, had family ties to the British Commonwealth establishment, and yet had also castigated the kind of hegemonic Western approaches to the Orient that Said inveighed against among Western orientalists?

Nevertheless, if Said was aware of Smith, he gave no indication of it. Certainly Smith's approach to Islamic or more generally to non-Western or "oriental" studies was not one that could have provided grist for Said's mill. What Smith had to say in his own criticism of attitudes among Western interpreters of "the Orient" toward "oriental" individuals and groups in his lectures and writings over more than three decades before Said's book appeared can be said to parallel the very kind of critique that Said makes, albeit from a very different perspective and in a different (decidedly not postmodern) idiom. (The same holds, as indicated above, for the positions Marshall Hodgson took in his efforts to look at the worldwide history of Islamic peoples and to argue the non-exceptionalism of European civilization; Said apparently knew nothing of his publications or his singular teaching career at the University of Chicago, both of which were cut short by his untimely death a decade before the appearance of *Orientalism*). I want to think that Said simply did not even attempt to canvass the field of American oriental studies; otherwise, one would have to conclude that Smith and Hodgson were excluded from consideration simply because they did not fit his paradigm of hegemonic orientalist scholarship.

Turning now to Wilfred Smith, I shall restrict myself in this brief exploration to considering Smith's *opera minora*, his lesser-known essays and articles, rather than drawing on his major, longer studies that bear on Islamic studies and Western colonialism and imperialism, since the latter have been widely read and cited.[4] To support my estimation of how little Smith's work fits Said's paradigm, I want to point briefly to some of the positions that Smith took that run counter to, or at least greatly complicate, the otherwise resolutely critical picture Said paints of prominent Western "orientalists" who studied and interpreted the non-West, its languages, cultures, politics, religions, and histories, going back at least to the late eighteenth century—and carried out their studies in the hegemonic context of Western societies that were systematically engaged in the despoilment, exploitation, colonization, and subjugation of non-Western societies around the world.

First, in his young adulthood, until perhaps the end of World War II, Smith was strongly socialist, even Marxist, and pacifist in his own politics—tendencies that we may speculate were only heightened by what he experienced during his six years in the British imperial India of the early 1940s. As a budding historian of Islam and India, he saw the grave consequences there of the "merchant" and then "industrial capitalism" that had exploited India under the East India Company and the British Raj. He was himself personally involved in some prepartition, Indian nationalist efforts to get rid of British rule, move beyond communalism, and find a way to a new, independent, unified India (he always regarded partition as a mistake and an unmitigated catastrophe). Smith's first scholarly monograph treated Muslim political and religious movements during what was to be the final century of British rule in the subcontinent. This book was completed in the middle of his time in India, in 1943, and submitted as his Cambridge doctoral dissertation. However (as H. A. R. Gibb had warned him[5]), it was turned down when presented during the war, apparently because of its unvarnished anti-British sentiments.[6] Published nonetheless in Lahore in 1943 as *Modern Islam in India: A Social Analysis* (2nd rev. ed., 1946), the book subsequently went through multiple editions and printings, the latest at least as recently as 2006. Although Smith, amid the ongoing disillusionments of communist dictatorships, abandoned his socialist and Marxist leanings, his moralist critique of Western imperialism, capitalism, and colonialism remained still strong in his writings of the 1950s and '60s especially. His first book had made clear above all that he would not make common cause with other orientalists in approaching the Orient, and Islam in particular, as a member of a Western tradition of either political and economic or intellectual hegemony, without a critical self-consciousness of that fact and a dedication to transcending it.

The first note sounded by Smith in his postwar work that I want to point to is *the rejection of any approach to Islamic, Hindu, or other Asian traditions that sees them as passive recipients or "victims" of a dominant "Western modernity" that has dealt them a blow either disrupting them or leading them to slavish imitation*. In a paper, "Traditional Religions and Modern Culture" in 1968, he says: "The impact theory has been widely held, usually without argument, perhaps especially by Western administrators, by political scientists, and by economic-aid men. . . . The impact idea often seems to suggest a somewhat massive assault under force of which the traditional system in this dichotomy is seen as reeling, bewildered, if not knocked down. . . . The impact metaphor also seems to suffer from a serious under-estimate of the dynamic, fluid quality of the so-called traditional religious systems."[7]

The chauvinistic, hegemonic idea of the Western, or the Western Christian, world as dominant and active, the subject, and of the oriental world of whatever type as submissive and passive, the object of the West's more "objective" knowledge and greater political power, is something that Edward Said later would associate strongly with "orientalism" in his book. More than two decades earlier than Said's book and a decade before his just-cited paper, Smith had spelled this out in a different manner in an interesting 1955 address to the American Oriental Society, which was published a year later as "The Place of Oriental Studies in a Western University."[8] In this address, in terms remarkably parallel to what Said would argue some twenty-three years later, Smith makes clear the danger that he sees of American or any Western study of the "Orient" becoming complicit in supporting political, economic, or any other domination of that "Orient":

> When an unexpected problem, an unfamiliar obstacle, confronts an ongoing activity, the universities are called upon to solve that problem, to manipulate that obstacle.
>
> It would be idle to deny that this principle underlies, and doubtless will continue to underlie, the stark and perhaps exhilarating expansion of oriental studies in our day. It is the source of money, of students, of whole new programs. But it would be equally idle to deny that it is full of danger, both to our studies and to the world. There is the danger of "being used"; of subordinating knowledge to policy, rather than vice versa. There is the subtler danger of acquiring seeming knowledge that is, in fact, false. For it happens to be a law of this universe in which we live that you cannot understand persons if you treat them as objects. You misinterpret a culture if you approach it in order to manipulate it. A civilization does not yield it secrets except to a mind that approaches it with humility and love. Knowledge pursued *ad majorem Americae gloriam* will, in the realm of oriental, as indeed in all human studies, fail to be sound knowledge. . . .
>
> [A] university cannot glibly subordinate its study of the Orient to the pragmatic desire of its society to cope with the Orient operationally.[9]

Here Smith points toward a second and enduring theme of his subsequent work, namely *the imperative for the scholar not to objectify what or whom she or he studies*. Later in the article he makes this more explicit:

> We shall have failed in our task as orientalists if our society continues to imagine that the problem is how we in the West can deal with the Orient. The practical problem is rather how man throughout the world can deal with the fact that he is separated from his neighbor by a cultural frontier.[10]

Smith expands on what is wrong with this kind of objectification of other societies, traditions, or persons somewhat more clearly in an address that he gave at Colgate University in 1975:

> To treat persons objectively, as if they were objects, is not merely morally wrong, but is intellectually wrong. It does not lead to accurate or penetrating understanding. Hence the Western university does its work badly if it interprets Asia in purely objective, behaviourist, impersonalist terms, on the one hand, under the pretention of being "scientific," or if, on the other hand, it simply presents it in its own Asian terms, uninterpreted, receiving at face value and uncritically the self-understanding of an alien culture.[11]

Over a decade earlier, Smith's 1964 inaugural lecture at Harvard, "Mankind's Religiously Divided History Approaches Self-consciousness," had broached the concept of "corporate critical self-consciousness" as an antidote to objectification of other religious persons and traditions. Here he calls for those who study "other" religious traditions to recognize that henceforward whatever one says or writes can no longer be about "them" or even "you" as opposed to "us," but only about "us" altogether as fellow human beings of all faiths and cultures.[12]

A decade later, in a 1974 article, "Objectivity and the Humane Sciences: A New Proposal,"[13] Smith expands on his solution to the problem of objectivizing the "other." Here he argues again, but in greater detail, for the development of a "corporate critical self-consciousness," which he sees as essential to "humane studies," and as "the proper goal of humane knowing." He defines it as a rational, inductive, and communal understanding that is subject to a "valid verification procedure." While his explicit definition of this understanding in the article is frankly somewhat impenetrable,[14] he does go on in the article to elucidate more simply what he means by the term. There he indicates that, first, "corporate critical self-consciousness" requires objective knowledge: namely, that in studying another culture or religious community, one must insure "that a first observer's understanding has done justice to what is observed" by testing it against the experience of further observers. Second, such self-consciousness involves the understanding "that no statement involving persons is valid . . . unless its validity can be verified both by the persons involved and by critical observers not involved."[15] In sum, this is a strong argument against the kind of objectification of the "other" that Said identifies as typical if not universal in the work of Western scholars studying things "oriental."

A third theme of Smith's work from the '50s through the '70s is also very much at variance with the "orientalist" hegemonic approach to the non-Western world that Said excoriates in his book. This is Smith's *objection to the idea, rooted in the evolutionary biases of the previous century of Western thought, that modernity is something being achieved by the Western world in the late nineteenth and especially the twentieth centuries that should be, and is being, emulated by the most progressive elements in "the Orient."* Smith debunks this notion in several places, not least in his three 1964 Annual Lectures of the Indian Council of World Affairs at Sapru House, New Delhi, published in pamphlet form as "Modernization of a Traditional Society."[16] Noting that "what 'modern' means is not really clear,"[17] he goes on to question whether the "traditional [W]estern state" is really "modern" or perhaps itself now an outmoded model for a sovereign nation. Then he argues trenchantly that "India, or any non-[W]estern community cannot just copy the West in its transformations, and cannot even find the meaning or content of modernization by simply inquiring from the West."[18] Even though India can learn from the West, "India's goal must be clearly an Indian goal, and the idea of imitating the West or imposing purely [W]estern solutions to India's problem is distasteful or laughable."[19] He subsequently remarks on the multiple ways in which India's circumstances differ from those in the West, even as he affirms that humanity is one, albeit a "multiform one."[20] He warns against treating "modernism" as a commodity to be acquired,[21] and he also points out that there is no single Western answer to the question of modernization to give to India or anyone else, for modernization has become a global process transcending the West. Hence "the fully modern West is no longer [W]estern"[22] at all but something more global: "The categories 'Western' and 'Oriental,' or more accurately 'Western,' 'Islamic,'

'Indian,' 'Far Eastern,' etc., have been exceedingly important—it is my professional business to say how important. Yet they are today in the process of being superseded, however incipiently, by a new cosmopolitanism. . . . The modernization of the West cannot be defined in terms of the West's future, for the West does not have a future of its own. It can look forward intelligently only to the [W]estern stand in the future of the world: a future that all of us must construct jointly, for good or ill."[23]

This line of argument is augmented in the same essay by statements such as "Afro-Asian resurgence involves not only a throwing off of [W]estern political control but also a refusal to think in [W]estern ways," following which he notes that that Afro-Asian "refusals" should not only be negative but involve active efforts to modernize on their own terms and, correspondingly, that Westerners must think of modernizing not only in old Western terms, but must rather develop a common global frame of reference within which to modernize.[24] Again, Smith pushes toward a future in which any group anywhere should think of itself and everyone else globally in terms of "we," not "we and they." This is the antithesis of the hegemonic treatment of the non-Western world for which Said indicts the Western orientalist tradition.

The fourth, and in many ways the clearest, testimony that I want to highlight from among Smith's attempts to move beyond older "orientalist" paradigms of Western academic study of the Orient comes not from his writings so much as from his pragmatic work in creating the Institute of Islamic Studies at McGill on the principle that *the study of anything Islamic in a non-Muslim institution must be pursued in conversation with, and under the critique of, Muslim as well as non-Muslim scholars*. Smith led the Institute from its inception in 1952 until he left McGill for Harvard in 1964. (It is particularly fitting, I think, to end on this note, given that the conference for which this paper was prepared was held under McGill auspices on its campus; while Smith pursued similar principles as director of the Center for the Study of World Religions from 1964 to 1973, it was at McGill that he first tried to implement his approach.) Smith's principle of demanding that there be mutual critique by both Muslim and non-Muslim scholars alike of any analysis of things Islamic was evident from the outset in the makeup of the Institute's membership. The ethos of the endeavor is well captured in a 1996 appreciation of Smith's work at the Institute by McGill's Salwa Ferahian:

> The Institute endeavors to offer to Westerners a serious encounter with a civilization other than their own. It recognizes

that such an experience, in order to be valid, may require a creative modification of one's own terms of reference. It strives to help Western students understand and appreciate an important, rich and varied civilization.

To Muslims, the Institute aspires to offer an opportunity to study their own society in a serious, disciplined, scientific, and sympathetic environment, and to understand the international setting in which their society is currently involved and the problems that in modern times their faith must face.

The Institute was founded for the purpose of engaging in the serious study of the modern Muslim world. The innovative element was Smith's conviction that this could not be done effectively by non-Muslims studying in a non-Muslim institution and without the participation of Muslims. The design for the Institute, including the design for the library, was the result of his creative response to the dilemma, as he saw it, of how to study Islam in a way that would involve Muslims and non-Muslims.[25]

Smith's commitment to such an approach in studying Islam at McGill is also demonstrated vividly in his approach to the first major book that he completed in his years at McGill, *Islam in Modern History* (1967). He submitted each of his chapter drafts for this book as the text for critical discussion in a session of a faculty seminar that included both Muslim and non-Muslim scholars currently at the university; he then made changes as needed on the basis of the discussions there.[26]

The approach instituted by Smith at McGill exemplifies what I am describing as his rejection of (in Said's terms) an "orientalist" orientation to the study of the history of religion in particular, which was, after all, at the heart of his work on both Islam and other religious traditions and cultures. This is clear from frequently cited references, both in his own work and in critiques and appreciations of his work, to "persons," as opposed to "religions," as the proper focus of historical and social inquiry. Near the end of his 1965 paper, "Traditional Religions and Modern Culture"[27] (which was the first of Smith's writings cited above), he delineates the proper scope of the study of religion by averring that "the subject matter of our study . . . is not merely tradition, but faith; not merely the overt manifestations of man's religious life, but that life itself."[28] He goes on to say, "my entire thesis can be summed up in the phrase, that the study of religion must be fundamentally a study of persons."[29] He makes clear in a short 1979 essay, "Thinking about Persons," that by "person" he does not mean "individual," "for the fact is that the individual becomes a person only in community. And a society becomes a community only through being personal."[30] He goes on to note that older outlooks, Western or Eastern, were characterized by a coherence or integrity in which the natural, the personal, and the transcendent orders were perceived as "part of a total pattern"; it has been the rise of "objectivism" in modern science in the West that has fractured that integration, and it is now imperative in the light of the crises of our time (he mentions the nuclear threat and oceanic pollution as examples) to deal with the lack of integrity and coherence in our approach to the world. Of possible solutions to the problem, Smith's choice is "to pursue integration through a larger rationality—available to us, I believe, through a study of human history: an intellectual vision, of wholeness, within which the scientific is a component explicitly subordinate, and partial, and even inadequate, yet important; in which the personal, done full justice, is central; and for which the realm of value, though higher than we, is recognized as real, and is rendered intelligible, and apprehensible, even if not (in our finitude) fully comprehensible."[31]

This personal emphasis is ubiquitous in Smith's writings, and it has been widely misconstrued to mean unscientific subjectivity rather than scientific objectivity, something that he, dedicated rationalist that he was, would never have dreamed of suggesting. I would argue that one of the things he was trying to get at with this emphasis is specifically the problem of objectification of the *human* "other" whom he as an orientalist scholar had dedicated his life to studying. He was convinced at a very deep level that any humane study of a Muslim, or Hindu, or any religious or cultural "other" (even including any "other" in our own society and culture) requires more than some imagined objective knowledge to do justice to him or her. It is precisely the objectification and the subordination to "our" higher Western scientific knowledge of the Orient and the oriental "other" later inveighed against by Edward Said that Smith also saw as dangerous and dehumanizing—not only to the "oriental" being objectified, but to the objectivizing occidental scholar, because of the inherent distortion and intellectual dishonesty of such an approach. As he put it in the passage cited earlier, "the Western university does its work badly if it interprets Asia in purely objective, behaviourist, impersonalist terms."

In this, Smith was in a very real sense arguing for scholarly study that could transcend the limitations of the orientalist approach that he himself must surely have seen as rightly excoriated by Said.[32] Like Said,

Smith had from the outset of his career, and primarily in the Indian rather than the Palestinian context, seen the linkage between Western economic and political intrusion into the Orient and the damaging force of an objectifying, much less than fully humane, scholarship focused on the indigenous cultural and religious traditions of that same Orient. Of course his book, *Modern Islam in India*, testifies to this, as did his anticolonial activism in India and, ultimately, his much-referenced "personalist" approach to Muslims, their faith and tradition and the wider world of Islamic cultures and civilization. The objectifying, culturally imperialist "orientalism" attacked so tellingly by Edward Said could hardly be said to be something Smith ever tolerated, let alone represented or fell prey to; in fact he actively fought against it, as the preceding should have demonstrated. It is unfortunate that Smith and Said apparently never shared with one another their very similar indictments of many lamentable strands of Western orientalism.

Notes

1. As seen in comments Said makes at the outset in *Orientalism*, such as: Orientalism is "a Western style for dominating, restructuring, and having authority over the Orient" (p. 3), and "The relationship between Occident and Orient is a relationship of power, of domination, of varying degrees of a complex hegemony." (p. 5). Edward Said, *Orientalism* (New York: Vintage Books, 1978).

2. Notably his much subtler book, *Culture and Imperialism* (New York: Knopf, 1993).

3. Not to mention the excessive repetition and generally sloppy editing of the book, which is particularly curious given the excellence and precision typical of Said's large corpus of scholarship otherwise.

4. E.g., Wilfred Cantwell Smith, *Modern Islam in India* (Lahore: Ripton Printing Press, 1945) and *Islam in Modern History* (Princeton, NJ: Princeton University Press, 1957), *The Meaning and End of Religion* (New York: Macmillan, 1962), etc.

5. Personal oral communication of W. C. Smith, ca. 1982.

6. Smith went to Princeton after the war and earned his PhD with a thesis on the content of the *Majallat al-Azhar*, the monthly journal of Al-Azhar in Cairo.

7. *Proceedings of the XIth International Congress of the International Association for the History of Religions* (held at Claremont, CA, September 1965), vol. 1: *The Impact of Modern Culture on Traditional Religions* (Leiden: E. J. Brill, 1968), pp. 55–72.

8. Wilfred Cantwell Smith, "The Place of Oriental Studies in a Western University," *Diogenes* 16 (Winter, 1956), pp. 104–11.

9. Ibid., pp. 108–9.

10. Ibid., p. 109.

11. Wilfred Cantwell Smith, "The Role of Asian Studies in the American University," plenary address of the New York State Conference for Asian Studies, Colgate University, October 10–12, 1975 (published in pamphlet form with support from the Fund for the Study of the Great Religions of the World, Colgate University, 1976), pp. 9–10.

12. Wilfred Cantwell Smith, "Mankind's Religiously Divided History Approaches Self-Consciousness," *Harvard Divinity Bulletin* 29 (1966), pp. 1–17.

13. Wilfred Cantwell Smith, "Objectivity and the Humane Sciences: A New Proposal," *Transactions of the Royal Society of Canada*, 4th ser., 12 (1974), pp. 81–102.

14. "that critical, rational, inductive self-consciousness by which a community of persons, constituted at a minimum by two persons, the one being studied and the one studying, but ideally by the whole human race, is aware of any given particular human condition or action as a condition or action of itself as a community, yet of one part but not of the whole of itself; and is aware of it as it is experienced and understood simultaneously both subjectively (personally, existentially) and objectively (externally, critically, analytically; as one used to say, scientifically)." Ibid., 84.

15. Ibid.

16. Wilfred Cantwell Smith, *Modernization of a Traditional Society* (New York: Asia Publishing House, 1965).

17. Ibid., p. 7.

18. Ibid., p. 12.

19. Ibid.

20. Ibid., p. 13.

21. Ibid., p. 18.

22. Ibid., p. 15.

23. Ibid., pp. 15–16.

24. Ibid., p. 43.

25. Salwa Ferahian, "W. C. Smith Remembered," MELA [Middle East Librarians Association] *Notes*, no. 64 [1996], viewed October 31, 2009, at the unpaginated website: http://www.mela.us/MELANotes/MELANotes64/toc64.html.

26. Personal communications in conversation with Herbert L. Bodman (who had taught previously at McGill with Smith) at UNC–Chapel Hill and with W. C. Smith in Cambridge, MA, both in the late 1960s.

27. Smith, *Impact on Traditional Religions*, pp. 68–72.

28. Ibid., p. 68.

29. Ibid., pp. 71–72.

30. Wilfred Cantwell Smith, "Thinking about Persons," *Humanitas: Journal of the Institute of Man* 15, no. 2 (May, 1979), p. 148.

31. Ibid., p. 152.

32. Here this author has to confess to an inability to remember any specific confirmation of this from discussions with Smith after his 1978 return to Harvard (and an adjacent office in the Study of Religion) from Dalhousie. I do remember Smith's general approval of the positive review of Said's book by Albert Hourani at the time.

Bibliography

Ferahian, Salwa. "W. C. Smith Remembered." *MELA* [Middle East Librarians Association] *Notes*, no. 64 [1996], viewed October 31, 2009, at the unpaginated web site: http://www.mela.us/MELANotes/MELANotes64/toc 64.html.

Said, Edward. *Orientalism*. New York: Vintage Books, 1978.

———. *Culture and Imperialism*. New York: Knopf, 1993.

Smith, Wilfred Cantwell. *Modern Islam in India*. Lahore: Ripton Printing Press, 1945.

———. *Islam in Modern History*. Princeton, NJ: Princeton University Press, 1957.

———. *The Meaning and End of Religion*. New York: Macmillan, 1962.

———. "Traditional Religions and Modern Culture." *Proceedings of the XIth International Congress of the International Association for the History of Religions*. Claremont, CA, September 1965. Vol. 1: *The Impact of Modern Culture on Traditional Religions*, 55–72. Leiden: E. J. Brill, 1968.

———. "The Place of Oriental Studies in a Western University." *Diogenes* 16 (Winter 1956), pp. 104–11.

———. "The Role of Asian Studies in the American University." Plenary address of the New York State Conference for Asian Studies, Colgate University, October 10–12, 1975. Published in pamphlet form with support from the Fund for the Study of the Great Religions of the World, Colgate University, 1976.

———. "Mankind's Religiously Divided History Approaches Self-Consciousness." *Harvard Divinity Bulletin* 29 (1966), pp. 1–17.

———. "Objectivity and the Humane Sciences: A New Proposal." *Transactions of the Royal Society of Canada*, 4th ser., 12 (1974), pp. 81–102.

———. *Modernization of a Traditional Society*. New York: Asia Publishing House, 1965.

———. "Thinking about Persons." *Humanitas: Journal of the Institute of Man* 15, no. 2 (May 1979), pp. 147–52.

Enabling Antinomies

Tensions and Tensile Strength in Wilfred Cantwell Smith

John Stratton Hawley

Wilfred Smith used to talk a great deal about transcendence, and there was something oddly transcendent about his presence. It was so in a physical way. I don't know exactly how tall he was, but he always seemed a little taller. And yet, for all its height, his body simultaneously bespoke a lifelong fondness for sitting and reading. There was something rounded in his torso, suitable for cradling a book. Even in his physical presence, then, there was a built-in contradiction. He was massively tall, thin, and assertive in some fantastically WASPish way, and yet at the same time he was stooped, rounded, inward-looking.

His verbal personality was similarly enigmatic. On the one hand there was his unrelenting insistence on precision: the sharply crafted phrases, the Edwardian manners, the overwhelming exactitude, the page-long polyglot footnotes and his fearsome willingness to check what appeared in the footnotes of his students' papers. Once I heard he had proposed to offer a workshop on the art of the memo. Yet for all this precision, things had a tendency to trail off as he moved through life, as if he was himself aware of how tenuous and fragile these verbal formulations actually were. How many times, listening to one of his lectures, did I wonder whether or not he had finished his thought? I often felt I was observing one of those celestial sages from Buddhist Dunhuang, with the robes that flow off into nowhere. Then suddenly he would be back—he'd not forgotten us after all; the sentence remained to be completed. Or perhaps aborted: he'd suddenly ask for a show of hands to determine how many students in the class considered themselves polytheists.

You could actually see him thinking. Enmeshed though he was in the fabulous web of words, you could still see the wind of thought blow through him. It was the same with his historical consciousness. Situated ever so definitely at Harvard or McGill and regarding the world from his carefully examined position in what he called "the modern Western academy," he nonetheless wondered aloud whether it might have been better to have lived in Baghdad in the tenth century, or Agra in the sixteenth, or Chang-an in the eighth. If these were imagined destinations, they were hardly random. They shared a telltale cosmopolitanism, a world-determining urban self-confidence that he certainly chose for himself. I never felt he was so transcendent that he could really imagine for himself a life spent in the desert or on a farm.

One could make an argument that Wilfred Smith was the first great postmodernist in the field of religious studies. He spent his life fighting essentialism ("reification," he called it); he was tireless in questioning the going notions of Self and Other; and he loved to point out how "constructed" our sense of the past actually is. Yet he managed to do all this in a distinctly old-fashioned way. He looked and often spoke like the past, and would have felt quite strange wearing the future on his sleeve. Still, in this volume we are doing just that—examining the future he anticipated and helped create.

A man of puzzles, then. In this essay I hope to pursue some of these puzzles by taking the word "contradiction" out of the paragraph with which I began and replacing it with "antinomy." The *Oxford English Dictionary* warns us that this is apt to be a meaningless exercise, for the word *antinomy* is all about contradiction. An antinomy is, I quote, "a contradiction in a law, or between two equally binding laws; a contradiction between conclusions which seem equally logical, reasonable, or necessary; a paradox; intellectual contradictoriness (After Kant)." And here's one Wilfred would have liked. According to the *OED*, antinomy is "an authoritative contradiction. *Obs.*" Those italics mark off something obsolete. As for me, though, I would focus on the "after Kant" part. The remarkable thing about Kant's antinomies was that—in the lineage of Hegel and Marx—they actually did lead somewhere beyond their own mutual contradiction: outside the box, as the familiar phrase has it. Wilfred Smith was acutely conscious of our intellectual and, one might say, dispositional boxes, and he had a great talent for pointing beyond them. I wonder whether Wilfred's entanglement in a particular set of antinomies may have been the key to the special brand of intellectual freedom that he enjoyed. If despite his staid appearance and genteel habits of speech he was indeed some sort of mental Houdini, perhaps an examination of the special set of ropes and chains that bound him will provide clues as to how he managed to escape—and take a few other jail-mates out of the box with him.

In the spring of 2001 I convened for the first time a graduate seminar at Columbia called World Religions: Idea, Display, Institution. Its purpose—remember, this was before the publication of Tomoko Masuzawa's famous book—was to investigate how that concept came into being and got institutional legs, and whether it made any sense.[1] We toured the Parliament of the World's Religions in Chicago and interrogated several of its participants; we followed P. J. Marshall as he sleuthed his way into *The British Discovery of Hinduism in the Eighteenth Century*; we examined the curators of the Buddha.[2] And inevitably, we watched as with great majesty the Center for the Study of World Religions at Harvard emerged from the wings and walked on for a crucial role. We read *The Meaning and End of Religion*—strange manifesto for such an institution—and wondered about what Wilfred Smith left behind at McGill when he went south of the border to become director of the Harvard center. Was this going to be way too much institution for the *End* part of his title to survive? How could Wilfred submit himself in service to the concept "religion"—and worse, to the concept "world religions," whose plural he found so especially odious? For a man of intellectual principle, someone who loved to think of Confucius straightening his mat as if gesturing to his great project of rectifying names, here was a minefield of contradictions. Confucius's own name had to be rectified to Kung Fu-tzu in Wilfred's speech. How then would he muddle through at the (from his point of view) distinctly misnamed Center for the Study of World Religions?

I hope that Wilfred would have liked the idea of mounting a course on the concept and practice of "world religions," where puzzles such as these were thrust into the limelight. When we came to the Harvard center in the course of our seminar, we tried to subject it and the thoughts Wilfred brought to it to the same effort of historicization that he himself pursued on a much grander scale. Needless to say, we read *The Meaning and End of Religion*, and we tried to talk it through. The discussion left me with a knot in my stomach. Something seemed unfinished, undigested. And the next morning, as if goaded by a large invisible hand, I set out to write a memo to my seminar companions about my discomfiture: "Dear all, I found myself this morning chewing over the issues that emerged for me in rereading parts of Wilfred Smith's oeuvre, and in thinking about the critical reactions to him that Talal Asad and several of you have offered. I came to feel that one way of displaying some of the issues involved (thought issues and doubtless life issues too) would be to think of them as tensions in his thought—or to put it in a stronger form, antinomies that are not quite soluble in their own terms. Here is how I would list them this morning. . . ."

That morning is now long gone, but in considering the nature of Wilfred's legacy I find myself going back to the list I drafted more than a decade ago. Deeply dug substance, sharply stated criticism, and a remarkable range of data are surely major aspects of Wilfred Smith's scholarly impact, but I would add to these a persistent element of tension or antinomy that colored so much of what he did. Often when Wilfred articulated some large theoretical point, there would be another side to it, hidden just beneath, and often he himself had articulated that contrary undercurrent in a different way somewhere else. By tacking back and forth across the water in this fashion, I believe, he amassed the buoyancy and tensile strength to keep going, to change and hold on at the same time, and to welcome others into the world of thought that he inhabited. I wonder if this may have been his greatest intellectual legacy. It wasn't that he got it all right. I think Talal Asad, in his classic memorial article of 2001, has shown with deep appreciation that he did not.[3] But the very plasticity of Smith's formulations, taken as a whole, and especially their devotion to process, have made his way of thinking endure to an extent that has been possible for only a few. Ah, how he loved a paragraph in which he uttered only a single declarative sentence! But was this not because so many other paragraphs were long and many-sided, even rigorously indeterminate?

Starting with the language of Wilfred's masterwork, then, *The Meaning and End of Religion*, let me name the ten antinomies that I circulated among members of my seminar as I tried to understand how this process worked. Or to be truthful, it's nine plus one: I have added the last on the list from another store. Of these, the first is doubtless the most important—the inspiration for all the rest. I take it to be Wilfred's vade mecum for an exercise such as this.

1. *Tradition vs. Faith.* This is the tension that Wilfred himself announced as the basic dynamic that made "human religiousness" work. He proposed this paired formulation as a way to escape from the term *religion* as used in modern European languages, and from the depth of human intellectual depravity that he saw it as representing: our cardinal sin as a species of language-users, the sin of reification. We trivialize

when we call this essentialism, as if were a plague that could be contained by levying that now familiar quarantine judgment. Intellectual name-calling of this sort doesn't quite do the work, for reification isn't an "ism," it's a process. We are all implicated in it, and it extends far beyond the zone we call religion. Yet it is worth considering whether religion is perhaps the realm that most perfectly facilitates this sin—here's the bad side of tradition—as well as the best means toward release from it, since it so often cultivates the growth of something Wilfred called faith.

Talal Asad has come to the judgment that these two terms, *tradition* and *faith*, are not a fair match for one another in Wilfred's system. He says that for Smith "the continuity of tradition depends on faith but not the other way around."[4] There is considerable truth in such an observation, and it was a truth that Wilfred himself once suggested by saying that he was most interested in the "better side" of human religiousness—the better side from his point of view. We can see this imbalance in a number of passages in Wilfred's writing, not just the one to which Asad particularly refers us. One that comes to mind for me is the following:

> Religious communities have been extremely important; but they are not final, either historically or conceptually. To be religious is an ultimately personal act. It is, to an important degree, an act that one makes in community; but it is not one that any community can make for one.
>
> Faith finds expression not only in community as such, but in a number of social institutions, from monogamous marriage to temple prostitution, from Sunday schools to the Caliphate. Such matters have come into historical existence and have remained there modified or developed, for a number of historical reasons, of which quite a fundamental one is that the particular religious faith of particular persons has found expression in them. These like other religious actualities have unquestionably existed not only in this world but of this world, within its imperfections and corruptions and ambiguities and drift. This fact is not precluded by, nor does it preclude, the other fact that they have expressed a partly unworldly faith within men's hearts.[5]

Even in a passage like this, however, where the personal "act of faith" is so palpably front and center, I would plead that the force of the other side of the antinomy—the tradition side—is also something seriously to be reckoned with. As he writes these paragraphs, Wilfred explores interconnections between religious communities and other social institutions—a wider "tradition" net than is captured in the term *religious community* itself—and he is eager not only to see faith as exceeding that which is "worldly" but bearing it at the same time. He is struggling to keep together the several institutions ("community" is only one) that come into relation if one takes seriously what he calls faith, and to insist, thereby, that faith is a necessary component in the making and reporting of history.

Thus even with regard to faith Wilfred was a deeply historical being, though of course he was not sufficiently practice-oriented in the way Asad and others would have liked him to be. One way of excusing this, if you had to put it that way, would be to say that he often had his eye on a wider realm of practice than the term "religious" usually designates. In any case, I would propose that his elaboration of what made traditions traditions actually *was* at the core of what he did; it wasn't all a flight to faith. Smith's attention to tradition was what made his observations about reification so powerful. True, he was sometimes obsessed with the importance of dimensions of history that he felt other historians had failed to appreciate, but that made him, so he hoped, more adequate as a student of tradition, not less so. At the same time, I think we have to concede that Wilfred was sometimes afraid that what he considered the true subject of human religiousness—transcendence or even (shhhhhh!) God—would disappear from view if he gave in to the power of practice, ritual, and discourse as much as his own bifocal orientation to religion may really have required. And that brings us to the next antinomy.

2. *Cultural history vs. the radical individual subject.* This antinomy is similar to the first, but the focus now is on the formation of the self. Here we meet a very intriguing question. Time and again Wilfred would point out how culturally determined our Western presumptions about the primacy of the individual self actually are. Every time I hear it said that an individual would do this or that—as against a person or simply someone—I hear Wilfred grinding his teeth. He joined McKim Marriott in thinking about the *dividual* as a counterweight to this uninterrogated New World monster, the autonomous solitary being called the *individual*.[6] But one might well ask whether Wilfred's faith commitments prevented him from going the second mile. Was he able to grant that selfhood

could be conceived entirely as a product of social-historical forces—a subjectivity constituted by discourse and practice? Or did he always have to insist, as Asad has put it, that "the man or woman of faith is . . . a split subject" with respect to the material and perhaps ritual world that she or he inhabits? Even the discursive, stylistic embarrassment of "she or he" points to the difficulty: Wilfred always spoke as if *Homo religiosus* could be genderless. Was this because at root he thought in terms of an ideal conscious subject unconditioned by social fact? Or should we give greater weight to his awareness that *Homo religiosus* was instead a species-specific thing, and as a matter of speciation, something that both challenged and bent toward the specific conditions of period, age, or place?

However we end up untangling this knot—if indeed we are able—I think it points us to the antinomy involved. I wonder whether Smith was able to feel the full force of the great flow of cultural history, as he insisted our increasingly global self-consciousness was forcing us to do, precisely because he took it for granted that we all stand as our own radical selves before God. Was this his Archimedean vantage point, and if so, did it unbalance the antinomy? Even as he ruminated in lectures about the meaning of what are usually called "prehistoric" physical remains—those having to do with burial practice, in particular—and cautioned against assuming that we knew what was going on in the minds of those responsible for leaving them behind, there was a sense of kinship in the endeavor. I think he cared about violating the conceptual space of these early examples of *Homo sapiens* not just because it was bad history but because it was an insult to subjectivity itself, something he somehow shared with these long-gone forebears. So there, then, the sense of tension was palpable. The general historian never gave up—no field was too large for him to gaze on—but neither did the radically conscious individual. Perhaps the one entailed the other, and it worked both ways.

3. *Formal verbiage vs. interior personhood.* This third antinomy offers another look at the same terrain—this time from the point of view of language. I love what Talal Asad does in this respect. He is happy to follow Smith from nouns to adjectives, but faults him for not proceeding on to adverbs.[7] Asad wants the transcendental subject to emerge—if emerge it can—not from a being, a nominalized entity, or even from the adjectival realm that logically depends on it (despite Smith's protestations about the important difference between "religion" and "religious"), but rather, within the realm of action itself. In this we hear the clear voice of the anthropologist.

Once again, however, before we simply affirm that Asad is right, there is another dimension of Wilfred's intellectual personality to be considered: his devotion to speech as such—speech as practice, speech as the distinctive, transcendental human action. Was there ever a man who cared so much about his words, finicky to the point of being fanatical, ever conscious of the fact that any word emerged in a language and that "the human" is littered with languages in a deeply ontological way? That may well have been the crucible that served to refine his exalted sense of the personal. Or was it also the Christian exaltation of the person as ultimate (person as human integer, that is, not Trinitarian mask) that shed the light of contrast on the equally determinative power of language? Whichever etiology seems more persuasive, truth as proposition emerged as Smith's formidable enemy—and Smith, antinomously enough, was at once its foe and its proponent.[8]

4. *Smith against the hegemony of Protestant "belief" vs. Smith unaware of the hegemony of Protestantism in the "faith" he espoused as universal.* Here we turn the kaleidoscope again and another question takes shape—one that arises from Wilfred Smith's own preoccupations: Was he able to submit the concept of faith to the same historicist rigor he trained on the idea of belief? Or did faith stand for something sufficiently transcendent in his own economy of purpose that he really couldn't go that far? Did Smith believe too much in faith?

We have already quoted a passage in which Wilfred makes sweeping remarks about the historical entailments of faith, but he had an even greater interest in exposing the extent to which the foregrounding of propositional belief in the Christian West was a fact of relatively recent history—and therefore, from his point of view, very likely an anomaly. Faith, by contrast, remained a more worthy universal. Smith was supremely conscious of cultural, linguistic, and historical differences that bore upon any comparative investigation of the role and concept of faith in human history, but he was far less interested in the same enterprise insofar as it might pertain to belief. The one had general value; the other was a provincial aberration. Of course, Wilfred tried hard to demonstrate that this contrast in his evaluation of faith as against belief was one that emerged from a careful study of changing patterns of language and thought. It was a principled difference in assigning value, one that seemed to proceed from historical facts. But one can be forgiven for wondering, as Asad did, whether this was not also a somewhat prejudicial reading of historical change. Did the modernist sin of belief against faith stem from the fact that modernity itself—at least,

Smith's modernity—owed so much to the Protestant Reformation, with its peculiar exaltation of faith?

In an equal and opposite way I have sometimes been impressed by the level of comfort Smith felt when he was in the fecund jungle (or forest, as he said) that goes under the name of Hinduism. He loved the fact that Hindus "have gloried in diversity" rather than insisting on any uniformity of perception.[9] Among Hindus, belief, being elaborated in such wonderfully and self-consciously symbolic ways, seemed to have a harder time getting in the way of faith than in the Abrahamic traditions. Once again, was it ironically Smith's Protestant belief in faith that caused him to see things this way?

5. *Smith against reification vs. Smith as representationalist.* With this fifth antinomy, the time has come to get a little more operational. The antinomy involved is one to which William Darrow draws our attention by recalling a familiar subject of conversation at the Center for the Study of World Religions.[10] Namely, if the idea of "religions" is the lamentable product of reification processes that Smith identified in *The Meaning and End of Religion*, then what could be the logic of assembling people at the Harvard Center under precisely that rubric?

Here the difficulty was twofold. First, in the Center as it was when Wilfred Smith was director, there seemed to be at least a provisional acceptance of the category "world religion" (or "world religions") in performing the selection process. Those of us who were associated with the Center frequently found ourselves being thought of as Buddhist, Christian, Jain, and so forth. Not that Wilfred was the only one to parse things that way, but the particular living and intellectual environment over which he presided seemed to encourage it. To work with religious plurality in this way was hardly to abandon the processes of reification that kept the system going—everything that went into setting out "the great religions" or "world religions."

Second, there was the problematic idea that one person could actually represent the religious collectivity out of which he or she emerged. This was the representationalist fallacy that Darrow calls to mind. Why was it allowed to flourish? Did Smith's exaltation of the person—we were interacting as living, breathing people, not disembodied propositions—make it intellectually possible for him to ignore the difficulties otherwise involved? We might well ask: Was this retreat to "world religions" in the form of individual persons—retreat as measured against the ideals enunciated in *The Meaning and End of Religion*—integrally a part of Smith's method, or was it merely a tactical retreat, all that convenience (read: finance) would allow? After all, you couldn't assemble the world under a single roof.

Whatever we decide, I'd hate to read out the element of antinomy or in this case, irony. Those of us who lived at the Center often came to see just how unrepresentative Ms. X was of "her" religion—just as unrepresentative as I was of "mine." For one thing, she would tell me so, and I would do the same. So if there was a problem here, at least to some extent it was a problem that had a good result. Living cheek by jowl forced us to see that the "world religions" were not in fact persons writ large. We felt the internal disparities as dimensions of ourselves, and it was easy enough to draw out the disparities in others as well, both by extrapolation from ourselves and by outright questioning the other. All to the good, but in another respect it is hard to dismiss a negative dimension. Let's call it the Harvard problem—that sense of floating along above the rest of the world and the need to justify oneself as somehow representing the world for precisely that reason. This launches us into the next antinomy on the list.

6. *Smith as warrior against the cancerous, reifying West vs. Smith happy as a lark at places like Harvard and McGill.* Here is the specter of unacknowledged elitism, even if it appears under the banner of utopianism. Columbia students were quick to pick up on this one.

One of the things I liked most about Wilfred Smith was that he was perfectly happy to call himself an intellectual. This was the work he did. It wasn't that he felt one could only think within the enclosure of the academy—*The Faith of Other Men*, whose chapters began as radio talks, exemplifies just the opposite mentality—but there was no built-in embarrassment about the idea that a person might think for a living. Still, it was in large part the intellectual commitments of places like Harvard and McGill that turned them into such efficient engines of the corrosive, globe-gobbling Enlightenment of the missionary West and made them able to cantilever their self-created world above whatever existed anyplace else. Here was a legacy of engagement that almost inevitably tended to favor the metropole over the field, and as students at Harvard we felt such processes as an almost inevitable consequence of life at the Center itself.

In their defense, one could certainly see the Institute of Islamic Studies at McGill and the Center for the Study of World Religions at Harvard as long-running efforts to stage a palace coup against "the West" as it was then experienced and practiced. Indeed, one could say a great deal in the cause of justifying such a claim. But if the Center for the Study of World Religions was an attempt on Smith's part to stage a palace coup of "the Western academy," we have to acknowledge how much he loved the palace. Maybe a palace coup always entails just that.

7. *Dialogues of difference vs. transcendent intellect.* A famous problem for "Dr. Smith's approach," as my teaching fellow Donna Wulff used to call it when I was taking Wilfred's introductory course on world religion, was the issue of assent. Whatever you said about the "faith of other men," according to Smith, should be recognizable to that other "man." (Issues of translation would certainly arise, but he was well aware of those.) Furthermore—a stronger form of the same dialogical impulse—that person should be able to assent to the accuracy of your statement even if he or she was not in full agreement with its intent. These were wonderful demands, and they were the sort of thing the Center for the Study of World Religions sought to put into daily practice. The presumption was that if disparities emerged, you could talk them out. It was not necessarily that the "believer" always had the last word, but the burden of proof lay on the outsider. It was often felt, though never urged as a limiting condition for entrance into the field, that being an insider in another context—another "faith"—might provide some grease to oil the engine of dialogue.

Well and good, but because of the verbal, almost propositional level at which so much of this occurred, it was sometimes hard to fend off the lurking suspicion that what was actually being prioritized here was a shared intellectualism—bluntly, "higher education," even higher education of a particularly elite, internationalist cast. After all, why should an educated member of a religious community have a specially sanctioned right to speak on its behalf? Shouldn't it be the opposite in certain instances? What guarantee was there that such a person could act as a reliable interpreter? This was a specific form of representationalism, and it pointed beyond dialogue to a shared confidence in transcendent intellect, which served to mute the starker realities of difference. Thus once again the Center acted out a fundamental tension. And then there was a particular aspect of its history to take into consideration: the missionary factor, we might call it.

8. *Missionary vs. convert.* Was the Center, covertly speaking, a missionary environment and unbalanced in that way? That charge was sometimes made, and sure enough, both Wilfred Smith and John Carman had missionary elements in their pasts. You could hardly accuse either of them of keeping the natives out on the veranda, however, or of failing to respect intellectuals whose educational formations had been different

from their own. Hardly! But there was perhaps a danger that related to something that caught Talal Asad's attention. He quotes Smith's observation that "the formalities of one's religious tradition are at best a channel, and at worst a substitute" for the real thing, and goes on to say that this "is in essence the missionary's standpoint. The missionary cannot re-form people unless they are persuaded that the formal ways they live their life are accidental to their being, channels for which other channels can be substituted without loss."[11] Indeed, Smith had spent some extremely important years at Forman Christian College in Lahore, and formally he was doing missionary work. But it would be fair to ask, I think, whether he ended up being a missionary not to Muslims but to the missionaries themselves, and in relation to Muslims less a missionary than a convert—a convert to intellectual Islam. Did *iman* become his faith? I do not know the answer, or what answer Wilfred gave to himself on this point, but at the very least we have to think about both sides of this antinomy if we are tempted to pursue the missionary rubric in thinking about Wilfred Smith's encounter with Islam.

9. *Marxian analysis vs. Hegelian idealism.* The other great conversion that descended on Smith in his Lahore years was his conversion away from Marxism and toward the intellectual frame suggested by the comparative study of religion. This whole aspect of Smith's life was, in my experience, something we students hesitated to ask him about too closely. But Kevin Reinhart, in his role as the youngest child, the one most leniently treated—Kevin was the last of Wilfred's PhD students at Harvard—says he did once have the chance to ask that question in the course of a seminar on Wilfred's work at Dartmouth to which he had invited the man himself. What about that famous book in the brown paper wrapper? What about Wilfred's first dissertation, the one they refused to accept at Cambridge, the work that was later published (with a strangely dissonant final chapter not of his authorship[12]) as *Modern Islam in India?* What had happened to that sort of intellectual commitment?

The answer Wilfred gave, to Kevin's report, was that it had been the terrible violence of the partition of British India that caused the young Smith to see the force of religion as a political reality. It seemed plain that the power of ideas—religious ideas—was at least as important to understand as the power of class and the entailments of materiality. By designating this (a little playfully) as a move to "Hegelian idealism," I mean to indicate a certain backwatering of the jib—back from Marx to Hegel—but also to point to what I suspect was in Smith's own life a reversion to the ideal. Of course, Hegel also points forward, and here I am thinking of the essay Wilfred entitled "Mankind's Religiously Divided History Approaches Self-Consciousness"—a mouthful, no doubt, but an exact statement of the battlefield on which he saw himself engaged in combat.[13]

But what about antinomy? Was anything left of Smith's Marxism after his conversion? Yes, I think: the sense that history really mattered, right down to the details, and that a good bit of it was a dismal science.[14] I'm not sure Talal Asad has caught that side of things fully. If Smith's retreat from Marxism was a retreat, it was a tragic one, not a journey that sailed off into the skies. Inside, I wonder, did the conversation between the Marxist and the humanist continue to rage? Again, a report from Kevin Reinhart about that Dartmouth seminar is helpful. Wilfred had been accompanied by Muriel on that occasion, and one night, seated on Kevin's deck, when the discussion turned to politics "they emphatically asserted that they were socialists."[15] For Canadians, Kevin rightly observes, this may not have seemed as radical an affirmation as it would have been for citizens of the United States, yet anyone who knew Wilfred and Muriel will know that they really meant it, even if they didn't think the world was going to change anytime soon.

10. *Mozart vs. Dukkha.* This brings me to my final antinomy, and it comes to mind as I recall two unusual occasions when I thought I heard Wilfred speak in a self-consciously oracular way. One was in his lecture on the Buddhist concept *dukkha* in the big introductory course I have already mentioned. By contrast to all those lectures in which he would speak from notes and wait long, exquisite intervals until the proper word crystallized in his consciousness, this was a lecture he read. He had written it out word for word. He spent this lecture reconfiguring the notions of pain and suffering that he supposed we held in our minds, hoping we would see that the dictum "all is *dukkha*" says less about subjective experience than about the fact that everything in this world is awry. And here's the oracular part. He took the liberty of predicting that long after we'd forgotten everything else he had said in his course, we would remember this one lecture and its sober yet strangely joyful affirmation. He had a deep sense of things being awry—hence his passion for the Confucian project of rectifying names—and somehow one sensed he knew a good bit about suffering. I don't think anyone forgot the lecture.

Wilfred's second prognostication was of a different sort—indeed quite opposite. Every so often he'd venture to forecast that in heaven they'd be playing Mozart. One time I said I couldn't see it: surely they'd be singing Bach. He breathed deeply and asked, "Really?," as if no one had ever thought to challenge this particular preconception. We talked of it for a while—the eloquent cantatas, the grandeur and depth of the B Minor Mass held up against the magic of *The Magic Flute*—and he seemed open to the idea that he might be wrong. But not really. In his heart it was always Mozart. I think he needed it to deal with the *dukkha*. Here too, though, we can perhaps also play the antinomy game. Could it be on the other hand that Wilfred needed the *dukkha* to stave off his inner Mozart? I am thinking of his loving, fully confident mother; of his beautiful, supremely talented wife; and of a life born to the manor of the mind. Did Wilfred need the Buddha's sober message to set all this in perspective? Only those much closer to him than I could possibly know.

In concluding, let us look back over the ten Un-Commandments we have uttered. I've called them "enabling antinomies" because to me Wilfred Smith was a man who wore his intellectual heart on his sleeve far more than most people dare to do, and he did it honestly. He had great convictions, and the importance of suspending one's convictions was one of them. Not to be set in his ways was precisely the way he wanted to be set in his ways. If you said something to him that he hadn't thought—or, more likely, hadn't thought of in just the way you had—he would stop and say, "Oh, do you think so?" He really meant it. He would actually stop and think about whatever it was right then and there, and then you might also get a memo after a while—months, even years—saying he'd been mulling it over again.

I believe a fair measure of this special aptitude was owing to the antinomies where Wilfred pitched his life. He thought as systematically as he could over a vast, troubled, and extremely detailed terrain, and he allowed himself to be questioned repeatedly. Those antinomies were in his limbs and bones. They were tensions that gave him the tensile strength to keep on changing and growing for as long as he lived.

At the end of his brilliant essay Talal Asad holds up for admiration "the kind of openness that anthropologists ideally try to assume in their inquiries." In relation to religious movements in the Middle East, Asad hopes such a stance will reveal "new social forms for experience and admiration that one hopes will help to reshape the idea of tolerance—tolerance neither as indifference nor as forbearance but as mutual engagement based on human interdependence." And he goes on to say that he is sure that is also what Wilfred wanted. "For Wilfred Cantwell Smith was a writer of remarkable sensitivity," he says, "a humanist who continued to develop his comparative understanding of religion in suggestive ways right until the moment that he died."[16]

Indeed, he didn't let go. He kept trying to make it come out better, even as he felt the odds lengthening within himself and perhaps in the world at large. I'd like to think it was not just his faith, or for that matter his devotion to tradition in its broadest sense—the two faces of religion he so famously pried apart—but his deeply embedded familiarity with the contradictions of life that gave him the strength to keep on growing, developing, altering in this way. But let's not call these contradictions. For Wilfred, I believe, these seemed instead to be antinomies, equal and opposite forces that promised someday to sublate themselves into another form as he experienced his own personal version of "mankind's religiously divided history approaching self-consciousness."

Or maybe I'm wrong. Maybe, in the end, these antinomies did not promise such a sublation—in this world, that is. As for the next, it may all be Mozart, but I bet Wilfred's busy composing some sort of celestial exposé even so.

Notes

1. I have written about the course in "Comparative Religion for Undergraduates: What Next?" in *Comparing Religions: Possibilities and Perils*, eds. Thomas Idinopulos, James Hanges, and Brian Wilson (Leiden: E. J. Brill, 2006), pp. 115–42. Cf. Tomoko Masuzawa, *The Invention of World Religions, Or, How European Universalism Was Preserved in the Language of Pluralism* (Chicago: University of Chicago Press, 2005).

2. P. J. Marshall, ed., *The British Discovery of Hinduism in the Eighteenth Century* (Cambridge, UK: Cambridge University Press, 1970); Donald S. Lopez, Jr., ed., *Curators of the Buddha: The Study of Buddhism under Colonialism* (Chicago: University of Chicago Press, 1995).

3. Talal Asad, "Reading a Modern Classic: W. C. Smith's *The Meaning and End of Religion*," *History of Religions* 40, no. 3 (2001), pp. 205–22.

4. Asad, "Reading a Modern Classic," p. 215.

5. W. C. Smith, *The Meaning and End of Religion: A New Approach to the Religious Traditions of Mankind* (New York: Macmillan, 1962, 1963), p. 177, or Mentor Books, 1964, p. 160.

6. McKim Marriott, "Hindu Transactions: Diversity without Dualism," in *Transaction and Meaning: Directions in the Anthropology of Exchange and Symbolic Behavior*, ed. Bruce Kapferer (Philadelphia: Institute for the Study of Human Issues, 1976), pp. 109–14.

7. Asad, "Reading a Modern Classic," p. 207.

8. W. C. Smith, "A Human View of Truth," *SR: Studies in Religion/Sciences Religieuses* 1 (1971), pp. 6–24.

9. Smith, The Meaning and End of Religion, p. 66 (1964: p. 63).

10. William R. Darrow, "The Harvard Way in the Study of Religion," *Harvard Theological Review* 81, no. 2 (1988), pp. 232–33.

11. Asad, "Reading a Modern Classic," pp. 216–17.

12. I owe this insight to a conversation with Rajeev Bhargava at Columbia University on October 2, 2010.

13. Wilfred Cantwell Smith, "Mankind's Religiously Divided History Approaches Self-Consciousness," *Harvard Divinity Bulletin* 29, no. 1 (1964), pp. 1–17.

14. In saying this, I think especially of Smith's introduction to *Islam in Modern History*, where the subject comes up explicitly (New York: Mentor Books, 1957, pp. 30–34), and of his article "Lower-class Uprisings in the Mughal Empire," *Islamic Culture* 20, no. 2 (1946), pp. 21–40, reprinted in *The Mughal State, 1526–1750*, eds. Muzaffar Alam and Sanjay Subrahmanyam (Delhi: Oxford University Press, 1998), pp. 323–46.

15. Kevin Reinhart, email communication, November 4, 2009.

16. Asad, "Reading a Modern Classic," p. 222.

Bibliography

Asad, Tasal. "Reading a Modern Classic: W. C. Smith's *The Meaning and End of Religion*." *History of Religions* 40, no. 3. (Feb. 2001), pp. 205–22.

Darrow, William R. "The Harvard Way in the Study of Religion." *Harvard Theological Review* 81, no. 2 (1988), pp. 232–33.

Hawley, John Stratton. "Comparative Religion for Undergraduates: What Next?" In *Comparing Religions: Possibilities and Perils*. Edited by Thomas Idinopulos, James Hanges, and Brian Wilson, 115–42. Leiden: E. J. Brill, 2006.

Lopez, Donald S., Jr., ed. *Curators of the Buddha: The Study of Buddhism Under Colonialism*. Chicago: University of Chicago Press, 1995.

Marriott, McKim. "Hindu Transactions: Diversity without Dualism." In *Transaction and Meaning: Directions in the Anthropology of Exchange and Symbolic Behavior*. Edited by Bruce Kapferer, 109–14. Philadelphia: Institute for the Study of Human Issues, 1976.

Marshall, P. J., ed. *The British Discovery of Hinduism in the Eighteenth Century*. Cambridge, UK: Cambridge University Press, 1970.

Masuzawa, Tomoko. *The Invention of World Religions, Or, How European Universalism Was Preserved in the Language of Pluralism*. Chicago: University of Chicago Press, 2005.

Smith, Wilfred Cantwell. *The Meaning and End of Religion: A New Approach to the Religious Traditions of Mankind*. New York: Macmillan, 1962.

———. "A Human View of Truth." *SR: Studies in Religion/Sciences Religieuses* 1 (1971), pp. 6–24.

———. "Mankind's Religiously Divided History Approaches Self-Consciousness." *Harvard Divinity Bulletin* 29, no. 1 (1964), pp. 1–17.

———. *Islam in Modern History.* New York: Mentor Books, 1957.
———. "Lower-Class Uprisings in the Mughal Empire." *Islamic Culture* 20, no. 2 (1946), pp. 21–40. Reprinted in *The Mughal State, 1526–1750.* Edited by Muzaffar Alam and Sanjay Subrahmanyam, 323–46. Delhi: Oxford University Press, 1998.

Who Cares If the Qur'an Is the Word of God?

W. C. Smith's Charge to the Aspiring Public Intellectual

Jonathan R. Herman

> Are those of us in this field not exceptionally fortunate to be involved in such a wonderful area of study and in introducing students to it? Coming to the end of my own days, it is a joy to see a new generation carrying the torch to new heights and broader circles.
>
> —W. C. Smith, 6 August, 1977

More than a dozen years after his retirement from Harvard, and a few short years before his death, Wilfred Cantwell Smith offered this astonishingly simple and candid reflection on the academic study of religion and the fortunes of those involved in it, simultaneously embodying both the wide-eyed enthusiasm of a novice seminarian and the quiet satisfaction of an inveterate elder statesman. But certainly, Smith was not unaware of the internecine struggles underway in his beloved study of religion, or of the sometimes contentious debates over exactly how this discipline—if it can, in fact, be correctly labeled a "discipline"—can and should be configured. Even this most rudimentary starting point, the question of whether our sector of the academic world should constitute a distinct discipline with well-articulated methods and objectives, or a broad interdisciplinary "field" accommodating a multiplicity of approaches and goals, shows little sign of being laid to rest any time soon. Closely related is the issue of whether religious studies is primarily a humanistic or social scientific enterprise, one that requires (in the former case) self-consciously cultivated intuition and aesthetic imagination or (in the latter) quantifiable data and falsifiable hypotheses. One issue very much implicit in all such discussions is the status of theology and religiously engaged scholarship. To put it bluntly, are theologians equal partners in the academic inquiry, or are they participants in an entirely separate discourse? Certainly, the joint affiliations of faculty at seminaries and secular religious studies programs throughout the country would reinforce the former view, although a number of contemporary gadflies challenge such arrangements and contend that theologians and their institutional contexts are the very phenomena that we should be studying and analyzing as "raw data."[1] Interestingly, the different positions are mirrored by the contrasting mission statements of the major North American scholarly societies dedicated to the study of religion. On the one hand, the numerically dominant American Academy of Religion (AAR) "welcomes all disciplined reflection on religion—both from within and outside of communities of belief and practice," while the upstart North American Association for the Study of Religion (NAASR) restricts its inquiry to "the historical, comparative, structural, theoretical, and cognitive approaches to the study of religion."[2]

There is certainly much at stake in such discussions, but perhaps nothing is more held in the balance than the tangible role of the public intellectual in religious studies, or, perhaps more basically, the responsibilities incumbent on those of us who have expertise in religious traditions and familiarity with academic discourses that others do not. That is to say, how one imagines the shape of this particular branch of learning probably embeds a more fundamental assumption about our overall intellectual telos, and it is here that the disagreements seem especially insurmountable. Even the seemingly "neutral" position, that our goal is simply to foster widespread religious literacy, is often criticized as being, alternately, unfeasible or insufficient. One might imagine that there is nothing contentious about working to give the public "a basic understanding of the history, central texts (where applicable), beliefs, practices, and contemporary manifestations of several of the world's religious traditions and religious expressions as they arose out of and continue to shape and be shaped by particular social, historical and cultural contexts; and the ability to discern and explore the religious dimensions of political, social and cultural expressions across time and place."[3] But at one end of the spectrum, in a curious irony, the former chair of the AAR Committee on the Public Understanding of Religion strenuously opposed the society's commissioning a task force on teaching about religion in the public schools, on the grounds that it simply "can't be done properly."[4] At the other end, those who have various normative investments maintain that mere translation or transmission of information does not go far enough, though they hardly agree on which alternative directions would be most warranted. Diana Eck, the architect of Harvard's Pluralism Project, insists that the role (or at least a significant role) of the religious studies educator is as a conduit to interfaith dialogue and to help facilitate mutual transformation in a religiously plural world,[5] while sociologist of religion Russell McCutcheon contends that the scholar should function primarily as a "cultural critic" who takes on the challenge of "laying bare the conditions and strategies by which their fellow citizens authorize the local as universal and the contingent as necessary."[6] Clearly, such questions lie at the heart of our work, and any scholar in the field will eventually need to confront them while constructing and refining his or her intellectual persona and mission.

It goes without saying that Wilfred Cantwell Smith has been invoked for his scholarship, and for his inspiration, in a number of different areas, including Islamic studies, theology, critical theory in the study of religion, comparative religion, and interfaith dialogue. Chapters in this volume also extend his work to discussions of matters such as postmodernism, contemplative education, hermeneutics, and religion and war. But very few analyses of Smith's work explicitly address his legacy as it relates to the role of the public intellectual, perhaps because Smith demonstrated no fondness for that particular language, perhaps because his primary contributions lay in other identifiable areas, or perhaps because he simply had his fingers in so many different pieces of scholarly pie that it would be nearly impossible to do justice to all of them. In any event, this essay directly examines the importance of Smith's work for this conversation, taking its cues from a much overlooked—and much misunderstood—entry in Smith's substantial scholarly corpus. By way of outline, this chapter summarizes what I take to be the central *problématique* of Smith's argument in that document, brings it to bear on a pair of historical events, and finally relates it specifically to our unique role as educators and scholars.

A Question of Religious Truth

Smith initially presented "Is the Qur'an the Word of God?" in 1963 at Yale Divinity School, as the first of three addresses that would comprise that year's installment of the Nathaniel W. Taylor Lecture Series, a biannual cluster of talks organized around specific theological themes. Working from his well-known conviction that "the arguments of a student of religion or of a particular religious or indeed any human community, should in principle be persuasive to other intellectuals, not only, but in addition also to intelligent and alert members of the group or groups about which he and she writes,"[7] Smith "road-tested" the lecture in India the following year. He first brought it to a Muslim audience at the National Islamic University (Jamia Millia Islamia), and then to a religiously mixed audience at the missionary Henry Martyn Institute of Islamic Studies (since renamed the Henry Martyn Institute: International Centre for Research, Interfaith Relations, and Reconciliation). The essay appeared in print shortly thereafter as one chapter of *Questions of Religious Truth* (1967) and was reprinted in other volumes over the next two decades.

Although he characterized the Yale presentation as his "first public appearance in the field of theology (as distinct from Islamics or comparative religion),"[8] Smith in the Qur'an essay does not attempt to offer a theological answer to the problem posed in the title, or for that matter, an answer of any type.[9] Rather, he puts forward a series of astute observations about the central issue that the question encapsulates. In the background throughout is Smith's contention that what may appear obvious on the surface is actually quite puzzling, and even a bit troubling. He begins by noting how, in a world that has long assumed the possibility of divine revelation ("a joyous proclamation or quiet assumption of religious faith"),[10] that world seems to have been historically divided into two lopsided halves, with each half so sure of the answer that it has never asked the question seriously. Smith writes, "Each of these answers has tended to be clear and straightforward. Some people have given one, some people the other; but whichever it was, it has been given with confident assurance, and even with force."[11] Of course, neither side has really arrived at its position through scrutiny of the text or formulated strictures on what constitutes revelation; rather, both the "yes" and the "no" are what Smith calls "pre-convictions," more often than not the result of inheritance, inculcation, and immersion in the traditions of family and community.[12] For whatever reasons, to be a Muslim historically has been to reply with an emphatic "yes"; even to ponder another alternative would tread dangerously close to infidelity. And likewise, the non-Muslim world has been equally emphatic in its "no," an a priori certainty that the text could not possibly be of divine stature. The division is striking, as what is self-evident to one side is anathema to the other, and vice versa.

More significantly, this is not simply a matter of abstract philosophical contemplation, or an idle difference of opinion about some obscure taste in food or art; the commitments of those involved have been very real, and the stakes for them have historically been very high. A great many people have cared, and do care, if the Qur'an is the word of God, but for different reasons. As Smith notes, the adoption of "yes" as a foundational truth informs a whole range of ethical and aesthetic corollaries, which have been tested pragmatically and expressed in the workings of historically rich cultural complexes. "Civilizations are not easy to construct, or to sustain; yet great civilizations have been raised on the basis of this conviction."[13] To invoke the language of contemporary comparativist William Paden, the "yeses" inhabit a distinct religious *world*,[14] a cultural and moral universe very different from that of the "nos," who are of course grounded in their own foundational truths and points of reference. "They, too," Smith avers, "are to be numbered in the hundreds or thousands of millions. They, too, have constructed great civilizations, have made great cultures dynamic."[15] Yet Smith is not chiefly interested in demonstrating that this divide exists, that one single issue can so richly symbolize how impenetrable discrete religious worlds may be to one another. Nor is he primarily interested in exploring the interpretive history or cultural roles of these respective *Urgrund*. Rather, what seems most to interest Smith, to put this somewhat playfully, is simply *that no one has ever found this issue particularly interesting*, or in his own typically understated words, that "we have also come to accept such a fact without disquiet."[16] This is the point that is well worth unpacking and examining carefully. On the one hand, civilizations have historically responded to religious divergence with militant absolutism, detached tolerance, or any of the varying shades in between. On the other hand, the academy has been content to observe and chronicle the reality of religious diversity without confronting the need to make intellectual sense of that reality. What does it, in fact, mean that people perceive and inhabit the same world so differently, and how does one craft an intellectually satisfying and honest resolution to those discontinuities without projecting one's own theology onto the discourse or deluding oneself into buying a premature resolution? Smith continues, "This is curious. The radical divergence might well make both groups more restless with their own answers than either has often thought it necessary to be. At the very least, there is an intellectual challenge:

how is one to rationalize the divergence, to conceptualize it, to interpret it intelligibly? (We leave aside for the moment the theological and the moral implications; this intellectual problem sufficing us, just now.) Are our minds to be content to accept lying down the total divergence, unreconciled, on a major issue?"[17]

An important subtext to Smith's work, in this essay and elsewhere, is a concern that with imminent advances in technology facilitating rapid shifts in demographics, with the world truly growing smaller, humankind could find itself in serious trouble if it fails to develop strategies for negotiating an increasingly complex religious diversity. Thirty years before widespread use of the Internet and email, forty years before such "viral" phenomena as YouTube and Facebook, the well-mannered Presbyterian minister who did not own a television set had a vision of a world where people of other ethnicities and religious traditions, people who speak different languages and observe different cultural habits, would no longer be merely the exotic subjects of liberal arts inquiry, but would be one another's neighbors, colleagues, friends, and sometimes adversaries. And for Smith, how we as a species respond to the "intellectual challenge" of religious diversity could make the difference between stability and unending conflict, which leaves him all the more puzzled at the apparent lack of urgency, the apparent lack of critical engagement with the reality of elemental theological differences. When one thinks of Wilfred Cantwell Smith, one does not usually think of religious conflict, but it is in thinking about religious conflict where Smith's voice can often ring most clear.

The New Religiously Plural World

In the decades since Smith wrote "Is the Qur'an the Word of God?," his observations in the essay have many times seemed to have been especially prescient, but I would like to draw attention to a pair of religiously charged episodes, both relatively recent, that have unfortunately done much to define the state of contemporary politics, interreligious relations, and general practical conceptions of self and other. Twenty-odd years ago, much of the world was in a state of profound agitation, prompted by the publication of and responses to Salman Rushdie's novel, *The Satanic Verses*. The events of late 1988 and early 1989—the violent demonstrations in some Muslim communities, the bomb threats against stores displaying the book, the fatwa issued by Ayatollah Ruhollah Khomeini calling for the death of both the author and the book's publishers, and

Rushdie's eventual flight into more-or-less permanent hiding—exposed an intercultural rift and a strain of resentment and outrage that blindsided much of the North American public. During this time, scholars of Islam publically scrambled to provide needed context and historical analysis of the situation, though they quickly learned that they had to contend with the possibility that they might be, on the one hand, targeted as Western proxies for Rushdie, or on the other hand, dismissed as liberal apologists for Islam. In the wake of this volatile environment, several Harvard Islamicists took the initiative to schedule an impromptu "teach-in" on the Divinity School campus. With similar events being threatened by disruptions or worse, this gathering was minimally publicized, and attended mainly by those who had heard about it through word of mouth.

Arguably, the most surprising contribution came from the Kenyan-born scholar of South Asian Islam Ali Asani, who began his contribution anecdotally. He imagined that in years to come, for him the single most memorable image from the whole ugly affair would be not of Khomeini pounding his fists into the air, not of angry crowds burning figures in effigy, but of an interview he had just seen on the BBC of an old man sitting in the corner of a mosque, weeping. When asked through an interpreter why he was crying, he replied that "the Prophet had been hurt."[18] Apparently, this was a revelation for many in the audience, who were almost exclusively non-Muslims and non-Islamicists, and who had only rudimentary exposure to the tradition. For the most part, the public discourse in the United States and Canada at that point had been dominated by discussions of literary freedom, religious tolerance, and the distinction between slander and fiction. With some exceptions, public opinion reflected a general consensus that however unwise Rushdie may have been in his literary exploits, religious outrage over a characterization in an overtly fictional document was palpably absurd. But while it had certainly been obvious that a significant Muslim constituency felt *angry* about the book, it was only after hearing Asani's remarks that many in attendance began to appreciate how "ordinary" Muslims may also have felt *injured* by it.

This single vignette was quite telling, because as the Rushdie episode unfolded further, it became clearer that both his most ardent defenders and his most passionate critics were utterly insular in their positions, and generally oblivious to the values and feelings of the other. For all the later hyperbolic talk of "clash of civilizations," this may more accurately have been a case of civilizations missing one another completely. When numerous literary figures stepped forward to engage in public readings of *The Satanic Verses*, in support of the author and of the principles of artistic freedom and freedom of expression, one wonders if they would have done the same with a new version of *The Protocols of the Elders of Zion* or other overtly anti-Semitic literature. Perhaps they would have voiced their support for artistic freedom, and perhaps even voiced their condemnation of attempts at censorship, but it also seems likely that they would have stopped short of public recitation, in the interest of sparing the Jewish community, of sparing people who were their neighbors and friends, and who presumably came by their religious sensibilities (and sensitivities) honestly. In any event, the two different perceptions of Rushdie's book, as with the different perceptions of the Qur'an, were, to echo Smith's words, "clear" and "confident." They also seemed in many ways mutually unintelligible, and I would suggest that most had, in Smith's words again, taken that mutual unintelligibility "lying down."

That was twenty-plus years ago, but Smith's words again seemed especially sobering during the aftermath of the mass murders of September 11, 2001. Certainly, the memories are fresh and raw enough that it is superfluous to rehearse the events of that day, but I do want to draw attention to one perspective on them, a perspective that casts the entire situation in a very different light. I am referring to historian-theorist Bruce Lincoln's astonishing—and disturbing—analysis of the final-day instructions found in the suitcase of Muhammad Atta, the apparent lead hijacker. Working from materials that would be pulled from public scrutiny shortly after transcripts of them first began to appear, Lincoln explicates the document as a *religious* text, saturated with Qur'anic allusions and other language that would be easily recognizable to one schooled in a particular strain of Islamic interpretation. Apart from the cold-bloodedness with which the most horrific admonitions were described, what is immediately striking from Lincoln's study is the relative coherence and internal consistency of the implicit religious worldview of the author or authors, as well as the lucidity of the rhetorical presentation. According to Lincoln, the "text" presupposes an orientation toward the world that is one of "religious maximalism"—a phrase he substitutes for the much-overused and morally charged term "fundamentalism"—characterized not chiefly by literalism or conservatism per se, but by "the conviction that religion ought to permeate all aspects of social, indeed of human existence."[19] Such a view is at odds with the predominant "minimalism" of the post-Enlightenment West, which "restricts religion to an important set of (chiefly metaphysical) concerns, protects its privileges against state intrusion, but restricts its activity and influence to this specialized sphere."[20] It also helps explain the response to *The Satanic Verses* in some Muslim circles, where the minimalist distinctions between aesthetic and religious discourse, between artistic license and blasphemy, are less obvious, if they exist at all. Moreover, Lincoln observes that the Atta document echoes ideas initially voiced by the controversial Egyptian scholar Sayyid Qutb, who judged that the modern West (which had already cast a long political shadow over the Middle East) was replicating the state of *jahiliyyah*, the chaos and idolatry of the pre-Islamic Arab world. That is to say, the working premise undergirding the al-Qaeda ideology—and motivating the September 11 attacks—is not simply a cartoonish rejection of "infidels," but actually a passionate and thoughtfully argued call to action against those who are in an "active state of rebellion against God's sovereignty on earth."[21]

For Lincoln to illuminate this is not only in direct contradiction to the conventional wisdom about Al Qaeda and others caught in the sweep of "Muslim fundamentalism" "or radical Islam," it is also in violation of what is virtually an unspoken taboo in the West against even considering the perpetrators as anything other than simply "terrorists." The refrains of the last decade surely sound familiar: "The hijackers were not brave; they were cowards." "These men were not true Muslims; they perverted Islam." And most ironically, "They were not religious; they were evil," as though such categories are self-evidently mutually exclusive. These types of tropes surely indicate the extent of the trauma felt by many Americans, but they also represent a kind of willful ignorance, *a construction of other by ideological fiat*. As Smith notes repeatedly, mutual understanding can be a formidable task under the best of circumstances; it certainly seems destined to fail when events conspire so cruelly against it, and when the drive is so strong to perpetuate the unintelligibility of the other.[22] If these two incidents—the Rushdie affair and the September 11 attacks—together illustrate anything, it is how far apart the "yes" and the "no" can be, and how untenable a posture it is simply to sit back and allow their respective trajectories to create further and further distance.

To Adumbrate a Whit . . .

Smith closes "Is the Qur'an the Word of God" by suggesting that the only satisfactory future for the question he posed at the beginning—and by implication, for the future of humanity—is not to be found in deliberating between the "yes" and the "no," not to be found in bargaining to agreement or in striking a relativist compromise. Rather, he imagines that the best hope lies in the construction of a different type of discourse, in the creation of a different type of solution to the question, one that moves beyond simple binary choices and yet somehow remains faithful and true to the living persons on both sides of the divide. Certainly many contributors to this volume, and many readers of it as well, could step up and testify that they have been hard at work for years at interfaith dialogue, seeking out religious diversity and fostering good-faith exchange—and no doubt Smith would applaud those efforts heartily. But if we take Smith at his word that the goal is "a new type of answer . . . some *tertium quid*, more subtle, more complex, tentative, yet to be hammered out,"[23] then I would suggest that he has something much more radical in mind.

What Smith is intimating is not (to borrow Diana Eck's language) a paradigm shift from religious exclusivism to religious pluralism, from contentious ethnocentrism to respectful disagreement; rather, he is envisioning a *wholesale reconstruction of public religious language*, where "a question such as that with which we began is becoming an open question, and to which the answer is not known but has to be discovered, and where the question itself is no longer simple, but has to be understood."[24] In a sense, Smith is proposing that the rules of the intellectual game, so to speak, need to be reformulated, and the implications of this would be profound. At the onset, even the most elemental terminology contained in or implicitly referenced by the initial question—*word*, *revelation*, *scripture*, *truth*, perhaps even *God* and *Qur'an*—would ultimately be subject to intellectual scrutiny. It is this desideratum that is Smith's charge to the aspiring public intellectual, that is, that our most pressing task—actually, our intellectual and teleological mission—is to *reconceive*, *reimagine*, and *redirect* the public discourse in a way that supersedes the limitations of "so irrationally conspicuous a dichotomy" of "a generic 'yes' or 'no' answer,"[25] and constructs "a theoretical answer more comprehensive, coherent, and unifying than the traditional ones."[26] Of course, such a process does not occur in isolation, but is inherently dialogical, as Smith envisions that "the best minds and most honest spirits" in the other religious communities will join us in "searching for a new answer to our question."[27] Ironically, Smith, the self-described Puritan, demonstrates here his basic affinity for classical Confucian thought, which foresees an intellectual vanguard taking a visible public role in transforming the social, moral, and religious well-being of the people. This, if one reads Smith carefully, is the real basis for interreligious dialogue.

I would suggest that it is this subtle, ambitious, and perhaps even intimidating vision that is the most frequently misunderstood and oversimplified aspect of Smith's legacy, a position that is too often caricatured by his detractors and sanitized by his defenders. In many circles, interfaith dialogue is synonymous with a naive "kumbaya" ideology, evoking images of smiling people from multiple ethnicities, bleached of all real diversity, who reach across their respective boundaries to hold hands in some kind of rarified unity. The irony here, of course, is that recent research has revealed that the well-known folk song by that name has undergone its own simplification and bastardization in the popular imagination. Just as Smith's call for a truly difficult series of religious encounters is often portrayed as a misguided belief that generic dialogue can provide a panacea for all of the world's ills, "Kumbaya" (most likely a white mishearing of the Gullah-inflected "Come By Here") was originally a local, specific expression that "appealed for divine intervention on behalf of the oppressed" that now plays in some circles as a "snarky shorthand for ridiculing a certain kind of idealism."[28] But however much Smith celebrated this "wonderful area of study," he was hardly blind to the types of historical circumstances that would lead Jonathan Z. Smith bold as brass to assert that "religion has rarely been a positive, liberal force," that "religion is not nice, (that) it has been responsible for more death and suffering that any other human activity."[29] The real challenge that W. C. Smith is issuing is not for us to facilitate affable conversations among Unitarians and Western-educated Buddhists, or to congratulate ourselves for having undergone liberating encounters with the "other." Rather, the real challenge is to forge something utterly new, something that, judged by today's sensibilities, may push the limits of tolerance well over the edge, something that can simultaneously speak to the liberal Christian modernist and to the white supremacist, that can simultaneously speak to Lincoln's Western religious minimalist and to the Islamic maximalist who may find the entire dialogical enterprise not only suspect but also as evidence of a basic corruptness of post-Enlightenment Western thinking.

Admittedly, Smith does not have a prefabricated solution for the puzzle he sets forth, and he more than once indicates that such initiatives must surely fall to the next generation, as he anticipates that during the coming century "the religious history of mankind will be taking a major new turn."³⁰ And yet, Smith does eventually drop some breadcrumbs suggesting where he thinks, or hopes, such a turn might lead. Or, to channel the language that he would employ with equal caution twenty years later in *Towards a World Theology*, he does volunteer "to adumbrate a whit more generically the direction in which it may be sought, and along which indications thus far have seemed cumulatively to point."³¹ One of Smith's more interesting ideas, one that he would continue to develop throughout his career, is that all of humankind has participated—and is participating—in a shared religious history, or rather a shared drama of human religiousness. Such a drama is inhabited not by religiously ossified individuals who belong to reified "religions" that are hermetically sealed off from one another, but by complex human beings living in complex human communities, whose religious sensibilities are informed by their own histories and the flexible networks of relationships with other equally complex beings living inside and outside of those communities.

For example, even in the most homogenous religious community, one's own Christian-ness has been shaped, perhaps indirectly and without the individual's knowledge, by the conversations and struggles and innovations that made up that community's history, as well as by the intricacies of Christian history itself, including the ongoing social and intellectual relations with Jews, Muslims, and others. For Smith, it might even be misleading to state that Christians and Jews are part of each other's histories; it would be more accurate to imagine that they are part of a single, collective religious history, in which some have been participating in a specifically Christian way, some in a specifically Jewish way, and so on. While this model of thinking about religious history does not directly address Smith's charge to intellectuals that they transform the public religious discourse, it does provide them with a kind of historical impetus to approach their task with a critical and corporate self-awareness. History is *already* teeming with the mutual religious transformations of those in implicit dialogue with one another; Smith's ideal religious studies scholar consciously chooses to participate in that process and attempts to influence it constructively.

More concretely, and a corollary to Smith's theory of religious history, is what he identifies as his "personalist" view of humanistic study. The earliest formulation of this, perhaps, is the memorably glib theological aside in *The Meaning and End of Religion*, that "God is interested in people, not things."³² Smith repeats this line, almost verbatim, in another one of the 1963 Taylor Lectures ("Can Religions Be True or

False?"), which would also appear in *Questions of Religious Truth*, remarking this time that "God is interested in persons, not in types."[33] This was, no doubt, the spark that inspired Smith's approach in his contemporaneous *The Faith of Other Men*, the laconic world religions primer that organized chapters around religious persons—"Hindus," "Buddhists," "Muslims," "the Chinese"—rather than the reified entities of Hinduism, Buddhism, and so forth.[34] Smith's personalism would eventually find its most mature articulation in *Towards a World Theology*, where he ventures to "adumbrate a whit" in the volume's "Interim Conclusion." It contains the single most concrete clue Smith ever offered for developing a new mechanism for assessing the veridicality of propositions like those either attesting to or challenging the revelatory status of the Qur'an:

> Truth, I submit, is a humane, not an objective, concept. It does not lie in propositions. (Propositions are not true or false—*pace* Tarsky and others; to treat them as if they were is parochially possible at best only within a highly circumscribed universe of discourse and a highly limited community of shared prejudgements; also, over a sharply limited period of history.) To it approximate not the propositions themselves but what these mean, have meant, to particular persons, and groups. In so far as truth is apprehended by persons, it is apprehended within history; yet in so far as it is true, it transcends history (and any particular formulation). It is therefore inherently a transcendent as well as a humane concept. (1981, p. 190)[35]

The epistemological needle Smith is trying to thread here is a delicate one, as he is trying to construct a nuanced understanding of truth that is not bound to a clinical objectivity, but can withstand accusations that he proposes only subjectivism or relativism in exchange. Whether or not he succeeds, there is no doubt that even those sympathetic to his thinking have had difficulty completely recognizing the territory Smith attempted to chart with the Qur'an essay and developed throughout his career. Scholarly reviews of *Questions of Religious Truth* were generally warm to the contents, but included slight misrepresentations—or at least what Smith would probably see as misrepresentations—of his position. Indologist Paul Younger portrayed Smith as "prepared to say that both these answers ('yes' and 'no') are right"[36] and theologian Eric Rust had Smith "contending that a religion's truth or falsehood is relative to those who profess it."[37] Interestingly, reviewers of Smith's works up to and including *Towards a World Theology* would continue to find a similar unresolved tension; theologian Richard Crouter expressed "puzzlement" and "bewilderment" that "religious pluralism is wholly accepted, along with its relativistic consequences."[38] And yet, in his climactic theological proclamation, Smith takes pains to head off any such interpretation. "A superficial reading of my present argument for comprehensiveness might tempt some to imagine that I am contending that all religion is true, or equally true; or all religious statements. That would indeed be silly." Smith's alternative view is the considerably more subtle and dynamic position that one's "religion"—he places the word in quotation marks to emphasize that he is not speaking of a reified system of propositions—"becomes more or less true in the case of particular persons as it informs their lives and their groups and shapes and nurtures their faith."[39] Again, this personalist understanding of religious truth is not offered as the only, or an inevitable, ingredient in the new discourse and understanding that Smith envisions the next generation producing. But it is one such possibility, and it illustrates the tremendous potential that exists for rethinking questions that previously seemed straightforward and binary.

The Public Intellectual: Whither and Why

Smith's Qur'an essay, like the historical episodes examined here, addresses relations between Muslims and non-Muslims, but it is obvious that this is merely a single case study that can be generalized to broader questions of religious diversity. In a final footnote, Smith appends one final coda: "It is perhaps unnecessary to add (I hope the point has been manifestly implicit throughout) that this whole discussion may presumably be transposed, whether on to parallel Hindu or Buddhist issues, or back into internal Christian terms. A consideration of the Western-Muslim divergence over the Qur'an is applicable at least in principle to a secular-Christian divergence over Christian positions."[40] Be that as it may, "Is the Qur'an the Word of God?" is light years away from being a quaint speculation over an odd theological riddle; it is an earnest charge to the aspiring public scholar of religion to take a leadership role in the unfolding of history yet to be made, across all religious traditions. And now, nearly a half-century after Smith first dropped the gauntlet, it seems fair to interrogate the reasonableness and relevance of his challenge, to assess the state of the public religious discourse, and to gauge what progress the "next generations" have made in steering the new century to its anticipated "major new turn." To all of these, it is tempting to confess some measure of despair, that the present religious conflicts are as fierce as ever, that the world is sitting on a proverbial powder keg, and that Smith's intellectual heirs—I strive to count myself as one of them—have simply proven unfit for the task. Indeed, during one of my last conversations with Smith, I confessed that I was eagerly on board with his desiderata, but could not really imagine, concretely, what the new discourse might look like, even embryonically.

Still, as one of the "next generation" who aspires to be the type of public religious studies intellectual that has been elucidated here, I have been forced to arrive at my own "interim conclusion," and it is one that my final correspondence with Smith suggests he would endorse. In short, I pass the problem on to my students; I force them to confront the challenges, much as Smith has done for me. This is actually not a difficult or uneasy step to take, and not primarily because it assumes a posture of abdicating responsibility. It is the current generation that has grown up amid the real religious diversity that Smith knew was coming, that is fluent in the expanding technologies that I can barely manage, and that had their youth marked not by the assassination of a president or a cloak-and-dagger Cold War, but by the specter of September 11 and the knowledge of religious conflict occurring simultaneously in all parts of the globe. And I remind them that even after a modest survey class in world religions, even after a fifteen-week whirlwind tour of Chinese or Japanese religion, they are in a position where they now know more about the religious traditions of their neighbors than do the vast majority of people around them, and with that they carry a special responsibility, a responsibility to know who cares if the Qur'an is the word of God, and why. In the sphere of religious studies, the role of the public intellectual is to demonstrate exactly how much is at stake in cracking the mysteries of religious diversity, i.e., "to rationalize the divergence, to conceptualize it, to interpret it intelligibly," and perhaps to assay some small movement in that direction. Thus, I keep returning to Smith's words in his final correspondence with me, where he acknowledged "coming to the end of my own days," but also celebrated feeling "exceptionally fortunate to be involved in such a wonderful area of study and in introducing students to it," and, most importantly, expressing optimism about "a new generation carrying the torch to new heights and broader circles." It will now be fascinating to see what light that torch can shed, and what fires it can help ignite.

Notes

1. According to the most recent catalogue, nearly two thirds of the faculty at Harvard's Committee on the Study of Religion are also listed as faculty of the Divinity School. For the critical view, see McCutcheon 2001.

2. Internet addresses change notoriously quickly, but as of publication of this book, the AAR and NAASR can be viewed at https://www.aarweb.org/about and http://www.naasr.com/about.html, respectively.

3. This is quoted from the "Guidelines for Teaching About Religion in K–12 Public Schools in the United Sates," produced by the AAR "Religion in the Schools Task Force," chaired by Diana L. Moore of Harvard University.

4. Personal correspondence from Dena Davis (10/9/2010), who chaired the Committee on the Public Understanding of Religion from 2000 until 2006, just before the Religion in the Schools Task Force was commissioned to undertake production of the "Guidelines."

5. Diana Eck, *Encountering God: A Spiritual Journey from Bozeman to Banares* (Boston: Beacon Press, 1993).

6. Russell McCutcheon, *Critics Not Caretakers: Redescribing the Public Study of Religion*. (Albany: SUNY Press 2001), p. 135.

7. W. C. Smith, *On Understanding Islam: Selected Studies* (The Hague: Mouton Publishers, 1981), p. 282.

8. Ibid.

9. It is interesting to note that, notwithstanding Smith's claims to the contrary, the essay would later be offered as dealing specifically with both Islamics and comparative religion, as it was reprinted in, respectively, *On Understanding Islam* (1981) and *Religious Diversity: Essays by Wilfred Cantwell Smith*, ed. Willard G. Oxtoby (New York: Harper & Row, 1976).

10. W. C. Smith, *Questions of Religious Truth* (New York: Charles Scribner's Sons, 1967), p. 39.

11. Ibid., pp. 39–40.

12. Ibid., p. 51.

13. Ibid., p. 42.

14. William Paden, *Religious Worlds: The Comparative Study of Religion* (Boston: Beacon Press, 1988).

15. Ibid.

16. Ibid., p. 44.

17. Ibid., p. 44–45.

18. Asani would later write about this in *Celebrating Muhammad: Images of the Prophet in Popular Muslim Poetry* (Columbia: University of South Carolina Press,1995). Ironically, Annemarie Schimmel's echoing of a similar sentiment, i.e., her statement that she had seen "grown men weep" when they learned of the contents of Rushdie's book, as well as her pointing out the extent to which ordinary Muslims felt injured by it, nearly cost her the German Booksellers' Trade Association's annual peace prize. Franz Kogelmann, "Germany and Aus-

tria" eds. David Westerlund and Ingvar Svanberg, *Islam Outside the Arab World* (New York: St. Martin's Press, 1999), pp. 315–16.

19. Bruce Lincoln, *Holy Terrors: Thinking about Religion after September 11* (Chicago: University of Chicago Press, 2003), p. 5.

20. Ibid.

21. Ibid., p. 4.

22. It is interesting to note how the search for intelligibility is, for some, laden with ethical implications. Several years ago, I had students in a first-year undergraduate class view *Blood in the Face*, a documentary film about the white supremacist movement in the United States. When asked to reconstruct the worldview of the people interviewed and shown in the film, i.e., to imagine how the world might actually look to them, the students unanimously rejected any responsibility for understanding them, claiming that such a task would take people who were overtly racist (and possibly mentally ill) too seriously, give them moral credibility, or both.

23. Smith, *On Understanding Islam*, p. 57.

24. Ibid., pp. 61–62.

25. Ibid., p. 61, p. 54.

26. Ibid., p. 55

27. Ibid., p. 59.

28. Samuel G. Freedman, "A Long Road from 'Come by here' to 'Kumbaya,'" *New York Times*, November 19, 2010.

29. Jonathan Z. Smith, *Imagining Religion: From Babylon to Jonestown* (Chicago: University of Chicago Press, 1982), p. 110.

30. Smith, *On Understanding Islam*, p. 60.

31. W. C. Smith, *Towards a World Theology: Faith and Comparative History of Religion* (Philadelphia: Westminster Press, 1981), p. 181.

32. W. C. Smith, *The Meaning and End of Religion: A New Approach to the Religious Traditions of Mankind* (New York: Harper & Row, 1962), p. 127.

33. Smith, *Questions of Religious Truth*, p. 71.

34. Wilfred Cantwell Smith, *The Faith of Other Men* (New York: Harper & Row, 1962).

35. The cryptic reference here is to Alfred Tarski, the Polish-born mathematician who wrote an influential, albeit clinical, essay on the relationship between language and truth.

36. Paul Younger, "Review of Wilfred Cantwell Smith, *Questions of Religious Truth*," *Journal of the American Academy of Religion* 38, no. 1 (1970), p. 79.

37. Eric Rust, "Review of Wilfred Cantwell Smith, *Questions of Religious Truth*," *Review & Expositor* 66, no. 1 (1969), p. 92.

38. Richard Crouter, "Review of Wilfred Cantwell Smith, *Towards a World Theology*," *Journal of the American Academy of Religion* 50, no. 2 (1982), p. 317.

39. Smith, *Towards a World Theology*, p. 186.

40. Smith, *Questions of Religious Truth*, p. 62.

Bibliography

Asani, Ali, et al. *Celebrating Muhammad: Images of the Prophet in Popular Muslim Poetry*. Columbia: University of South Carolina Press, 1995.

Crouter, Richard. "Review of Wilfred Cantwell Smith, *Towards a World Theology*." *Journal of the American Academy of Religion* 50, no. 2 (1982), pp. 316–17.

Eck, Diana. *Encountering God: A Spiritual Journey from Bozeman to Banaras*. Boston: Beacon Press, 1993.

Friedman, Samuel G. "A Long Road from 'Come by here' to 'Kumbaya.'" *New York Times*, November 19, 2010.

Kogelmann, Franz. "Germany and Austria." In *Islam Outside the Arab World*, eds. David Westerlund and Ingvar Svanberg, 315–36. New York: St. Martin's Press, 1999.

Lincoln, Bruce. *Holy Terrors: Thinking about Religion after September 11*, 2nd ed. Chicago: University of Chicago Press, 2006.

McCutcheon, Russell. *Critics Not Caretakers: Redescribing the Public Study of Religion*. Albany: SUNY Press, 2001.

Paden, William. *Religious Worlds: The Comparative Study of Religion*. Boston: Beacon Press, 1988.

Rust, Eric C. "Review of Wilfred Cantwell Smith, *Questions of Religious Truth*." *Review & Expositor* 66, no. 1 (1969), pp. 91–92.

Smith, Jonathan Z. *Imagining Religion: From Babylon to Jonestown*. Chicago: University of Chicago Press, 1982.

Smith, Wilfred Cantwell. *The Meaning and End of Religion: A New Approach to the Religious Traditions of Mankind*. New York: Harper & Row, 1962.

———. *The Faith of Other Men*. New York: Harper & Row, 1962.

———. *Questions of Religious Truth*. New York: Charles Scribner's Sons, 1967.

———. *Religious Diversity: Essays by Wilfred Cantwell Smith*, ed. Willard G. Oxtoby. New York: Harper & Row, 1976.

———. *Towards a World Theology: Faith and the Comparative History of Religion*. Philadelphia: Westminster Press, 1981.

———. *On Understanding Islam: Selected Studies*. The Hague: Mouton Publishers, 1981.

Westerlund, David, and Ingvar Svanberg, eds. *Islam Outside the Arab World*. New York: St. Martin's Press, 1999.

Younger, Paul. "Review of Wilfred Cantwell Smith, *Questions of Religious Truth*." *Journal of the American Academy of Religion* 38, no. 1 (1970), pp. 79–80.

Towards a Hermeneutic of Humanity

Wilfred Cantwell Smith and the Study of Muslims

AMIR HUSSAIN

I am honored, delighted, and humbled to be a part of this volume honoring our teacher, Wilfred Cantwell Smith. Let me begin with the words that Wilfred delivered over sixty years ago (December 8, 1949) in his inaugural lecture, "The Comparative Study of Religion": "There are two elements in the feeling, close to awe, with which I am touched in assuming the charge that has been entrusted to me here. . . ."[1] For Wilfred, those two elements were honor and gratitude. Like him, I am honored and grateful to be included in this volume. A very simple and sincere "thank you" to Dean Ellen Bradshaw Aitken (of blessed memory) for inviting me to be a part of this project, and to Professor Arvind Sharma for editing this volume.

I am from Los Angeles, so forgive me for writing about, well, me. I do this not to be self-indulgent, as I know people from LA are prone to self-indulgence, but to mention something of my connections to Wilfred and Muriel. And it is important to mention both of them, as the life lived by Wilfred was shared with Muriel. On January 24, 2010, Muriel MacKenzie Struthers Smith passed away in Toronto. I was privileged to be asked by her family to be one of the speakers at her memorial service on February 7, and I began my remarks with the Chinese communist saying, "Women hold up half of the sky." That line was appropriate on both Chinese and communist counts, because Muriel began life in China, the daughter of missionary parents, and she and Wilfred both had youthful indiscretions with communism. I will return to Muriel at the close of my chapter.

I had the privilege of working with Wilfred and Muriel in Toronto, after their retirement from Harvard. Surprisingly for someone from LA, in many ways, I am a traditionalist, not a modernist. I certainly count myself as one who is steeped in the past, one who respects and honors the elders. As Confucius is reported to have said, "I am a transmitter, not an innovator. I believe in antiquity and love the ancients" (*Analects* 7:1).

The last decade has seen the deaths of many of our grandmothers and grandfathers in the study of Islam. In 2003 we experienced the losses of Annemarie Schimmel of Harvard, my own thesis supervisor Willard Oxtoby, Franz Rosenthal of Yale, and Edward Said of Columbia. In September 2009 we lost Michael Marmura of the University of Toronto, one of the finest scholars in the world of Islamic philosophy. In September 2010 we lost Mohammed Arkoun, one of finest scholars of the Qur'an. I dedicate this chapter to the memories of all of them, and particularly to the two who had the most profound influence on my work, and indeed my academic life. For the lives and work of Wilfred Cantwell Smith and Willard G. Oxtoby, I am profoundly thankful.

In remembering all of them, I am reminded of the words of Bill Reid, one of the most famous artists from the Haida nation, who passed away in 1998. The Haida live in what we call the Queen Charlotte Islands in the Pacific Northwest, but they are known to the Haida as the Haida Gwaii, "the Islands of the People." In a collection of Haida stories, *The Raven Steals the Light*, Bill wrote:

> I consider myself one of the most fortunate of men, to have lived at a time when some of the old Haidas and their peers among the Northwest Coast peoples were still alive, and to have had the privilege of knowing them. Protected by the sure conviction of who they were, they survived terrible assaults on the way of life which had served them so well for so long, and they responded to the rigours of an arrogant, often unfriendly, disdainful world with dignity and courtesy, embodied in inbred instinct for doing the right thing. I certainly shall not see their like again in my time.[2]

Dignity and courtesy, embodied in inbred instinct for doing the right thing. That sentence is just as descriptive of my elders as it is of the Haida teachers of Bill Reid. Unfortunately, Bill's phrase "an arrogant, often unfriendly, disdainful world" is also an accurate depiction of much of the academy. I learned a great deal from my teachers, and one of the greatest things that they taught me was how to *be* in the world. To act, always, in a dignified and courteous manner. I rarely live up to the model that they provided me with, but I am so grateful to have their model to follow.

From the Study of Islam in the Twentieth Century to the Study of Muslims in the Twenty-First Century

To understand where we are going, it is necessary to know where we have been. Let me discuss the study of Islam in the twentieth century. I contrast that later with the study of Muslims. At the beginning of the previous century, the study of religion was concentrated in departments of religious knowledge or theology. Within theological institutions, if Islam was studied, it was not for its own sake, but largely to train missionaries who would spread the gospel to Muslim lands. In secular institutions, the study of Islam was subsumed under Oriental or Near Eastern Studies. The world of Islam was largely confined to the Near East, even though the majority of the world's Muslims live in South and Southeast Asia.

From Professor Smith I learned not only about scholarship, but about humanity and social justice. At the time that he began his work, before World War II, the study of Islam consisted almost entirely of the study, by non-Muslim scholars, of texts written by Muslims. His undergraduate degree, from the University of Toronto, was in oriental languages. Growing up in Canada, where there were very few Muslims, he went to India, which at the time was the country with the largest number of Muslims. This was a revolutionary idea: to actually live with Muslims, and to actually ask them what they thought, and then to actually write about it. Predictably, Cambridge, where he was enrolled for his doctorate, wanted nothing to do with his dissertation, and rejected it. Imagine the audacity of writing about what Muslims actually thought and did and passing that off as "scholarship," when everyone knew that "scholarship" meant writing a lengthy treatise on an obscure Arabic or Persian text that most Muslims had never heard of, let alone read. And, of course, everything old is new again. Nowadays, the current thinking is that, to do proper ethnographic scholarship, one must have a deep knowledge of the culture that one writes about. Professor Smith was doing this in 1941, over seventy years ago.

When he set up the Institute of Islamic studies at Montreal's McGill University in 1951, he wanted Muslims to be involved with it. Again, this was a radical idea for North American and European universities, Muslims being involved in the study of Islam. To quote from his obituary, "He recruited Muslim scholars and students to the faculty and graduate student body, involving them in a joint venture of scholarship formerly carried on largely by Western orientalists. By giving emphasis to numerically dominant South and Southeast Asian Islam, he also balanced earlier reliance on classical Arabic, Persian, and Turkish texts."[3]

In 2003, I taught a capstone course for religious studies majors at California State University, Northridge, on the work of Professors Smith and Said, a course called Religion, Description and Empire. My inspiration for that course and that combination of scholars came from a line by one of this volume's contributors, William Graham, who wrote of Wilfred, "He was the critic of 'Orientalism' years before Edward Said, a critic of intellectual colonialism long before the post-colonial debates, and these ethical and scholarly stances came from his moral and his intellectual rigorism."[4]

Professor Said was a scholar of comparative literature, but he wrote several books that had a direct impact on the study of Islam. One was *Covering Islam: How the Media and the Experts Determine How We See the Rest of the World*. Another was *Orientalism*, which although problematic, remains an important text. When I assign it to students, I always pair it with the review by Malcolm Kerr in the *International Journal of Middle Eastern Studies*.[5]

Like Professor Smith, Professor Said was never shy about speaking the truth to power. In an interview during the first Gulf War, he said:

> Re-engagement with intellectual process means a return to an old-fashioned historical, literary and, above all, intellectual scholarship based upon the premise that human beings, men and women, make their own history. And just as things are made, they can be unmade and remade. That sense of intellectual and political and citizenly empowerment is what the intellectual class needs. . . . For the American intellectual, that means, at bottom, that the relationship between the United States and the rest of the world, now based upon profit and power, has to be altered to one of coexistence among human communities that can make and remake their own histories and environments together. This is the number one priority—there's nothing else of that magnitude.[6]

In the twenty-first century, I envision a return to the serious, traditional intellectual scholarship advocated by Professors Smith and Said. At Loyola Marymount University, I am fortunate to have colleagues who study Islam and Muslims in different disciplines, and I hope that having multiple experts on Islam in the same university is a trend that will continue at other universities. In far too many institutions of higher learning, the study of Islam is left to one person. In and of itself, this is not necessarily a bad thing. Professor Smith was famous for his disapproval of "interdisciplinary studies," thinking instead that we should be able to use every discipline in the university to understand our subject. In 1981's *Towards a World Theology*, he wrote: "The recent concept of 'interdisciplinarity' is an attempt to construct a ladder by which to climb out of a hole into which genuinely humane studies never fell."[7] However, he was certainly in favor of having a group of scholars work on problems, rather than single scholars working in isolation.

What other trends do I see in the future aside from more collaborative scholarship? At least five come to mind. First is the involvement of Muslims, as Muslims, in the academic study of Islam. This is the case in the study of most other religious traditions in the world, yet somehow Muslim scholars of Islam are seen as suspect in a way that, for example, their Christian colleagues who study Christianity and their Jewish colleagues who study Judaism are not.[8] Second is less concentration on traditional languages and classic texts as the only way to study Islam. Let me be unambiguous here. I do not mean to deemphasize the study of languages. I think source languages and languages of modern scholarship are crucial to any serious study. That said, knowing only a language or a particular series of set texts does not indicate deep knowledge of a particular religious tradition. I see more concentration on cultural studies, gender, politics, art, history, and contemporary culture in the study of Islam, which is in fact a common trend more generally in the study of religion. Third, I see the need for more scholarship on cultural and national diversity among Muslims. Fourth, I see more studies on North American and European Muslim communities. Fifth is the awareness by scholars of the relationship between knowledge and power. Ours is the generation that came of age after *Orientalism*, and recognizes much of the colonial context and subtext of Islamic studies in the past century. To quote from the words of a latter-day prophet, the Honorable Robert Nesta Marley, sometimes also known as Bob, "We're forwarding this generation triumphantly."

A Hermeneutic of Humanity

The title of my chapter includes the phrase "hermeneutic of humanity." This phrase encapsulates for me the methodological advances that Professors Smith, Oxtoby, and Said brought to the study of Islam. Where our sisters offered to us the much-needed "hermeneutic of suspicion," let me offer alongside it the hermeneutic of humanity as my guiding principle for the study of Muslims in the twenty-first century. To value humanity, of course, does not mean to be unscholarly. Bill Graham's reminiscence of Professor Smith for the *Bulletin of the Harvard Divinity School* was entitled "The Scholar's Scholar."[9] And Professor Smith was certainly that, the greatest scholar of us all. But he was also one of the kindest men, one of the most human of human beings that I have ever met. I elaborate on his humanity later in my chapter. And so the basic meaning of a hermeneutic of humanity is to come to the scholarly study, the serious scholarly study, of Islam with humanity.

Let me elucidate what I mean by a hermeneutic of humanity with four points. The first is a deep knowledge of the subject. The second is an honest and critical evaluation of that subject, which does not at the same time do violence to the subject. The third is in spreading information about that evaluation. And the fourth, simply, is a way of being in the world that honors one's colleagues and students. Let me explain, briefly, how Professor Smith exemplified these four points.

The first point is a deep knowledge of the subject. Professor Smith certainly had a deep knowledge of Islam and Muslims. For six years, he and Mrs. Smith lived in Lahore. They learned about Muslims not simply through the study of texts, but from living with Muslims. And they did this over sixty years ago, decades before the current scholarly trend towards long-term participant observation. I am reminded of words that Edward Seidensticker (the first translator of the Nobel Prize winner Kawabata Yasunari) spoke about Kawabata at a lecture in New York City on October 18, 1990: "He stands at the cutting edge of the traditional, or at the point where the traditional and the new and modern intersect, or at the head of the march pulling the traditional into the future."[10] Professor Smith studied the texts that Muslims wrote, and the languages that we speak. This was the traditional scholarship of his day. The dissertation that was accepted by Princeton University (in 1948) was on the Azhar journal in Cairo. But Professor Smith also studied what it was that Muslims did. It was here that he was an innovator. The dissertation that was rejected by Cambridge University was a Marxist critique of the British in India that became his first book, *Modern Islam in India*.

This first point about a deep knowledge of the subject, particularly if that subject is Islam or Muslims, is, after the attacks of September 11, 2001, and the wars in Afghanistan and Iraq, even more salient. Suddenly, all sorts of people who have never done any serious study of Islam and Muslims are now expert commentators. In the years since the attacks, I have missed more than ever my conversations with Professor and Mrs. Smith about the Muslim world. It is the study of Muslims, not just Islam, that is important here. Let me return to his inaugural lecture sixty years ago. He said:

> Religion in any vital sense—or anyway, religion as the subject matter of our study—is not the rites, symbols, doctrines, etc., of the system; but what these mean to a man. What he does with them: and what they do to him. Religion lies somewhere in the interaction between men and their religious material. . . . Furthermore, for those who will join me in discarding the essentialist view, to enter the continuing community is to accept the past tradition not as binding, but simply as past tradition. That tradition is open: the future is ours. The future of Christianity lies with Christians; the future of Islam with Muslims.[11]

This leads me to my second point, about an honest and critical evaluation of the subject. I am surprised at how, unfortunately, some people seem to equate criticism and being critical with being rude. These are two very different beasts. Professor Smith was, for me, the paradigm of critical scholarship. From his deep knowledge, he was able to offer critique when it was needed. He was not a Muslim. He was not an apologist for Islam. Yet his critique never did violence to what it meant for other people to be Muslim. Let me quote something from *Islam in Modern History*: "A true Muslim, however, is not a man who believes in Islam—especially Islam in history; but one who believes in God and is committed to the revelation through His Prophet."[12] Those words were published in 1957. In 1962's *The Meaning and End of Religion*, he continued: "the essential tragedy of the modern Islamic world is the degree to which Muslims, instead of giving their allegiance to God, have been giving it to something called Islam."[13] Those words could have been written today with equal force and validity. It is a mark of Professor Smith's genius that those words were written over fifty years ago and yet they continue to inform us today.

The third point concerning a hermeneutic of humanity is in the spreading of the information that one has discovered. This process is usually referred to in the United States as "dissemination," but the feminist in me is uncomfortable at the use of that word. The works that Professor Smith produced remain models for me, for us, to this day. Humane scholarship, that is, both scholarly and humane. In the spring of 1992, the Centre for Religious Studies of the University of Toronto organized a conference in honor of Professor Smith. One of the participants in that conference was John Hick, one of the preeminent philosophers of religion. Of Professor Smith's scholarship, Hick wrote: "An outstanding feature of Wilfred's work is that it is on the highest level of technical historical scholarship and yet it is at the same time driven by involvement in and concern for the world-wide human community, with a keen sense of the threatening disasters and the amazing possibilities before us. This human involvement goes back to his work in India before Partition and has continued ever since, as a constant thread running through all his writings."[14]

The fourth point is perhaps the most important to my understanding of a hermeneutic of humanity. Many other academic enterprises comprise the first three points. What distinguishes this approach is the way of one's being in the world, how it is that one treats one's colleagues and students. In this, Professor and Mrs. Smith were without equal. Anyone that knew them had stories to tell. And one would never know from Professor Smith's humility that he was such an outstanding scholar. Let me tell my own story. The first time I formally met Professor Smith was almost thirty years ago, in 1989. I had written a paper that had been accepted for the annual meeting of the Canadian Society for the Study of Religion, and as an MA student about to make his first major presentation, I was excited and nervous. The meeting was in Victoria, British Columbia, and we had a small conference in Toronto preceding the meeting to first test out our papers. My paper, as part of its methodology, used some ideas from Professor Smith's magnum opus, *The Meaning and End of Religion*. Just before I was to present my paper, in he walked. I was mortified. What was he going to say about my use of his ideas? I had no idea. I presented, and thankfully, the paper was well received. At the reception afterward, Professor Smith came up to me. He thanked me for my paper, and asked if he could shake my hand.

I will never forget that gesture of humanity as long as I live. Here was Wilfred Cantwell Smith, *Wilfred Cantwell Smith*, and he was asking if *he* could shake *my* hand. That's the first time I thought I might be able to make it in this profession. In the years after that, as I got to know Professor and Mrs. Smith, I understood that this was simply how they were. Kind and decent people in a world in which humanity and decency are in such short supply.

That humanity was passed along and through those who came into contact with Professor Smith. Out of respect for Professor Smith, who would be deeply embarrassed at my use of the word in reference to him, I will not refer to it as his *baraka*, the Arabic term for an "intangible holiness that is sometimes tangible." But there is something there that he passed on to all of us. And if he would be embarrassed by my speaking of his *baraka*, I can only imagine what he would say about my usual ritual when I am at McGill, performing seven counterclockwise circuits around the Institute for Islamic Studies.

Professor Smith continued to live out the hermeneutic of humanity until the end. After he and Mrs. Smith moved from the large house on Brunswick Avenue in the Annex section of Toronto to the small apartment in Fellowship Towers, they gave their books on Islam to the library of California State University, Northridge, where I was teaching at the time. The books could have gone to Harvard University or McGill University, but those schools already had those books. At Northridge, they increased our holdings on Islam by about a third and benefited another generation of students. And I think they also thought about aiding another young Canadian at the beginning of his academic career. There they were yet again, Professor and Mrs. Smith, helping a new scholar out.

Let me turn here to Muriel and the story that I promised at the beginning of this chapter. In any discussion about humanity, we, particularly when it is a male "we," have to keep at the front of our minds the crucial roles of women. I was reminded of that at Muriel's funeral. Born in China, she was educated in English Canada. When Wilfred was hired at McGill in 1949, they moved to Montreal. At that point, they had three small children, Arnold, Julian, and Heather, with a fourth, Brian, born in 1951.

So there was Muriel, an English Protestant woman in a French Catholic city with a husband at work and four small children at home. And in those days, new professors did not command the princely sums that we currently enjoy, and so there were economic hardships as well.

And I thought for the first time about the shared experiences, the shared culture, of Muriel and my own mother, Feroza. My mother is a Muslim woman from Pakistan, who found herself in Protestant Toronto, raising two small children on the working-class salary of my father, Iqbal, who worked in factories. Until that moment, I had always thought of Muriel as a white woman of privilege, with no connections to a poor immigrant woman of color like my mother. Although living in very different cultures, these two women shared in both faith and culture. Women, we need to remember, hold up half of the sky.

Let me close with Salman Rushdie, who in 1982 published his magisterial essay about colonial and postcolonial literature, "Imaginary Homelands." Rushdie ended that essay with a reference to a book that Saul Bellow published that same year, *The Dean's December*: "There's a beautiful image in Saul Bellow's latest novel, *The Dean's December*. The central character, the Dean Corde, hears a dog barking wildly somewhere. He imagines that the barking is the dog's protest against the limit of dog experience. 'For God's sake,' the dog is saying, 'open the universe a little more!' And because Bellow is, of course, not really talking about dogs, or not only about dogs, I have the feeling that the dog's rage, and its desire, is also mine, ours, everyone's. 'For God's sake, open the universe a little more!'"[15]

This is my hope for the study of Muslims in the twenty-first century, that we open the universe a little more.

Notes

1. Wilfred Cantwell Smith, "The Comparative Study of Religion," *Inaugural Lectures: McGill University Faculty of Divinity* (Montreal: McGill University, 1950), p. 41.

2. Bill Reid and Robert Bringhurst, *The Raven Steals the Light* (Vancouver, BC: Douglas & McIntyre, 1996), p. 13.

3. Available on the web at: <http://www.ageofsignificance.org/people/wcsmith/index.html>.

4. William A. Graham, "The Scholar's Scholar: Wilfred Cantwell Smith and a Collegial Life of the Mind," *Harvard Divinity Bulletin* 29, no. 2 (Summer 2000), p. 7.

5. December, 1980 (12, no. 4), pp. 544–47.

6. Gauri Viswanathan, ed., *Power, Politics, and Culture: Interviews with Edward W. Said* (New York: Vintage Books, 2001), p. 366.

7. Quoted in Kenneth Cracknell, ed., *Wilfred Cantwell Smith: A Reader* (Oxford, UK: Oneworld Publications, 2001), p. 123.

8. I have written about this in "Teaching Inside-Out: On Teaching Islam," in *Method and Theory in the Study of Religion* 17, no. 3 (2005), pp. 248–63.

9. Graham, "The Scholar's Scholar," pp. 6–7.

10. Edward Seidensticker, *Kawabata and Snow Country: The Limited Editions Club Lecture Series: Number One* (New York: Limited Editions Club, 1990), p. 5.

11. Smith, "The Comparative Study of Religion," pp. 51, 55.

12. Wilfred Cantwell Smith, *Islam in Modern History* (Princeton, NJ: Princeton University Press, 1957), p. 146.

13. Wilfred Cantwell Smith, *The Meaning and End of Religion* (Minneapolis: Fortress Press, 1991 [1962]), p. 126.

14. John Hick, "On Wilfred Cantwell Smith: His Place in the Study of Religion," *Method and Theory in the Study of Religion* 4, nos. 1 and 2 (1992), p. 5.

15. Salman Rushdie, *Imaginary Homelands: Essays and Criticism 1981–1991* (London: Granta Books, 1991), p. 21.

Bibliography

Cracknell, Kenneth, ed. *Wilfred Cantwell Smith: A Reader*. Oxford, UK: Oneworld Publications, 2001.

Graham, William A. "The Scholar's Scholar: Wilfred Cantwell Smith and a Collegial Life of the Mind." *Harvard Divinity Bulletin* 29, no. 2 (Summer 2000), pp. 6–7.

Hick, John. "On Wilfred Cantwell Smith: His Place in the Study of Religion." *Method and Theory in the Study of Religion* 4, nos. 1 and 2 (1992), pp. 5–20.

Hussain, Amir. "Teaching Inside-Out: On Teaching Islam." *Method and Theory in the Study of Religion* 17, no. 3 (2005), pp. 248–63.

Kerr, Malcolm. "Book Review: *Orientalism*." *International Journal of Middle Eastern Studies* 12, no. 4 (December, 1980), pp. 544–47.

Reid, Bill, and Robert Bringhurst. *The Raven Steals the Light*. Vancouver, BC: Douglas & McIntyre, 1996.

Rushdie, Salman. *Imaginary Homelands: Essays and Criticism 1981–1991*. London: Granta Books, 1991.

Seidensticker, Edward. *Kawabata and Snow Country: The Limited Editions Club Lecture Series: Number One*. New York: Limited Editions Club, 1990.

Smith, Wilfred Cantwell. "The Comparative Study of Religion." *Inaugural Lectures: McGill University Faculty of Divinity*. Montreal: McGill University, 1950.

———. *Islam in Modern History*. Princeton, NJ: Princeton University Press, 1957.

———. *The Meaning and End of Religion*. Minneapolis: Fortress Press, 1991.

Viswanathan, Gauri, ed. *Power, Politics, and Culture: Interviews with Edward W. Said*. New York: Vintage Books, 2001.

Wilfred Cantwell Smith in Lahore 1940–1951

Sheila McDonough

> When I was a questioning undergraduate in the Depression, God spoke to me more effectively through the words of Amos than He did through Christ. This was not so ten years earlier.[1]

> One may remember the Fellowship for a Christian Social Order. Some of us tried to do our little bit to make life Christian in that significant sense.[2]

> Relatively few have thought the thesis [that non-Christian faith is partial, whereas Christian faith is final, perfect] through carefully, and self-consciously defended it. [One who has is H. H. Farmer.][3]

These three quotations indicate something of what Smith wanted his readers to understand about his own background. He had been a questioning undergraduate, a person whose conscience was stirred up by the Biblical prophet Amos; an admirer of the Fellowship for a Christian Social Order; and a graduate student in England reflecting on whether the Christian faith should be considered partial or final and perfect.

While an undergraduate, Smith became committed to the left-wing perspectives of the Christian social gospel movement. This is the implication of his comment about the importance of the prophet Amos for him as a young man. As an active member of the Student Christian Movement during his undergraduate days at the University of Toronto, he had moved away from the conservative theological and political attitudes characteristic of the members of the Knox Presbyterian Church that his family had attended. His father seems to have represented to him somewhat stern Presbyterian values. His father had opposed joining other Presbyterians in the new United Church of Canada that was established in 1925. Smith's mother, Sarah Cory Cantwell Smith, came from an American Methodist background and seems to have communicated to her son a feeling for religious poetry and an interest in foreign missions. He had visited Egypt with his mother when he was seventeen. His mother was descended from the Cory family, which had suffered persecution during the witch trials in Salem, Massachusetts, at the end of the seventeenth century.[4]

During his Student Christian Movement days, the young Smith developed a readiness to ask questions. One of his professors, Stewart McCullough, had trained him in careful study of ancient Near Eastern history and religion. During his undergraduate days, he had wrestled with the conflicts between science and religion; Arthur Eddington's writings on the two topics had led the young Smith into new ways of thinking about the size and mystery of the cosmos.[5] Biblical scholarship also influenced his mind, notably through participation in comparative study of the gospel records by the Sharman method, which was widely used throughout Canadian Christian student movements in the 1930s and 1940s. Further, Smith's father had lost much of his money as a result of the Depression, and the young Smith was receptive to the criticisms of the capitalist system characteristic of the Christian social thought of the time. The Scottish moral and political philosopher John MacMurray played a significant role in shaping the thinking of the young Christian socialists of Smith's undergraduate days.[6]

The book by Smith's friend and later colleague, R. B. Y. Scott, *The Relevance of the Prophets*, tells us something of how the Canadian Christian socialists of the 1930s viewed human history and society.[7] The imperative was to think about contemporary society in the manner of the Hebrew writing prophets, such as Amos and Jeremiah, to express judgment on corruption, and to call for a transformed future. Smith went to Cambridge in 1938 with all these ideas in his mind, and found there an even more radical critique of the forces at work in the world. He did not join the Communist Party, but he accepted much of the socialist analysis as to how class shapes ideas. His mental state was probably much like that of many of his contemporaries who went off to fight against fascism in the Spanish Civil War. It was a time when the threat of evil and the promise of a transformed future were perceived intensely as an "either-or" choice. He later told me that the tense state of mind that he had encountered among students at Cambridge had affected him greatly.

Many of the students at Oxford and Cambridge in the late 1930s were very disturbed about the rise of fascism, the Spanish Civil War, and the threat of impending war. The poet Stephen Spender has characterized the era as the "Pink Decade," a time when many young people felt that the conflicts between fascism and socialism were reaching epic proportions.[8] Wilfred Smith had gone to England in 1938. He was studying Christian theology at Cambridge; H. H. Farmer was his tutor. He was also taking classes in Islamic history with H. A. R. Gibb at Oxford. His family reports that he used to bicycle between the two universities.

Smith was a pacifist, as was his Canadian contemporary George Grant, who was also in England at the time. Smith and Grant had been contemporaries in their secondary-school studies at Upper Canada College in Toronto. In their secondary-school days, a group of students advocated pacifism as the best response to the problem of modern war. Grant remained in England to do volunteer ambulance work in London during the bombing raids. He later established, at McMaster University, one of Canada's main centers for the comparative study of religion.[9] Smith, however, opted to go as a missionary to Lahore in 1939, where he hoped to aid the Indians in getting rid of British imperialism. He believed that World War I had been a conflict between greedy imperialist powers; he hoped that the outbreak of another European war might provide an opportunity for India to free itself from exploitation. He saw himself at that time as devoted to Nehru's cause of working to create a new, free, and socialist India. He thought that if the imperialist powers destroyed themselves in the coming war, a better future might become possible for the former colonies.

In Lahore, the young Canadian taught Islamic history at the Forman Christian College; he also took part regularly in discussions with a group of young Indian intellectuals—Hindu, Sikh, Muslim, and Christian—who shared his hopes for the future. Some of them taught at Government College, Lahore, or were civil servants. Many of these people remained his lifelong friends. Several of them had studied in British universities before returning to Lahore. It was a milieu that Smith loved. The stimulation of the struggle to articulate the grounds for a better future remained with him always, in spite of much later discouragement and disillusion. Furthermore, for the rest of his life, he continued to see the struggle as one in which people from different traditions could, and should, talk to each other about directions for the future.

This background of the Canadian Christian social gospel, the Cambridge "Pink Decade," and the socialist intellectuals of India is readily discernible in the pages of Smith's first book, *Modern Islam in India*, published in Lahore in 1943. The book is a vigorous statement by a young man in his midtwenties of his passion for the immediate implementation of progressive ideals in India. The young man's mentor was Nehru; he was also fascinated by the Muslim poet, Iqbal, and he was committed to a scientific socialist revolution. Quotations from Nehru, Iqbal, and Smith himself may help illuminate the perspectives of the time.

Nehru

"The *avatars* of today are great ideas which come to reform the world. And the idea of the day is social equality. Let us listen to it and become its instruments to transform the world and make it a better place to live in."[10]

Smith's friends, the progressives of Lahore, were, like Smith himself, pro-Nehru. In 1907, Nehru was a student at Cambridge, where he had become interested in the Fabian Society.[11] Back in India, Nehru, in the heady excitement of the anti-British struggles of 1919 to 1922, joined the movement for national independence and was several times imprisoned by the British. During his visit to Russia in 1926 and 1927, the Congress leader had been impressed by much of what he saw.

This Indian reformer was very impatient with all forms of traditional religious thinking because he considered religious leaders to be generally passive about social change, or else as supporters of feudalism. He perceived the religious revivalism of Hindus and Muslims in the 1920s and 1930s as primarily reactionary. Nehru wanted to move India into a better future by, first, getting the British out, and then by using the power of the state to encourage and guide a form of industrialization that would promote economic and social justice. He did not want to copy the forms of government of the USSR, but rather wanted to use democracy to promote socialism. He thought of religion as largely irrelevant, or hostile to, the kinds of changes he envisioned for India. Wilfred Cantwell Smith, and the other socialist Indians in Lahore in the early 1940s, understood Nehru to be their leader in the struggles against imperialist control, against feudalism, and against the exploitation of the Indian poor. After the outbreak of World War II, the Congress leaders made their support of Britain in the conflict contingent on the departure of the British from India. The leaders of the Congress, including Nehru, were imprisoned. In 1941, Smith and his wife visited Nehru in Lucknow, where he had been imprisoned.[12]

Iqbal

Iqbal wrote in the poem "God's Command to His Angels": "Rise, and from their slumber wake the poor ones of My world! /Shake the walls and windows of the mansions of the great! /Kindle with the fire of faith the slow blood of the slaves!"

Lahore was the city in which the Muslim poet-philosopher Muhammad Iqbal (1877–1938) had spent most of his life. Iqbal had just died two years before Smith arrived in the city. As the above-quoted lines indicate, this Muslim poet also believed that the Indians must throw the British out and start work on creating a better society. Iqbal was older than Nehru and Smith; he had been a mature adult at the time of World War I.

Smith's friends in Lahore were representative of many Indians of that time who were enthused by, stimulated by, angry about, and in diverse ways reacting to the impact of Iqbal's life and work. It is not surprising that the intellectually alert young Canadian Christian socialist encountered Iqbal's ideas as omnipresent in the Lahore of the time. Smith reacted to Iqbal as his friends had. Smith's first book is largely about Iqbal and indicates the complex mix of admiration and exasperation that many Lahore socialists felt toward the poet. Iqbal had admired Lenin and the Russian Revolution. However, he also wrote a poem, "Lenin before God," that indicated that abolishing religion would not help to make the world better.[13] The point of Iqbal's poem on Lenin is that, if religious leaders support reactionary and feudal political leaders, as the Russian Church had supported the tsar, the fighters for social justice may abandon religion. Iqbal is warning the Indian Muslims that if they equate their religion with reactionary social forces, the religion itself may be destroyed. His message is a warning against using religious symbols to oppose social change.

On the other hand, Iqbal also thought that getting rid of religious life entirely would not do much to improve the world. The thesis of the poem is that the equation of the Russian Church hierarchy with the tsarist regime does not in itself prove the nonexistence of God. Iqbal was much more critical of the extremism of the Russian Revolution than was either the young Smith or the young Nehru. In the poem, Lenin, after his death, is surprised to find that God has all along existed.

In one of Iqbal's open letters to Nehru, he argued his point as follows: "He [Nehru] thinks, wrongly in my opinion, that the only way to Indian Nationalism lies in a total suppression of the cultural entities of the country through the interaction of which alone India can evolve a rich and enduring culture. A nationalism achieved by such methods can mean nothing but mutual bitterness and even oppression."[14] Iqbal thought that any effort by the state to suppress religion entirely would just make religious people more violent and irrational. The Muslim poet wrote several times to Nehru trying to explain this point of view.

Wilfred Smith

Smith said in the Preface to his *Modern Islam in India*: "I am a socialist with pronounced ethical convictions; and I believe in the scientific method."[15] This firm statement is an example of a manifesto from Smith, who thought of himself as a scientific historian who could discern the class struggle at work in any human situation. In this book, Smith says that otherworldly idealism is bad in religious thought because it diverts attention from the real problems of life. It makes no difference whether people are Hindus, Sikhs, Muslims, or Christians. From Smith's perspective at this period, the good people shared a common view of the problems and possibilities of their immediate situation and worked together with the immanent forces of progress in history. In other words, the good ones in Lahore in 1940 followed Nehru, and the bad ones did not.

In *Modern Islam in India*, Smith argues that a good scientific understanding of religion should demonstrate that the ideas of all religions are shaped by the class struggle. The historian of religion can recognize through what stage each religious group is currently passing. He can see what objective changes are taking place in society and how the religious persons in question are relating to those changes. These religious persons either oppose, ignore, or work constructively with the changes in question.

Smith said that, while the objective changes occur in the conditions of material existence as a culture moves from one phase of development to another, the minds often do not change quickly or accurately. Only the people who properly understand the objective realities at work in the historical process can adequately understand what is happening in their milieu. In this book, the word *liberal* is consistently used to indicate an objectively wrong way of understanding how human beings should relate to the will of God. Conservatives, reactionaries, and liberals all misunderstand the historical process. Only the socialists understand how the will of God is working. That will is best understood to be the unfolding of the immanent processes at work in human history. In discussing the Indian Muslims of his time, Smith wrote: "Naturally, it must be borne in mind that the social background has been constantly developing. Accordingly, the religion has changed slightly in harmony with that development. But in so far as it [the religion] has not changed sufficiently, its objective role in society has been transformed. Whereas it was once a progressive movement, it has passed through a passive, liberal phase, and has finally become conservative; it was ready recently even to become reactionary."[16]

This is the perspective that Smith, in Lahore in the early 1940s, thought was characteristic of the changes taking place in the thinking of representatives of all the major world religions. It was the perspective that he used to measure the lives and thoughts of the Indian Muslims in the modern period. Doubtless, in his student days at Cambridge, he had held that these were the phases through which the Christian world, as he understood it, had been passing in the nineteenth and twentieth centuries. From this perspective, religious persons in any tradition can be understood in their own contexts as reactionary, conservative, passive liberal, or progressive. Smith thought that each of these particular stances has a distinct relationship to the immanent processes at work as the objective conditions of life in the world go through their inevitable phases of development. The reactionaries in all religious traditions fight change actively and want to force society back into an earlier phase. The conservatives try to resist change by clinging to a status quo. The passive liberals allow change to move them but take no decisive actions. The progressives accurately understand the immanent forces at work as history progresses through inevitable stages, and they actively strive to work with these immanent forces to bring about the good society on earth.

It was by these criteria that Smith measured the major religious thinkers and religious movements within Indian Islam from 1800 onward. A measuring rod like this is characteristic of any intellectual system that assumes that one worldview is correct—or orthodox—and that all unorthodox, or heretical, positions have recognizable characteristics. One knows in advance what the heretics are like before one even meets them. The orthodoxy in this case was a religious Marxist view of history, namely, that the unfolding of human history toward a classless society is the plan and work of God. The intellectual challenge, for one who holds such a perspective, is simply to recognize which heresies are present and who the typical reactionaries, conservatives, liberals, and progressives are. The adherent of the orthodoxy already possesses the labels; the question is just which label to stick on which phenomenon.

However, Smith had trouble finding an appropriate label for Iqbal. The Canadian scholar wrote:

> Theologically . . . he [Iqbal] wrought the most important and the most necessary revolution of modern times. For he made God immanent, not transcendent. For Islam, this is rank heresy; but for to-day it is the only salvation. The revolution of immanence lies in this, that it puts God back into the world. Iqbal's God is in the world, now, with us, facing our problems from within, creating a new and better world with us and through us. Religion is life. And life, this mundane material life, is religious. The present world, of matter, time and space, is good. God himself, and all the values, rewards, ideals, and objectives of religion become transferred to the empirical universe. Correspondingly, the will of God is not something imposed from without to be accepted resignedly, but surges within, is to be absorbed and acted upon.
>
> All the religions have gone through world- and life-denying phases, in times of social decadence or unprosperous stagnation. Iqbal scornfully rejected these aspects from Islam as alien and evil, and insisted that his religion said "yes" to the material world.
>
> Iqbal, as we have seen, in deploring the old static other-worldliness of religion, now certainly a sin, denounced it as un-Islamic and inherently evil. . . .
>
> Religion performing this service for mankind has been called an opiate. It could equally be called a stimulant; for without it man could never have carried on. Man has had in his religions, in their vision of eternity, the only thing that has kept him going through thousands of years of non-achievement.
>
> But when good can be really attained, then that religion which still tries to preserve good in ideas, in some other world, *instead of* realising it in this world—that religion becomes reactionary and evil. It has become so attached to the metaphysical values that it actively resists the attempt

to put those values back into actual life. . . . Iqbal, John MacMurray, the Communist Party, and all social progressives, attack traditional religion for the same reason: namely, that by diverting attention by its idealism from the real situation and real opportunities, it to-day impedes right action.[17]

This passage is a significant key to Smith's thinking in the 1940s with respect to criteria for measurement of any religious thinker or movement. His heroes and mentors, as he clearly says, were Iqbal, John MacMurray, the Communist Party, and all social progressives. The Canadian was vigorously opposed to any kind of "pie in the sky" talk. As noted earlier, his passion was not unlike that of those who went off to fight in Spain—a feeling that immediate action was essential. In this case, the action was to make India free and strong and to ignore or oppose those adherents of traditional religions who did not share these values. Smith was somewhat baffled by Iqbal since he understood that the poet wanted the liberation of India and the abolition of feudalism but was against getting rid of religion. Smith found this to be an unintelligible paradox.

Inefficient Ideology

One of Smith's characteristically sharp statements in this volume is: "The trouble with a wrong ideology is that it is inefficient."[18] This was written with reference to the Khilafat movement in India, a movement that took place among Indian Muslims right after the end of World War I. These Indian Muslims wanted to restore the Turkish caliph to power as a way of ensuring the safety of all Muslims throughout the world. Smith did not note that neither Iqbal nor Jinnah was much interested in the Khilafat movement, whereas Gandhi was an active supporter of that cause. In any case, the relevant point is that Smith believed, at this time, that all religious ideas should be looked at in terms of their probable efficiency as instruments for making the world a better place. Restoring the Turkish caliph to power did not strike him as a useful, practicable, or efficient goal.

Iqbal and Smith were probably not far apart in their attitudes to the Khilafat movement. However, the clash between Iqbal's and the young Smith's views of history lay precisely in how each envisaged the threats and possibilities of post–World War I India. We have already indicated where Iqbal differed from Nehru. At this stage of his development, Smith did not comprehend Iqbal's point.

On the other hand, in many ways Iqbal also admired his fellow Kashmiri, Nehru; he put images of Nehru and his father into the epic poem *The Jawid-Namah*, which was dedicated to Iqbal's young son as a symbol of the Muslims of the future.[19] This means that the ideal of Nehru's life, a rich man's son who put all his energy into working for social justice, was an ideal Iqbal wanted all the future Muslims to understand and to internalize. Iqbal agreed with Nehru on many matters, but not on the ignoring of religion. Smith's position in the early 1940s was pro-Nehru, but he also responded to Iqbal's call to the Muslims to wake up. The young Canadian wrote:

> Muhammad Iqbal summoned the sleeping Muslims to awake.... Throughout his life he devoted himself to inciting activity, to insisting eloquently that life is movement, that action is good, and the universe is composed of processes, and not of static things. He bitterly attacked the attitudes of resignation and quiet contentment, the religious valuation of mere contemplative, passivity, and withdrawal from strife.... Above all, his Islam repudiated the conception of a fixed universe dominated by a dictator God and to be accepted by servile men. In its place he would put a view of an unfinished growing universe, ever being advanced by man and by God through man. Iqbal's prime function was to lash men into furious activity, and to "imbue the idle looker with restless impatience." Life is not to be contemplated but to be passionately lived.[20]

Thus, Smith responded with considerable personal intensity to the passionate dynamism of the Muslim poet. Smith had found friends in Lahore among the Indians from different religious backgrounds who shared his view of the necessity of social revolution. One of the Muslims he particularly admired was K. G. Saiyidain, author of a seminal book, *Iqbal's Educational Philosophy*. Iqbal had personally approved of this book as an excellent exposition of his ideas and had written a foreword to it.[21] Smith said of Saiyidain:

> He has been acutely aware of the stupidity ... of capitalism; and he has pointed them out with scorn. Not only does competitive society produce major evils from time to time, such

> as war, but it is bad throughout; and it must go. ... The perversion of personality, the frustration, the meaninglessness of life, the individual hopelessness, the fear, worry, and insecurity, the mutual competition and antagonism—all these products of capitalism are evil. Anyone who supports such a system is wicked. Similarly the "over-production," the destruction of commodities, the poverty in the midst of plenty, the wars—all these things are also stupid. Anyone who supports such a system is dull and unintelligent.
>
> On the other hand, Saiyidain, inspired by Iqbal, and understanding the potentialities of science, has looked forward to a new social order, in which man shall develop gloriously and flourish. The new personality which Iqbal proffered for attainment shall be attained: the strong and life-affirming individual; courageous, tolerant, disciplined; free, active and powerful; and dedicated to the service of God, with whom and with its fellow-men it shares the task of creating a better world. This ideal is not impossible of achievement, provided society is reconstructed—with co-operation instead of competition, production for use instead of production for profit, more equal distribution, and the full exploitation of technology—and provided education is reconstructed.[22]

One can readily see that this dislike of capitalist competition was Smith's own worldview, learned partly from John MacMurray and from the exponents of the Christian social gospel. The young Canadian was happy to have found friends in Lahore who shared this perspective on the threats and possibilities of the modern world. The fact that he and his friends achieved so much of a common mind helped to determine Smith's lifelong commitment to the possibility of mutual comprehension among persons from different religious backgrounds. He remained close to friends such as Saiyidain throughout his life.

Nevertheless, many of Iqbal's provocative images irritated and puzzled the young Smith. Smith thought that many of Iqbal's ideas were likely to be used by reactionary forces. Chapter 4 of Smith's book is entitled "The Movement in Favour of a New Culture of the Future: Reactionary." Since Smith had come out of the antifascist milieu of a British university in the 1930s, he was very alert to anything that looked protofascist. He arrived in India well aware of the struggles taking place in the Spanish Civil War and of the fierce conflicts between socialists and fascists in Germany at that time. He distrusted, as many people of his time did, any talk of supermen as profascist. Smith wrote:

> Of Iqbal, we can say that he himself was unable to see the full implications of his thought partly because he was not an economist and partly because of his natural prejudice in favour of the traditional Platonic idea of a primarily spiritual universe. This inability to carry this thought to its correct conclusions led him into innumerable reactionary potentialities and several reactionary actualities; and recently a full-fledged fascist tendency took advantage of these same errors to represent itself successfully as his following.[23]

The label "reactionary" was thus pinned by Smith on aspects of Iqbal's thought that were seen as detrimental to the cause of bringing about the required social revolution in India. Smith commented:

> In order to achieve anything valuable, it is important to know how to achieve it. Iqbal stirred the Muslims and pointed out to them the goal; but not being aware of the path to it, he left himself and his followers open to being misled by anyone interested in misleading them provided he could talk the same jargon. To-day events have been moving rapidly through a crisis, and the whole force of the old order has been directed to confusing the people and to promising them Utopia in idea while working in fact for reaction. At such a time it is not good enough merely to have the right ideals.[24]

This is a very clear statement of Smith's own beliefs in the early 1940s. He knew that India and the world were in crisis. He thought that he and fellow Indian socialists clearly understood the reasons for the crisis, the nature of the forces at work in the world, and the path to take, and that all they needed to do was to ally themselves with the immanent will of God, the inevitable movement of history toward a classless society, and follow that power into the future. At this time, Smith thought that all Muslims, Hindus, Buddhists, Sikhs, Jews, and Christians could, and should, jump on the same bandwagon and get moving in their efforts to bring about the objectively correct future. There is always passion in Smith's writings; this time it was antifascist passion. Smith wanted to engage himself in the war of ideas and help to speed on the social revolution he hoped to see arise in India. Many sensitive people at that time felt the imminence of crisis, the threat of collapse of the European social order. This awareness made many people conscious of a need to act fast.

Since Iqbal had not been ready to jump on Nehru's bandwagon, Smith saw the poet's ideas as dangerously vulnerable to misuse by Indian protofascists. Nehru had visited Iqbal in 1937, on the latter's invitation, and reported that they liked each other and enjoyed talking together.[25] Nehru seems to have warned Iqbal that his ideas might be misused by the feudal powers in India, and Iqbal presumably tried to explain yet again why he feared the notion of a strong central state with an antireligious bias. Smith followed Nehru and the other Indian socialists in just dismissing Iqbal's anxieties as reactionary. Smith knew, and said, that Iqbal himself was not reactionary, but maintained that Iqbal's view of the "spiritual nature of the universe" made the poet's images vulnerable to misuse by reactionary forces. At this point in time, Smith did not fully comprehend why Iqbal had said that Lenin would be surprised when he met God. The Canadian thought that such imagery just meant a reversion to feudalism. For "spiritual nature of the universe," Smith read "pie in the sky"—pie that distracts from clear thinking about social goals. Smith's view, as stated in this first book, was that it did not matter what religion a person belonged to; what mattered was whether that person understood the objective forces at work in history. He wrote:

> It is the world crisis facing all religions to-day. It lies in the fact that the objective conditions of the modern world are so radically new that to act religiously, to realise objectively and actually the values at which the religions have constantly aimed, means to act in a way that is no longer recognisably— that is, nominally, religious. To choose real righteousness is to spurn imagined morality. This fact Iqbal recognised; but he did not see the crisis that it involves. The world is so basically new that is no longer possible to have both the substance and the appearance of any religion.
>
> Once the crisis has been reached, the religious men split into two groups. The progressives, religious and righteous in fact, go on their way regardless of whether their acts and attitudes are superficially Muslim—or Christian or whatever. . . . The others, who choose to maintain religion in

idea, to be nominally and recognisably Muslim, etc. become the reactionaries.[26]

One can perhaps best think about the encounter of Smith with Iqbal as an instance of two disciples of historical theology crashing into each other. Both Smith and Iqbal thought that religious imperatives should be articulated in the context of actual situations; the imperatives should make sense in terms of what was going on in the world. Both of them acknowledged the futility of attempting to shape reality in terms of unworkable ideals, such as the folly of the Khilafat movement. Both acknowledged that, to make the world better, one would have to have an accurate appraisal of what forces were at work in a particular context and would have to give up the illusion of retreat into the past. Smith and Iqbal agreed on this point. Smith affirmed that one should take a positive attitude toward the possibilities of making life better in the world; he knew that Iqbal shared this perspective. Smith, however, explicitly talked in this 1943 book about the objective forces functioning in particular situations. Like many socialists of the time, he was convinced that right-thinking people could clearly see, if their thought was objectively correct, the forces at work in the world; they could accurately predict the future.

Iqbal also had affirmed the reality of process and constant change, but he never spoke of the "objective" realities of social change. The Muslim poet thought one could make a human judgment in a particular context as to what should be done to make things better for everyone, but he did not speak of God's will as an immanent process inevitably working in a particular direction. Iqbal's Lenin could be seen as a symbol of all persons who fail to acknowledge that they themselves live under judgment; humans are not infallible. Iqbal's perspective was closer to what is sometimes called "prophetic" faith. One can discern the judgment of God at work in a particular context. But one cannot see God working as part of an inevitable immanent process. One can discern what the good might be in a specific situation and make decisions based on that discernment. But a long-range view as to what exactly will happen next is not possible. "Prophetic" faith attempts to judge the potentialities for good[27] and evil in a specific situation, but it does not assume an immanent purpose in history that human beings can fully comprehend. Smith later acknowledged that he had learned to appreciate the Qur'an from the perspective of Iqbal. The poet taught him to recognize that the Qur'an conveys a dramatic imperative to choose rightly in all historical contexts.[28] Iqbal was an historical theologian in the sense that he understood the Qur'an to mean that wrong choices in history would lead ultimately to failure. The Muslim poet-philosopher understood himself to be following the perspective of Ibn Khaldun in this respect. Iqbal wrote: "The point of interest in this view of history is the way in which Ibn-i-Khaldun conceives the process of change. His conception is of infinite importance because of the implication that history, as a continuous movement in time, is a genuinely creative movement and not a movement whose path is already determined."[29]

Humans are free to choose, but, if they choose wrong values, they will face destruction. Iqbal often emphasized that time is real. He meant by this that good conditions of life for all persons could be created within time, if the believers understood the possibilities of the time in which they lived and chose to work rightly in the present to make the future better. But Iqbal also said that Marxism was a delusion of twisted minds who naively believed that they comprehended and could control the future and the universe. In his poem, "Satan's Parliament," Iqbal has Satan observe that he thinks that communists are his tools. Satan says: "When Nature's hand / Has rent the seam, no needleworking logic / Of communism will put the stitches back. / I [Satan] be afraid of socialists?— street-bawlers, \ Ragged things, tortured brains, tormented souls!"[30]

Iqbal had made several long speeches in English addressed to the Indian Muslims in the crisis period of the early 1930s.[31] He advised them to hold to a vision of what a good world should be. He quoted the biblical phrase—"Where there is no vision, the people perish."[32] He knew that negotiations were taking place between the Muslim League, the Congress, and the British with respect to the future of the subcontinent. In the context of ongoing negotiations, no one can reasonably hold a precise idea of what the end results will be. Iqbal had just warned the Muslims to hold fast to their basic values. Smith, in 1943, interpreted this perspective of Iqbal as reactionary because it was not a blanket approval of Nehru's socialist vision.

1947: The Impact of Partition

World War II ended; the two new nations of India and Pakistan gained independence. Widespread violence broke out in South Asia as millions of persons got involved in chaotic transfers of populations. Smith and Iqbal's friend K. G. Saiyidain remained with India, but after the troubles of the partition, the Indian Muslim wrote an open letter to Nehru warning him against the dangers of permitting communal forces to work unchecked. In 1947, Saiyidain wrote:

> It was the memorable night preceding the 15th of August when India was to attain her political freedom. . . . Then the midnight hour struck and the Radio was switched on and they all listened in to the historic ceremony. . . . and thrilled to your deeply moved and moving voice as you took the oath of office: "I, Jawaharlal Nehru. . . ."
>
> They went to bed that night full of joy and exaltation and the hope of a new earth, a new heaven and a new dawn. . . .
>
> It was almost exactly three months later. . . . during this short period, tragedy had stepped close on the heels of tragedy. The Punjab had gone up in flames: Delhi had its gruesome bath of blood; Calcutta had flared up twice. . . . in many other parts of India and Pakistan, life and peace and decency were trembling on the verge of a breakdown. The rosy glow of Freedom's dawn had turned blood-red. . . .
>
> You [Nehru] know more fully than I can possibly describe the extent and the intensity of the suffering which partition and the exchange of populations have brought in their train. But that is not the worst. What is even more ominous than murder and arson and loot and the disruption of families is the reaction to these happenings among those who have survived and on millions of others in different parts of the country. These bitter experiences and their reports—which some papers took delight in playing up—have induced in their hearts *not* feelings of pity and charity and commiseration . . . but bitterness and fanaticism and the mad craving for revenge. . . . this alarms me even more than the cold-blooded acts of inhumanity committed by goondas and hooligans.
>
> How can this fire be put out? . . . The declarations of faith published at the time on behalf of writers, artists, poets and other workers in the field of culture—in India as well as in Pakistan—are a small but welcome sign of hope.[33]

Smith regarded Saiyidain as one of the most lucid interpreters of Iqbal whom he had known in his early years in India.[34] Smith shared much of the horror and concern that his friend Saiyidain was expressing in this postpartition letter to Nehru. Saiyidain went on to spend most of the rest of his life working to help develop good training in the humanities and social sciences in the educational system of India.[35]

Smith returned to Canada. Like Saiyidain, he understood that the problem of South Asia after partition was not just one of recovering from the outbursts of violence. The more serious need was to recover some kind of basis of mutual respect between those who had inherited the results of the violence. This was to be one of the driving motives behind Smith's future efforts. He has told us that the violence at partition had affected him profoundly. He wrote: "One of the things that has burned itself most deeply into my consciousness is the Hindu-Muslim cataclysm of 1947, the time of the partition of India: the terrifying upheaval of hate and violence, when ten million persons were uprooted and perhaps one million were massacred, many brutally."[36]

It was this experience, *burned deeply* into Smith's consciousness, that directed his future concern to think through more carefully how to help people comprehend the strengths and weaknesses of religious thought and practice. He wanted to work toward a future in which such a cataclysm would not occur again. He eventually came to believe that transforming the ways in which we think about religion may be one of the best ways to help us discover more positive directions for thought and practice.

Smith left Lahore from 1947 to 1948 to pursue doctoral studies at Princeton. His first book had been intended as a doctoral dissertation for Oxford, where his tutor had been H. A. R. Gibb, but Smith thought it had not been accepted.[37] The difficulties of communication during wartime had interfered with the mutual understanding of Gibb and Smith. The latter thought his work had been refused because it was so anti-British. At Princeton, Smith wrote a thesis on the differences between the perspectives of two Muslim editors of the Arabic *Azhar Journal*, the publication of Egypt's leading Muslim theologians. He received his doctorate and accepted the position of Birks Chair of Comparative Religion in the Divinity Faculty of McGill University in Montreal, Canada.

As a result of the impact on his mind of the horrors of the violence that had accompanied the independence of India and Pakistan, Smith went through a radical change of perspective in many of his key ideas. He had returned briefly to South Asia after partition and had personally interviewed persons who had been working with the refugees. He wanted to find out for himself the causes and fruits of the violence. His conclusion was that Muslims, Hindus, and Sikhs had all taken part in destructive outbursts against persons from other communities.

Just four years after partition, he published in Lahore a small book entitled *Pakistan as an Islamic State*, in which he acknowledges his earlier errors. In these few years, he had undergone a revolution in self-awareness. He had to grapple with the realization that he had been seriously wrong in his judgment as to what might happen in South Asia. This small book can be read as a communication intended for Smith's Indian and Pakistani friends to help them think through what had happened and to find new directions for building the future. Smith's brother had been the Canadian ambassador to the USSR during World War II and had helped to convince Wilfred of the realities of the Gulag camps and other forms of Soviet tyranny. In this new book, Smith tells his readers that his earlier trust in an immanent force in history working inevitably in the Marxist way to a future good society had been just wrong—*that God had failed*.

A number of other Western intellectuals, who, like Smith, had become very left-wing during the era of the Cambridge "Pink Decade," later published a book entitled *The God that Failed*. The English poet Stephen Spender was one of the authors who explained the hopes and fears of many of his generation who found that their trust in the Communist Party, or their confidence that immanent forces for good were automatically driving history, was shattered by events. These disturbing events included the brief alliance between Hitler and Stalin, the revelations about the brutal tyranny of the Stalinist state against its own citizens, and the discovery of the hypocritical role of the communists in the Spanish Civil War.

George Orwell's *Homage to Catalonia* became the classic statement in English literature of disillusionment with what Stalin's forces had done in Spain.[38] The different authors of *The God that Failed* had shared the hopes of a bright new world, even though they came from many diverse backgrounds with different problems, such as racism in America, poverty in rural Italy, and the miseries in the industrial centers during the Depression. These authors had shared the dream of revolution. When their dream disintegrated in light of actual historical events, they also took different paths. They had in common the conviction that their trust had been betrayed. Smith was not explicitly part of this group, but he was of the same generation and had many of the same experiences. In his case, the discovery of the evils of the Stalinist system and the horrors of partition had both worked to shatter his confidence that he had infallible knowledge about the future direction of history.

In Smith's first book, published in 1943, the word "immanent" meant "good," and the word "transcendent" meant "bad"; in the second book, published after 1947, and subsequently, the reverse is the case. The idea of a knowable immanent force in history working to a comprehensible end becomes equated in Smith's later thought with an arrogant intellectualism, namely, the delusion that any human mind can comprehend exactly what is going on at a particular point in history and can be sure of the results of human action. One could say that the disasters of the partition violence and the horrors of Stalinism were shocks experienced by Smith as attacks against his intellectual conceit. We can better understand his later fulminations against simple-mindedness in methodology if we recognize that his model of "what not to do," when studying religious phenomena, is what he himself had done in his first book. His later message is: never be as arrogant in your assumptions as I was.

He talks more explicitly in this book of 1951 about the mistakes he now sees in Marxist thinking. Presumably, he was consciously trying to explain his new perspective to his Indian and Pakistani socialist friends. He wrote:

> We should note especially the profound and crucial distinction that while Communism treats ideals as instruments for attaining political power [Note 1], Islam treats political power as an instrument for attaining ideals.
>
> [Note 1] This is a serious indictment, and should therefore be documented. Cf. "Lenin defined Marxism as the revolutionary theory and tactics of the revolutionary class struggle of the proletariat." V. Adoratsky: *Dialectical Materialism, opening sentence. Indian edition.* . . .
>
> Cf. also: "Communist ethics. But is there such a thing as Communist ethics? Of course, there is. . . . We deny all morality taken from superhuman or no-class conceptions. . . . We say that our morality is wholly subordinated to the interests of the class struggle of the proletariat. We deduce our morality from the facts and needs of the class struggle of the proletariat. . . . For us morality is subordinated to the interests of the proletarian class struggle."—Lenin . . . as reprinted in V. I. Lenin, *Religion*, Burmon Publishing House, Calcutta, n.d.[39]

This is the core insight of Smith's subsequent reaction against belief in an immanent process in history, namely, that such a conviction knows no standard of judgment outside the success of the particular cause. Anything was justified in the cause of the victory of the proletariat. He wrote:

> In a Marxist state, such as the Soviet Union, whose rulers recognize, they claim, no ideals, opposition groups have precisely no rights. It is official Marxist doctrine that a person as such, "man in general," does not exist; persons exist only as member[s] of a social class. Consequently, an individual condemned as being "an enemy of the working class" is regarded in the USSR, as having literally no rights whatever, and is treated accordingly. It is difficult or even impossible for a Christian or democratic idealist to *conceive* such an attitude; and difficult therefore for him to believe the stories coming out of the Soviet Union about treatment of those out of favour. . . .
>
> Slowly, however, the outside world is beginning to discern the importance of transcendent ideals, and to realise that it is better to have ideals, even when not lived up to, than to repudiate them outright. It is important that practice be good. It is equally important that, when practice lapses, good ideals be acknowledged; so that there be something to which one can appeal.[40]

This passage neatly sums up the position Smith accepted after he had digested the shocks of partition and of Stalinist tyranny. There can be little doubt that one of the Christians who had trouble accepting the dark view of Stalinism was Smith himself. From now on, he regards his first book as full of dangerous error, not least because he had failed to comprehend the necessity of transcendent ideals as a way of keeping society sane.

In all of Smith's subsequent books and articles, the holding up of transcendent ideals is stressed as essential for sane functioning in the actual contexts of existence. It is sane to hold transcendent ideals because one needs to recognize that the actual implementation of justice, for instance, will always be imperfect. But one needs also to recognize that more justice is always possible. This perspective is required in order to keep people moving toward implementing more justice even though they never fully succeed. Smith became convinced that, without the acceptance of transcendent ideals, such as justice, people would sink into nihilistic destructiveness. Unless we think we could be better than we are and work toward that goal, we are likely to decay and revert to worse behavior. In the case of Pakistan, the transcendent ideals of Islamic justice and peace would be, Smith believed, useful guides for the creation of a better future. He writes: "That Pakistan is Islamic is given; its interpretation of Islam is free. And it will be on its interpretation that it will, by the world, be judged. The decisive question, in the village and in the country, is, as in all villages and all countries, what does that people in fact consider good, and how effectively do they pursue it?"[41]

In studying any religious tradition, therefore, Smith now says that we need to ask of persons in any context, what do they consider good, and what are they doing to make that good tangible and fruitful? He no longer thinks it is adequate just to characterize religious persons as reactionary or progressive.

To impose a preexisting theory on a particular context causes intellectual confusion. Smith now recommends that scholars be more open to the people involved in the context and just ask them what it is that they think they are doing and why they have such ideas. He now knows that his problem with finding a label for Iqbal had been that the label itself was too simplistic.

Smith was invited back to Lahore in 1974 to give a lecture on Iqbal. He told his Muslim audience that they could scarcely imagine how much the Muslim poet had meant to him. Reading *Bang-i Dara* in Urdu when he was first in Lahore had enthralled him.[42] He said that he was not going to write more about Iqbal but would rather try to do what he believed Iqbal said should be done. In part, this meant establishing the Institute of Islamic Studies so that Western scholars could learn a better appreciation of Islam by having Muslim teachers and fellow students. It also meant carrying on the tradition initiated by Sayyid Ahmed Khan and Shibli, and furthered by Iqbal, of helping Muslims understand how to reconstruct more effectively their traditional modes of religious thought and practice in light of the demands and challenges of the modern world.[43]

Many readers of Smith's books and articles seem to have trouble with his use of the word "transcendent." We can probably understand him better if we recognize that his personal rejection of the intellectual perspectives of his own former self is a significant key to understanding what the term came to mean to him. He came to see that no one could have final knowledge as to the forces at work in a particular situation.

Thus, to move from stressing immanence to stressing transcendence became a way of indicating the fallible nature of human thinking.

All the major religious traditions try to uphold transcendent ideals. Smith's later view is that the various cumulative religious traditions of the world usually function to transmit practicable visions of the potentialities for good in specific situations. As he said about the challenges of the new Pakistan, the Islamic goals of peace and justice already existed in the tradition. The challenge was how to implement those goals effectively.

In studying religious life and thought in the modern world, Smith's new focus was on letting people speak for themselves. One should ask people, like the Pakistanis, what they see as good and what they see themselves as doing to implement that good. In 1951, Smith wrote this little book called *Pakistan as an Islamic State* for the citizens of the new Pakistan who were struggling to articulate what they should do about their new challenges. He used the poetic image of a kite pulling them. The image came from a Muslim friend, who said that Pakistanis should move forward, always trying to act in the light of transcendent standards of goodness and justice. The kite was the symbol of the transcendent, pulling, but not entirely controlled by, or fully comprehensible to, humans.[44] In Smith's words:

> Living in the mundane present is itself no mean task; as we have insisted, Pakistanis may not for a moment neglect the matter of making their nation viable. Yet for them, as for all men, living wholly within the mundane present is unworthy of human dignity, as well as disruptive of human history. They, as are the rest of us, are faced in the embattled world of the latter twentieth century with the massive problems of living at all. In addition, as have been all communities since the dawn of history, they are faced with the concurrent question of living well.[45]

Notes

1. Wilfred Cantwell Smith, *Questions of Religious Truth* (New York: Scribners, 1967), p. 92.

2. Smith, *Questions of Religious Truth*, p. 110.

3. Wilfred Cantwell Smith, *Faith and Belief* (Princeton, NJ: Princeton University Press, 1979), 328, 329, n. 1.

4. Marion Starkey, *The Devil in Massachusetts* (New York: Anchor Books, 1969), pp. 64–75, 106, 207.

5. Arthur Eddington, *The Nature of the Physical World* (London: Everyman, 1935).

6. Roger Hutchinson, "The Fellowship for a Christian Social Order: A Social Ethical Analysis of a Christian Socialist Movement," PhD dissertation, Emmanuel College, University of Toronto, 1975. See also Roberta Cameron, "The Making of Wilfred Cantwell Smith's 'World Theology,'" PhD dissertation, Department of Religion, Concordia University, Montreal, 1997. The most influential of John MacMurray's books was *Freedom in the Modern World* (London: Faber and Faber; first published 1932). This book was delivered in a series of lectures over the BBC and received a widespread public response. It helped shaped the antifascist attitudes in the English-speaking world of the 1930s.

7. R. B. Y. Scott, *The Relevance of the Prophets* (New York: MacMillan, 1944).

8. Stephen Spender, *World Within World: The Autobiography of Stephen Spender* (London: Allen and Unwin, 1952).

9. William Christian, *George Grant: A Biography* (Toronto: University of Toronto Press, 1993).

10. Jawaharlal Nehru, as quoted by P. C. Joshi in "Nehru and Socialism in India," in *Socialism in India*, ed. B. R. Nanda (New Delhi: Vikas Publications, 1972), p. 122.

11. Ibid., pp. 122–39.

12. Reported by Muriel Smith to John Coleman.

13. V. G. Kiernan, *Poems from Iqbal: Renderings in English Verse with Comparative Urdu Text* (Karachi: Oxford University Press; Lahore: Iqbal Academy Pakistan, 1999), p. 114.

14. S. A. Vahid, ed., *Thoughts and Reflections of Iqbal* (Lahore: Ashraf, 1964), p. 258.

15. Wilfred Cantwell Smith, *Modern Islam in India, A Social Analysis* (New Delhi: Usha Publications, reprinted 1979; first published 1943), p. viii.

16. Ibid., p. 61.

17. Ibid., p. 122–26.

18. Ibid., p. 248.

19. *The Javid Nama*, trans. A. J. Arberry (London: Allen and Unwin, 1966), p. 121.

20. Smith, *Modern Islam in India*, p. 119.

21. K. G. Saiyidain, *Iqbal's Educational Philosophy*, revised and enlarged edition (Lahore: Ashraf, 1965; first published 1938).

22. Smith, *Modern Islam in India*, pp. 144–45.

23. Ibid., p. 155.

24. Ibid.

25. Iqbal Singh, *The Ardent Pilgrim*, 2nd ed. (New Delhi: Oxford University Press, reprinted 1997), p. 152.

26. Smith, *Modern Islam in India*, p. 147.

27. Wilfred Cantwell Smith, *On Understanding Islam* (The Hague: Mouton, 1981), pp. 111–12.

28. Ibid., pp. 112–22.

29. Muhammad Iqbal, *The Reconstruction of Religious Thought in Islam* (Lahore: Ashraf, 1977 reprint; first published [six lectures] 1930, then [seven lectures] 1934), p. 141.

30. Kiernan, *Poems from Iqbal*, p. 240.

31. Vahid, *Thoughts and Reflections of Iqbal*, pp. 161–220.

32. Ibid., p. 195. For the biblical verse, see Proverbs 29:18 (KJV).

33. K. G. Saiyidain, *Education, Culture and the Social Order* (London: Asia Publishing House, 1963 reprint), pp. 266–73.

34. Smith, *Modern Islam in India*, p. 142.

35. K. G. Saiyidain, *The Humanist Tradition in Indian Educational Thought* (Bombay: Asia Publishing House, 1966); *Islam, the Religion of Peace* (New Delhi: Islam and the Modern Age Society, 1976); *The Faith of an Educationist* (New York: Asia Publishing House, 1965); *Universities and the Life of the Mind* (New York: Asia Publishing House, 1968).

36. Smith, *Questions of Religious Truth*, p. 108.

37. Oral communication from W. C. Smith.

38. George Orwell, "Homage to Catalonia," *The Orwell Reader* (New York: Harcourt, Brace, first published 1956).

39. Wilfred Cantwell Smith, *Pakistan as an Islamic State* (Lahore: Ashraf, 1951), p. 26.

40. Ibid., pp. 87–88.

41. Ibid. In Smith's later book, *Islam in Modern History* (Princeton, NJ: Mentor Books, 1959), a similar approach is used to discuss many other modern Muslim societies, including India. The chapter on Pakistan in this later book is similar to the small 1951 volume.

42. Wilfred Cantwell Smith, "Faith and Belief: Some Considerations of the Islamic Instance," *Iqbal Memorial Lectures* (Lahore: University of the Punjab publication, 1975).

43. For Iqbal's tributes to Shibli, and Sayyid Ahmed Khan, see M. A. K. Khalil, trans., *Call of the Marching Bell* (Lahore: Iqbal Academy, 1997) p. 108, 308. For Iqbal's ideas about religious education, see Vahid, pp. 103–9, 234–37.

44. Smith, *Pakistan as an Islamic State*, p. 66.

45. Ibid., p. 109.

Bibliography

Cameron, Roberta. "The Making of Wilfred Cantwell Smith's 'World Theology.'" PhD dissertation, Department of Religion, Concordia University, Montreal, 1997.

Christian, William. *George Grant: A Biography*. Toronto: University of Toronto Press, 1993.

Eddington, Arthur. *The Nature of the Physical World*. London: Everyman, 1935.

Hutchinson, Roger. "The Fellowship for a Christian Social Order: A Social Ethical Analysis of a Christian Socialist Movement." PhD dissertation, Emmanuel College, University of Toronto, 1975.

Iqbal, Muhammad. *The Reconstruction of Religious Thought in Islam.* Lahore: Ashraf, 1977. Reprint; first published [six lectures] 1930, then [seven lectures] 1934.

———. *Call of the Marching Bell.* Translated by M. A. K. Khalil. Lahore: Iqbal Academy, 1997.

The Javid Nama. translated by A. J. Arberry. London: Allen and Unwin, 1966.

Joshi, P. C. "Nehru and Socialism in India." In *Socialism in India*, edited by B. R. Nanda, 122–39. New Delhi: Vikas Publications, 1972.

Kiernan, V. G. *Poems from Iqbal: Renderings in English Verse with Comparative Urdu Text.* Karachi: Oxford University Press; Lahore: Iqbal Academy Pakistan, 1999.

MacMurray, John. *Freedom in the Modern World.* London: Faber and Faber, 1932.

Orwell, George. "Homage to Catalonia." *The Orwell Reader.* New York: Harcourt, Brace, first published 1956.

Saiyidain, K. G. *Iqbal's Educational Philosophy.* Revised and enlarged edition. Lahore: Ashraf, 1965; first published 1938.

———. *Education, Culture and the Social Order.* London: Asia Publishing House, 1963.

———. *The Humanist Tradition in Indian Educational Thought.* Bombay: Asia Publishing House, 1966.

———. *Islam, the Religion of Peace.* New Delhi: Islam and the Modern Age Society, 1976.

———. *The Faith of an Educationist.* New York: Asia Publishing House, 1965.

———. *Universities and the Life of the Mind.* New York: Asia Publishing House, 1968.

Scott, R. B. Y. *The Relevance of the Prophets.* New York: MacMillan, 1944.

Singh, Iqbal. *The Ardent Pilgrim.* 2nd ed. New Delhi: Oxford University Press, reprinted 1997.

Smith, Wilfred Cantwell. *Questions of Religious Truth.* New York: Scribners, 1967.

———. *Faith and Belief.* Princeton, NJ: Princeton University Press, 1979.

———. *Modern Islam in India, A Social Analysis.* New Delhi: Usha Publications, 1943. Reprinted 1979.

———. *On Understanding Islam.* The Hague: Mouton, 1981.

———. *Pakistan as an Islamic State.* Lahore: Ashraf, 1951.

———. *Islam in Modern History.* Princeton, NJ: Mentor Books, 1959

———. "Faith and Belief: Some Considerations of the Islamic Instance." *Iqbal Memorial Lectures.* Lahore: University of the Punjab publication, 1975.

Spender, Stephen. *World Within World: The Autobiography of Stephen Spender.* London: Allen and Unwin, 1952.

Starkey, Marion. *The Devil in Massachusetts.* New York: Anchor Books, 1969.

Vahid, S. A., ed. *Thoughts and Reflections of Iqbal.* Lahore: Ashraf, 1964.

Diagnosis Rather than Dialogue as the Best Way to Study Religion

Robert A. Segal

Long before it became de rigueur, Wilfred Cantwell Smith challenged the appropriateness of the term *religion*. He maintained that the term fits only the modern West and is ethnocentric when applied elsewhere.[1] His objection was not political, the way the standard objection has since become, but theological. For him, *religion* refers to outer, formal trappings. *Faith*, his preferred term for his preferred focus, refers to inner conviction. Somehow the way to study faith is through dialogue, or conversation. Smith proposes that the term *religion* "be dropped—at least in all but the . . . personalistic sense,"[2] which means in all but the sense of religion as faith.

Smith never claims that dialogue is the sole way to study religion. He never claims that adherents, or insiders, know all there is to be known of their religion. He never claims that what he calls the "externals" of religion—"symbols, institutions, doctrines, practices"[3]—are irrelevant. He never claims that academic expertise is useless. He himself was a distinguished scholar of Islam.

What Smith does claim is that dialogue is the key way to study religion. There can even be dialogue with adherents of a dead religion: "Personalization can be achieved also . . . in the case of the religion of an historical community that has ceased to exist."[4] The dialogue here must be reconstructed rather than recorded.

Smith's claim rests on many assumptions. The first assumption is that the study of religion is reciprocal. It is not merely my studying you but also your studying me: "Several years ago I had occasion to characterize the study of comparative religion as moving from talk of an 'it' to talk of a 'they'; which became a 'we' talking of a 'they'; and presently a 'we' talking of 'you'; then 'we' talking 'with' you; and finally—the goal—a 'we all' talking together about 'us.'"[5] Smith even calls the relationship between scholar and believer an "encounter."[6]

The second assumption is that from dialogue we learn not just about the other party but also about ourselves. The third assumption is that with sufficient good will and sensitivity, dialogue will succeed. The fourth assumption is that the study of religion is a hermeneutical exercise: the goal is not explaining but "understanding" religion.

The fifth assumption is that the heart of a religion is to be found in its adherents: "The study of a religion is the study of persons."[7] The heart is what religion "means" to adherents. The heart of a religion is not to be found either in its texts, which was once the conventional view, or in its practices, which, starting with William Robertson Smith's pioneering Lectures on the Religion of the Semites (1889), has come to be the present-day view.[8] The sixth assumption is that adherents are the best judges of what religion means to them.

The seventh and final assumption is that, with some qualification, adherents cannot be wrong about what religion means to them: "no statement about a religion is valid unless it can be acknowledged by that religion's believers."[9] Adherents thus hold veto power over any outsider's proffered interpretation. If adherents can decide which interpretations are wrong, then they can decide which ones are right. The meaning of religion becomes like sense data for old-fashioned epistemologists: it is veridical.

I question all of these assumptions, and as an alternative to dialogue as the proper analogy for the study of religion, I propose diagnosis. I contend not that religion is a disease but simply that the analogy of patient to doctor is more appropriate for the study of religion than the analogy of conversation partner to conversation partner. Taken as diagnosis, the study of religion denies all of the assumptions underlying dialogue.

There is nothing reciprocal in the relationship of adherent to scholar. Just as the patient has the disease but is not thereby the authority on it, so the adherent has the religion but is not thereby the expert on it. The scholar, like the doctor, has ordinarily studied the topic far more fully than the adherent. True, the scholar and the doctor are both beholden to their subjects, but only for information. And if the adherent is uninformed or silent, the study can still proceed. Even when, conversely, the patient has inexhaustible information to offer, the doctor still typically conducts tests. A patient can also be a doctor, and an adherent also a scholar. But the roles are distinct, and it is the patient as doctor or the adherent as scholar who knows better.

Smith himself concedes that adherents may know less than experts. He thus denies that he is suggesting that "a personalist epistemology is infallible. It is possible to be inadequately informed, and even misinformed."[10] He even acknowledges that "personal explanations must be checked against or co-ordinated with texts and other overt data."[11] But if all he is asserting is that the "personalist approach . . . cannot fail to supplement" an impersonal approach,[12] against whom is he arguing? The issue is one of proportion. Smith needs to justify the clear nod he gives to the personalist approach.

To take an approach to religion that could not stand more opposed to Smith's, anthropologist Roy Rappaport, in *Pigs for the Ancestors* (1968), argues that religion is merely the human means of maintaining the ecosystem we share with animals.[13] For Rappaport, the ritualistic killing of pigs by the Tsembaga Maring farmers of New Guinea serves to keep an increasing number of pigs from damaging the ground and making planting harder. The ritualistic eating of pigs provides protein to keep the people healthy. Rappaport's resolutely materialist view of religion in *Pigs* is supported by heaps of data accumulated over fourteen months of fieldwork and years of thinking. I would not be prepared to assume that he learned less about the meaning of religion for his natives than a session on Papua New Guinea of the world's parliament of religions would have yielded.

In twentieth-century literary criticism, authorial intent was ever more dismissed. In 1946 the identification of the meaning of a work with its author's intent was formally pronounced fallacious by New Critics William Wimsatt and Monroe Beardsley in their essay "The Intentional Fallacy." The shift of focus away from the author peaked in the 1970s and 1980s with the reader-response criticism of Stanley Fish, Roland Barthes, Wolfgang Iser, and the Freudian Norman Holland. The authority of the reader replaced that of the author. Moreover, in literature the author is not merely a practitioner but the creator, yet scant deference to the equivalent of the religious founder remained. There have been rear-guard defenses of authorial intent by, notably, E. D. Hirsch, but they have hardly reversed the trend.

In the social sciences the rise in the twentieth century of, especially, functionalism shifted the focus of explanation from intent to effect, and commonly to unintended effect. The analysis of religion in

Durkheim, Radcliffe-Brown, Malinowski, and Merton replaced conscious intent on the part of individuals—as, for example, in Tylor and Frazer—with byproduct on the part of the group. Structuralism, which succeeded functionalism, dispensed with intent even more. The structure of a myth or a ritual is supposedly programmed mechanically in the mind of the creator and is projected unconsciously onto the outer world.

In the psychology of religion the depth psychology of Freud and Jung replaced the introspective psychology of Wundt and the conscious psychology of James. "Depth" means the unconscious, which may (Jung) or may not (Freud) be credited with an intent of its own but which in any case is wholly unknown to its subjects and forever remains unknown, short of psychoanalysis. Unconsciousness aside, the believer may be ignorant, deluded, or in Sartrean denial, which Sartre ironically calls *bad* faith. In short, Smith's deference to the meaning provided by the adherent is naïve.[14]

The doctor learns about the patient. The patient does not learn about the doctor. Doctor and patient need have nothing in common save anatomy and billing. Smith himself allows sceptics to study religion. True, the doctor may suffer from the same ailment as the patient, but that kinship is merely coincidental and scarcely affects the diagnosis. Smith stresses that we are all humans. So what? Are all humans religious? Even if for Smith, as for Eliade, all are, are all thereby authorities on their religiosity? Lay believers who interpret religion for themselves are like nonlawyers who in court have themselves as clients.

Some diseases are hard to detect, even with the most up-to-date technology. Some diseases are asymptomatic. Diseases have varying prognoses. Treatments can vary. As Susan Sontag (1978) showed, cancer in the twentieth century used to have the same stigma that tuberculosis had had in the nineteenth: that it was a character defect.[15] Today the sufferer is no longer blamed. Even claims that outlook affects recovery have been exposed as false.

A retort might be that however innocent the victim is with most physical ailments, the patient is surely at least partly at fault in AIDS, in lung cancer, in diabetes, in melanoma, and in the consequences of alcoholism and obesity. A stronger retort would be to switch from physical to mental illness. Yet even here the relationship between the mind and the body gets ever blurrier. Psychiatrists tend to dispense drugs for mental problems. Only analysts dispense talk exclusively. While the relationship of mind to body is ultimately a conceptual and therefore a philosophical issue, the total autonomy of the mind, where intent lies, is a position, known as "substance dualism," that is held by few, if any, philosophers today.

Just as no twentieth-century literary critic would rely on biography as the guide to interpretation, and just as no twentieth-century social scientist would rely on polling to determine why members of society stick together, and just as no twentieth-century depth psychologist would rely on conversation to determine motivation, so no twentieth-century scholar of religion should rely on what adherents report to decipher what makes them tick. Adherents are informants, but informants have no complete or incorrigible access to their own minds. Extending to them good will is akin to wishing a patient well before surgery.

The goal in medicine is not "understanding" but explanation: classifying the patient's symptoms as symptoms of an illness, determining the origin of the illness, and predicting the course of the illness. The goal is not to pry loose what it feels like to a patient to have cancer. The goal is figuring out what ailment a patient has, how the patient became ill, and how the ailment can be treated.

Religion should be studied the same way. Eliade blocks explanation by proclaiming as innate either religion or, more precisely, the need that religion is created to fulfill: the need to encounter the sacred. Smith denies that he himself is going this far: "I do not mean that man is inherently religious."[16] But what he offers in place of the innate religiosity of humans is indistinguishable from it: "I mean rather that religion . . . is inherently human."[17] His declaration that "Man is everywhere and has always been what we today call 'religious'"[18] rests on conviction, not proof.

If religion is inherently human, then for Smith, as for Eliade, all humans are religious. What is Smith's evidence? Since he himself accepts, if bemoans, the influence of secularism, how does he account for its existence?[19] He does not seem to maintain, as Eliade does, that secularism masks religiosity. Nor does he seem to duplicate Paul Tillich's reliance on a definition of religion so broad that by it everyone is religious. Certainly he enlists no faculty psychology à la Schleiermacher.

Rather, Smith appeals to the view of apparently all non-Westerners that religion *for them* is more than an "add on" to their humanity: "A just discernment of Asian religious history makes manifest that common modern-Western secularist mistake, of supposing that man is basically man but that for some strange reason he and she have here and there tacked on to their simple humanity one or another of these various bizarre addenda. To see things this way is to misunderstand the world, we can now see."[20]

But why is the modern Western view wrong? So what if it is at odds with the view of non-Westerners? Are they, the equivalent of patients, automatically right in their diagnosis of themselves? Why is the modern Western separation of church and state or of the private and the public sectors wrong? Contrary to Smith, confining religion to a separate sphere need not make it "bizarre" or marginal. Religion set off as a private activity can give it the freedom to thrive.

For my part, I take religion to be an acquired taste, but not thereby an insignificant or unfortunate one. Like disease, religion has a cause, and the social sciences strive to find out what it is. The pervasiveness of religion is not the issue. Religiosity is not innate even if it turns out to be universal. The definition of religion must be narrow enough for the spread of religion across humanity to be unclear until measured—that is, measured rather than known a priori by a definition like Tillich's "ultimate concern." A disease that afflicted every human being would not somehow be in less need of a diagnosis.

Like the explanation of disease, the explanation of religion should be comparative. Far from treating the patient as an individual, the doctor puts the patient in the category of all those with the illness. Studies of other patients with the illness dictate the treatment of the patient at hand. Smith himself definitely wants the study of religion to be comparative, but he deems comparison optional and at most beneficial, but never mandatory.

Yet mandatory a comparison is, and the broader the comparison, the better. A comparison of all religions is superior to a comparison, however intimate, of just two. Even to "understand" Buddhism is to categorize it as one religion among all the others. To categorize Buddhism as a religion is to put it in a global camp that far transcends the "meaning" of Buddhism for Buddhists. Buddhism is undeniably a specific religion, but its distinctiveness begins only where the similarities between it and all other religions end. The Buddhist is best understood not by being set in a dialogue with the Christian but by being lined up with all other believers. The distinctiveness of any one religion is overshadowed by the similarities among all religions. The theorist, by virtue of being a comparativist, has superior insight to the practitioner unless the practitioner also knows about other religions.[21]

I do not see why the meaning rather than the origin and function is the heart of religion. I do not see why the "explanation" of religion—to use an admittedly confusing term—is less revealing than the "interpretation" of it—to use the equally confusing counterpart term.[22] In fact, the origin and function can be a guide to the meaning. For theorists of religion, the meaning is indeed the given, and what theorists are trying to figure out is why religion has the meaning for adherents that it does. Like Eliade, Smith mischaracterizes social science, which ordinarily denies neither the reality of God nor the reality of religiosity. Social science commonly limits itself to accounting for why any or all humans are religious and sidesteps considering whether what believers devote to themselves is real. If social science denied the reality of religiosity, what would it be left with to explain? Few social scientists are the equivalent of philosophical eliminativists.

Put another way, even if one maintains that the meaning is the heart of religion, the origin and function are a helpful and maybe even indispensable route to it. Smith, whose disdain for social science matches Eliade's, continually invokes a false divide between social science and sheer conversation: "The application of theories and methods and outlooks from the natural sciences to the study and organizing of man and society has contributed much to affluence, something to prediction and manipulation, less to understanding, and least to understanding human beings specifically as persons, or to understand human history."[23] In other words, subjects are like the teenagers in *Rebel Without a Cause*: hopelessly misunderstood by adults.

In actuality, what patients report, if they report anything at all, is not the diagnosis of their ailment but just part of the data for making the diagnosis. Why assume that what religious adherents report is any different? Outward expressions of religiosity—texts and practices—are like medical tests. They supplement patients' reports and are at least as important. Why separate the inner from the outer? Why not take the outer as the equivalent of X-rays—as a way of detecting the inner?

Smith's division between outer and inner is artificial: "That is why I have spoken of it [religion] as at two levels: one of external facts, one of interpretation and meaning. . . . It is one thing to know, for instance, that in Christian worship there is a cross; it is another to know what the cross means to the Christian who is worshipping."[24] Who claims otherwise? What *is* claimed otherwise is that the inner meaning can be gleaned from the outer. Smith permits an outsider "by diligent scholarship" to "discover things that an insider does not know and may not be willing to accept."[25] Yet he then asserts that an outsider cannot "go beyond the believer" "about the meaning that the system has for those of faith."[26] He is thereby waxing tautological, for the meaning of faith for Smith is what the believer takes it to be.

Patients often offer their own diagnoses, but their diagnoses are at most part of the data themselves and are not the assessment of the data. The same should hold for adherents' interpretations of their religion. Religion belongs to a believer the way a disease belongs to the patient. Neither believer nor patient is automatically an authority on what each harbors. To make the believer or the patient an authority is to confuse roles. To carry a disease is not thereby to be an expert on the disease. Would a taxpayer claim the authority of an accountant just because the taxpayer is paying the tax?

Eliade strives to isolate religion from the rest of life in order to preserve its autonomy. To link religion to seculardom is for him to risk collapsing religion into seculardom. Antithetically to Eliade, Smith strives to dissolve the divide between religion and seculardom—a divide that he blames on the modern West: "This division of life into two spheres, religious and secular, is a characteristically Western pattern."[27] Smith prefers the phrase "the Indian way of life" to "Hinduism" to convey the view that religion, rather than being "one item in our social life," is in fact "the form in which the items cohere."[28] But unless Smith is prepared to argue that all of the Indian way of life is Hindu, then he is asserting only that religion is the most important factor in life. But to be so, religion for him, too, must be distinguishable from the rest of life.

Surely many "secular" theorists of religion would agree. Durkheim and Weber, for example, give religion as much clout as Smith does. Both see religion and society as interacting. And both are as troubled by the rise of seculardom as Smith, and exactly because of the importance for them of religion on the rest of life. Smith's social scientific nemesis is a straw man.

In conclusion, dialogue is neither necessary nor sufficient for the study of religion. At most, it amounts to data collection. The social sciences themselves often enlist this kind of data gathering—through interviews and fieldwork, for example. Yet social scientific techniques have been developed to ensure that the information garnered is far more reliable than that gleaned from chatting. More important, the social sciences rely on much more than subjects' reports. Overall, I think that, to paraphrase Pope (not the Pope), the proper study of religion is religion and not just faith.

Notes

1. On the term *religion*, see, for example, Wilfred Cantwell Smith, *The Meaning and End of Religion* (New York: New York American Library, 1964),

pp. 21–22, 23–49, 109–38; Wilfred Cantwell Smith, *Towards a World Theology* (London: Macmillan, 1981), pp. 51–52.

2. Smith, *The Meaning and End of Religion*, p. 48.

3. Wilfred Cantwell Smith, "Comparative Religion: Whither—and Why?" in *The History of Religions*, eds. Mircea Eliade and Joseph M. Kitagawa (Chicago: University of Chicago Press, 1959), p. 35. Reprinted in Smith, *Religious Diversity*, ed. Willard G. Oxtoby (New York: Harper & Row, 1976), pp. 138–57.

4. Smith, "Comparative Religion," p. 36

5. Smith, *Towards a World Theology*, p. 101. On the reciprocity of dialogue, see also Smith, "Comparative Religion," p. 34.

6. Smith, "Comparative Religion," p. 47.

7. Ibid., p. 34.

8. When W. C. Smith announces at the outset of his *Belief and History* that the thesis of this book is radical because it exposes as merely modern "The idea that believing is religiously important" (Smith 1977, v), he is unaware of what William Robertson wrote back in 1889: "And here we shall go very far wrong if we take it for granted that what is the most important and prominent side of religion to us was equally important in the ancient society with which we are to deal. In connection with every religion, whether ancient or modern, we find on the one hand certain beliefs, and on the other certain institutions, ritual practices, and rules of conduct. Our modern habit is to look at religion from the standpoint of belief rather than of practice; for, down to comparatively recent times, almost the only forms of religion seriously studied in Europe have been those of the various Christian Churches, and all parts of Christendom are agreed that ritual is important only in connection with its interpretation. . . . But the antique religions had for the most part no creed; they consisted entirely of institutions and practices" (W. R. Smith, *Lectures on the Religion of the Semites* (London: Black [1894] (1889), p. 16).

9. Smith, "Comparative Religion," p. 42.

10. Ibid., p. 40, note 18.

11. Ibid.

12. Ibid.

13. Roy A. Rappaport, *Pigs for Ancestors* (New Haven, CT: Yale University Press, 1968).

14. In his introduction to the Festschrift for Smith, editor Frank Whaling, to his credit, criticizes Smith for limiting himself to "faith" and spurning "wider sociological and other factors of which the believer may not consciously be aware." See *The World's Religious Traditions* (Edinburgh: T&T Clark, 1984), pp. 18–19.

15. Susan Sontag, *Illness as Metaphor* (New York: Farrer, Strauss and Giroux, 1978).

16. Smith, *Towards a World Theology*, p. 53.

17. Ibid.

18. Smith, *The Meaning and End of Religion*, p. 22.
19. On secularism, see Smith, *The Meaning and End of Religion*, pp. 113–14.
20. Smith, *Towards a World Theology*, p. 52.
21. On the superiority of comparativism, see Robert A. Segal, "In Defense of the Comparative Method," *Numen* 48 (2001) pp. 339–73.
22. On the varying meanings of these terms, see Robert A. Segal, *Explaining and Interpreting Religion* (New York: Peter Lang, 1992).
23. Wilfred Cantwell Smith, *Belief and History* (Charlottesville: University Press of Virginia, 1977), p. 30.
24. Wilfred Cantwell Smith, *The Faith of Other Men* (New York: New American Library, 1963), pp. 15–16. Reprinted: New York: Harper Torchbooks, 1972.
25. Smith, "Comparative Religion," p. 42.
26. Ibid.
27. Smith, *The Faith of Other Men*, p. 101.
28. Ibid., p. 102.

Bibliography

Rappaport, Roy A. *Pigs for the Ancestors*. New Haven, CT: Yale University Press, 1968.
Segal, Robert A. *Explaining and Interpreting Religion*. New York: Peter Lang, 1992.
———. "In Defense of the Comparative Method." *Numen* 48 (2001), pp. 339–73.
Smith, William Robertson. *Lectures on the Religion of the Semites*. New ed. [First ed. 1889.] London: Black, 1894.
Smith, Wilfred Cantwell. "Comparative Religion: Whither—and Why?" In *The History of Religions*, edited by Mircea Eliade and Joseph M. Kitagawa, 31–58. Chicago: University of Chicago Press, 1959. Reprinted in Smith 1976, 138–57.
———. *The Faith of Other Men*. New York: New American Library, 1963. Reprinted: New York: Harper Torchbooks, 1972.
———. *The Meaning and End of Religion*. New York: New American Library, 1964.
———. *Questions of Religious Truth*. London: Gollancz, 1967.
———. *Religious Diversity*, edited by Willard G. Oxtoby. New York: Harper & Row, 1976.
———. *Belief and History*. Charlottesville: University Press of Virginia, 1977.
———. *Towards a World Theology*. London: Macmillan, 1981.
Whaling, Frank, ed. *The World's Religious Traditions*. Edinburgh: T. & T. Clark, 1984.

Wilfred Smith's Prophetic Sense of History and Proposal Regarding Verification

Peter Slater

In what follows, I revisit Wilfred Smith's—to some, notorious—privileging of "insider's" judgments on religious faith and reading of history. I concentrate on his global sense of a comparative history of personal faith and cumulative tradition and his conception of corporate critical self-consciousness. To him, the opposite of "impersonal" is "personal," which means always intending to include the social and corporate, but necessarily homing in on individual responsibility. The job of cultural historians of faith and tradition is to understand how God/Truth/the eternally Transcendent touches particular people's lives in the process we call history. The job of historians of specific traditions is to help us understand what it means to be Muslim, Buddhist, or whatever, learning to see the world through such concretely faith-traditional eyes. As an aid to understanding, historians draw on the social sciences to explain how different traditions have shaped events, for better or worse. But a proper assessment of the sciences, he declared, is that they are part of our history; it is not history that is part of the social sciences.[1] Whether we share these conclusions often turns on how much we accept of his definitions of key terms.

Often, WCS's critics exhibit just as suspect a privileging of their definitions and presuppositions on these topics as he did, while missing the subtleties of his mature positions.[2] Consequently, they are not always our best guides when addressing real problems with his formulations of issues and positions on them. As H. R. Niebuhr insisted, we should pay more attention to what authors affirm than to what they deny.[3] That admonition holds for readings of both WCS and his critics. What he denied was the adequacy of naturalistic social sciences for university-disciplined studies of personal involvement in religious traditions and studies of the distinctively human dimensions of universal history. What he affirmed was a colloquial—I would say dialogical—academic entrée to human responses to "the Transcendent," which became his locution for what he deemed the critical referent of any relevant history or histories of faith-based texts and institutions.

There is no doubt that WCS used the "inside-outside" dichotomy when depicting his position, even though he exhorted us to move "beyond" such bifurcations. In his Royal Society of Canada address, "Objectivity and the Humane Sciences: A Proposal," he declares that "human experience . . . appears differently, and in fact *is* different, from the inside and from without" (B 125). In what follows I shall draw often on this text, as his most considered final statement on issues raised, noting that these include contemporary concerns regarding meaning, verifiability and falsifiability among traditions that sway us in times of war and peace. I shall concentrate on (1) experience, (2) meaning, and (3) possible verification of matters of faith.

Experience

WCS was a wordsmith—if you'll pardon the expression—who chose his terms very carefully. Unlike most of us, he and Paul Tillich, as I knew them, actually used words for the most part the way they defined them, sharing what is now regarded as an inadequate, essentialistic, classical theory of meaning crafted in the heyday of European "gymnasium" education.[4] They expected their readers and hearers to accept what they considered the "proper" uses of terms, as the only authorized usage in their context. Until his daughter persuaded him to bow to changing usage, for instance, WCS used to insist that by "man" he meant both women and men and, therefore, did not have to modify his locutions, even after feminists heard a gender bias that he did not intend.[5] With this in mind it is important to parse his formulations carefully.

From the outset, a critical term in WCS's work and conception of his profession was *experience*. He regarded himself primarily as an historian of developing expressions of religious faith in historic traditions, originally specializing in Islam. This he studied at Cambridge University under Sir Hamilton Gibb, who tried to warn him off his undergraduate

Marxist proclivities.[6] These, he told me, were simply what anyone with a conscience who witnessed the Great Depression adopted, until dissuaded by further experience (in his case, hearing John Macmurray lecture in Toronto on personalism and modern communism).[7] The Cambridge take on experience-based history, as I learned it from three "Cambridge men" (my theology supervisor Henry Chadwick, my father and McGill theology professor, WCS's colleague Robert Lawson Slater; and his contemporary at Cambridge and their colleague at Harvard, Arthur Darby Nock), was to master all "the facts" on a particular subject by immersing oneself in all available sources. Chadwick, for instance, once commented during a tutorial that he just "smelled" Philo in the Prologue of the Fourth Gospel, but he could not document a direct influence. Nock, in the days when this was imaginable, set out to know all there is to know from the fourth century "BC" to the fourth century "AD."

WCS's reach was even more ambitious—to undertake a global "comparative history of religion."[8] He taught us to aim high, not to settle for simplistic explanations of lowest-common-denominator pieties. Mark Heim remarks on the breathtaking "mixture of humility and hauteur" in WCS's pronouncements, harking back to the expansive, inclusive vision of eighteenth-century Enlightenment authors with, at bottom, a Muslim-tinged Protestant account of personal faith.[9] Historians of theology point to Schleiermacher as the liberal progenitor of starting with experience. But British scholarship has more philosophical roots in the empiricism of Locke and Hume.[10] Less important than their fixation on "sense data," as Kant realized, was their denial of any necessary rational link from one idea to the next, when observing what goes on in history. For those weaned on British empiricism, causal connections are intuited, and the best historians are those recognized by fellow practitioners as having the best summation of and feel for "the facts" in their chosen field.

Among "manifest facts" for WCS in our common history he lists that "the human is patently different . . . from material objects," and such human qualities "as self-transcendence, a sense of justice, a creative and destructive imagination, a capacity to respond to and to create beauty, a capacity for wickedness and also for dignity, freedom, rationality . . . (and) the pursuit of truth; a sense of remorse" and "moral responsibility" (B 126). Another "massive fact" is that science cannot tell us all that is worth knowing about the moon (B 129). Regarding a famous temple in South India, he remarks that "the reality that the temple constitutes in the life of the pious devotee . . . is after all the primary reality of the temple as a fact in human affairs." (B 131–32).

In similar vein, he insisted that the Center for the Study of World Religions at Harvard is the people who are its members, not the building. The fact that, without the endowed building, the Harvard Center might have been abolished, in the years before he was invited to direct it, would not have changed his thinking.

Among European rationalists, the closest to a Humean account of human experience was Edmund Husserl's phenomenology. It was the approved method for historians addressing the data of "living religions," when the Center was established at Harvard.[11] It is not surprising, therefore, that Russell McCutcheon's critique of WCS's assumption of "insider" privileges in the assessment of relevant data is subsumed under a wider critique, aimed primarily at Eliade's phenomenology of "the sacred" and "the profane."[12] In more recent work, McCutcheon acknowledges the weak thinking engendered by such bifurcations. But in the works cited he accepts the insider/outsider distinction, objecting only to the privileging of "insider" as opposed to "outsider" perspectives in the establishment of university-based studies of religion, on the grounds that officially "objective" academic institutions should make "outsider" perspectives their norm.

Part of the dispute had to do with familiar nineteenth-century attempts to distinguish between *Geisteswissenschaft* and *Naturwissenschaft*, making empathetic understanding the goal of the former and causal explanation the goal of the latter. Both were reductionist—not just the latter. In practice, *any* theoretical model requires some abstraction, so that is not the issue. Shifting from appeals to ontology, as in Tillich, to narrative explications of events and situations, as in WCS, does not avoid all the problems, since any narrative leaves much out and frames what is put in. The dispute does in fact turn on definitional issues regarding what dimensions or aspects or angles on experience of purportedly religious significance have to be included for any account to be on topic. In particular, is experience of "the transcendent" veridical, or mistakenly assumed to be such by faith-based religiologists?

For WCS and Tillich, when faith is involved, the subject is necessarily personal or "transpersonal," and the referent is our human relation to "the Transcendent" or the God "above God." For McCutcheon and others, who regard that referent as nonempirical, the actual referent is theologians' use of such markers to delineate academic turf, whether in centers or departments for the study of religion or on faculties of divinity. That was certainly part of WCS's agenda—legitimately so, some would argue. But for him and his backers, the stakes were much higher, since getting our histories wrong on this subject can foster fratricide, as in the 1947 division of India into India and Pakistan.

Ironically, McCutcheon's rule, following Donald Wiebe, that theologians and crypto-theologians count only as "native speaker informants" regarding data for the study of religion, not colleagues in framing critical theories, has the effect of privileging theologians' accounts of the relevant history, at least in the first phase of data-gathering.[13] One consequence, as we encounter it in the work of J. Z. Smith, is that the Protestant privatizing of faith and its political ramifications in the U.S.A. are taken as givens, not secondhand selective histories. We shall note shortly WCS's different take on the impetus to privatization.

For both WCS and Tillich, the relevant experience is both individually self-involving and global in scope. WCS spent years in India before the 1947 partition, in dialogue with leaders on both sides who invoked their corporate faith or cumulative traditions in support of political conflicts. Tillich experienced the defeat of his homeland twice and the failure of the majority of his fellow Lutherans to defend their Jewish colleagues from Hitler: he was ever thereafter dismissive of Christian triumphalism and secular utopianism. In the process, both WCS and Tillich personally experienced the failure of naturalistic and neo-Marxist explanations to deal with the demonic depths of the powers that be, including those of our own plutocracies parading themselves as democracies. The issue for them was not whether religious movements have political ramifications. All politics have a religious dimension. The issue is which priorities make for clearer thinking, when wrong choices may lead to war. For Tillich, the answer lay in a dialectical version of Augustinian warnings against misplaced absolutes.[14] For Smith, the answer lay in religious insights into what makes human beings fully human. Their difficulty with their atheistic critics often had more to do with the latter's eschatological myopia than with their methodological reductionism.

Not surprisingly, given his Protestant orientation and specialization in Islamics, WCS's baseline when assessing religious traditions was prophetic experience. A comprehensive study must reckon with what temple-going means to Vaishnavas or Shaivites in India, for instance.[15] But divorcing personal meaning from social, economic, and political ramifications was, in his view, due in Euro-American academic culture to the influence of the Graeco-Roman, not the Palestinian biblical, strand of our inheritance, in the juxtaposition—never synthesis—of these two major traditions in "Western" history. He comments:

> Western secularism . . . developed the concept "religion" to designate the other of these two traditions—and to designate also other movements round the world which it has named "Hinduism," "Buddhism," and the like, and Islam. Western secularists are profoundly convinced that religion either is a fallacy . . . or . . . in any case to be distinguished from the rest of culture and separated from most of it, and especially from politics, law, and economics. Islam, however, is not a religion in this sense . . . [Misled by this misconception,] Westernizing liberals in the Islamic world lacked a moral foundation for their liberalism. (B 93)

Notice here that WCS attributed the privatization of faith to the influence of Renaissance secularists, not Protestant reformers.[16] The Shah's failure in Iran, he remarked in an earlier paragraph, was at bottom a moral failure, due to the fact that his liberalizing agenda was, in the end, "effete" and "vacuous," lacking a grounding in faith. "In Muslim countries, the only basis for morality and morale is—has been—Islam." American officials' failure to recognize this accounts for American blindness to the consequences of their pro-Zionist stance throughout the Muslim world (B 90–91).

Also notice here that WCS is explaining events on the basis of his understanding of Muslim faith and American liberal secularism. He is not rejecting the need for explanation, when doing history, but making appropriate understanding of the relevant history its prerequisite. If we invoke a "covering law model" for explanations in political history,[17] in this instance, then the relevant law for WCS was moral, which is why I dub his conception of religious experience "prophetic." His primary test for truth was what rings true to this experience. (How to account for moral law after Hume was, we recall, a major challenge for Kant, which scientific exponents of religious studies mostly neglect.)

Meaning

In a widely endorsed proposal for a "cultural-linguistic" model of postliberal theories of religious doctrine, George Lindbeck argued on Wittgensteinian grounds against what he deemed to be the two major alternatives—the "traditional-propositional" and the "experiential-expressivist." He cites one side of Bernard Lonergan's work as representative of the experiential-expressivist model, among whose proponents he counts both WCS and Tillich. Pondering modern debates about "other minds," Wittgenstein concluded that there is no such thing as "private language." The principal lesson drawn from this by Lindbeck is that the causal connection between meaning and experience is the reverse of that assumed by "experiential expressivists." They tend to portray us in Augustinian fashion as starting with deep, inner experiences of self and God, then groping to give these, necessarily inadequate, overt expression.[18]

A key question is whether "inner" experiences are phenomenologically and logically prior to "outer" expressions of these. According to the cultural-linguistic model, "[i]nstead of deriving external features of a religion from inner experiences, it is the inner experiences which are viewed as derivative."[19] Again here the inner-outer dichotomy is invoked and the genealogical line of thought runs from phenomenology, through Schleiermacher, back to Kant and the modern "turn to the subject." However different exponents describe the experiential-expressivist position, "all locate ultimately significant contact with whatever is finally important to religion in the prereflective experiential depths of the self and regard the public or outer features of religion as expressive and evocative objectifications (i.e., nondiscursive symbols) of internal experience."[20] In interreligious dialogue, Lindbeck notes, one effect of this conclusion is to relativize differences of doctrine among traditions.

Typological contrasts are always oversimplified for the sake of argument. Lindbeck is well aware that the prereflective experiential baseline, as articulated by Rahner, for instance, is logically prior to any subject-object dichotomy. Lindbeck also recognizes that behind the romantic emphasis on symbolic expression is an idealist metaphysic, harking back to Christian Platonism. (His own Thomistic-leaning preference is for Christian Aristotelianism.) But he glosses over Tillich's Augustinian-Schellingian insight that, religiously, the inner encounter is with a qualitatively uniquely other "Godself," not just finite selves, and that theologically this Self is just as much behind outwardly derived experiences as introspective ones. By using William A. Christian's gloss on Schleiermacher/Tillich to identify as religious what is "finally important" for our ways of life (p. 21), not what is of absolute or unconditional concern, Lindbeck glosses the classical divide between finite and the qualitatively infinite that situates "the" infinite beyond both finite experience and finite expression, as the source of the religious significance of both. This gloss makes it easier to suppose that, when we look within, all we encounter is our finite selves.

For both introspective and other-directed models of philosophizing, classically in theology, the source of meaning is the Divine Word, however projected. Lonergan allows for this by having a place for revelation, but, according to Lindbeck, its articulation is treated in Lonergan as traditional-propositional. In WCS these nuances are generally left implicit, not made explicit. His focus is on human responses to "the Transcendent," which, according to him, are always "symbolic." Contra Jung and Eliade, varying in meaning from community to community and from age to age, symbolic understanding "is never quite precise: like a poem, only much more so . . . a symbol in principle never means exactly the same thing to any two persons (nor even necessarily to any one person at different times)" (B 129). Given the misunderstandings that the term engenders, he remarked later that perhaps a better word would be *sacramental*.[21] That would make more explicit what Tillich always maintained, regarding living symbols, that they "participate" in the reality being symbolized. Even so, what Lindbeck objects to is the assumption in WCS, Tillich, and others, that while they use very different symbols, different religious traditions are invoking or evoking the same Reality.[22]

On the cultural-linguistic model, what abide despite contextual differences are the rules governing meaning in particular "language-games" or ways of life. Between referents among different games, there are "family resemblances." Against the tradition that we grope for different words to express the same root experience is the contention that, without words, we cannot even name experiences as experience. Different words denote different experiences. Every fact is value-laden and every experience is theoretically shaped, when it is registered as such. When I reported this Wittgensteinian wisdom to my mother—a religious poet as well as a medical doctor—she replied, "Nonsense." Her experience was of groping for just the right word to convey the transforming insight that a poet's mystical context demanded. I. T. Ramsey tried to flag the "logically odd" character of "religious language" in this connection by describing it in terms of models and qualifiers.[23] In his dissertation on Burmese Buddhism, my father made a similar point, concluding that religious locutions regarding "ultimate terms" are necessarily paradoxical.[24] As Bakhtin might have pointed out to Wittgenstein, had they met, part of ordinary discourse is being meaningfully or ironically ungrammatical on occasion. As much may be missed by the grammar model as by the groping-for-expression-of-"deep"-experience model. We shall revisit this point below.

In actual practice, WCS, in his major works on "religion," "faith," and "belief," exemplified the etymological approach common among his contemporaries in biblical studies and epitomized by the Kittel Wörterbuch series, used by his generation when studying texts. His comparative historical practice, concerning "truth," for instance, was typically to examine three Arabic words—*haqqa*, *ṣaddaqa*, and *ṣaḥḥa*—and look at what their translations, in terms of "true"/"real"/"trustworthy" and so forth, suggest about "a human view of truth." His historian's conclusion is that "A price we have paid, for divorcing objective truth from sincerity, is to divorce subjective emotionalism from all discipline—and from community cohesion. We have made truth amoral . . . This makes for social disorder, and personal loneliness, and lostness" (B 117). His agenda, as elsewhere, was to point up consequences from regarding truth as the property of propositions rather than of more than objective personal and institutional relationships, especially in modern universities. His concern, as always, was more with morality than with semantics.

In his later work on "Scripture," the methodology is similar. But in that instance WCS did not want to return to the "original," etymologically derived meaning. His account of the changing usage in the context of it and cognate terms, such as *biblia*, would be quite consonant with the cultural-linguistic model emanating from Wittgenstein. Variants regarding oral and written, translatable or untranslatable, rules for usage in different communities, he shows, do not privilege any of them. His argument from the evidence is that "scripture" is not an attribute of texts but "a characteristic of the attitude of persons—groups of persons—to what outsiders perceive as texts."[25] Again the "inside-outside" mindset is invoked and endorsed. The primary alienating agency is still modern ideological institutionalizations of "objectivity" at the expense of subjectivity. But history also includes alienating "insider" rules for usage among fundamentalists, such as the ultraconservative Presbyterians of WCS's youth in Toronto.

Regarding WCS on the meaning of words, it seems, the fairest assessment is that of Talal Asad. He notes that WCS correctly objected to reifying "religion," but that his argument relied on confusions concerning the meanings of words. He still assumed a model of meaning keyed to nouns naming objects, which is intrinsically reifying. The thing named in religious traditions, WCS contended, is the person of faith and the Person in whom theists put their trust. His conclusion reflects an essentialistic anti-essentialism regarding meaning, which mutes the action-oriented thrust of Arabic terms and the Muslim ban on identifying

Allah as a person.[26] To this we may add that the primary Wittgensteinian insight had to do with classical models of linguistic usage privileging the notion of nouns as names of things. As WCS acknowledged, he was primarily a cultural historian, not a philosopher or systematic theologian, and his theory of meaning in general was less consistent than his use of key terms in specific contexts.

Verification

The divergences noted so far reflect intraacademic debates about privileging—theories, definitions, modes of knowing or testing—on the assumption that there are no neutral observers able to adjudicate our disputes. Despite appeals to revelation, most now acknowledge that none of us has a "God's eye view" of everything. Revelation requires explication in the language of its receivers. As David Kelsey has shown, with reference to such modern Protestants as Barth and Tillich, diverging theologies follow from adopting different paradigms. Correct conclusions are not simply read straight off the pages of "Scripture." Groups of scholars may engage in "scriptural reasoning" to render judgment on the relevance of revered texts for contemporary situations. But all judgments and interpretations rely on (1) philosophical-theological, (2) traditional-biblical, and (3) phenomenological-ecclesial or communal-experiential presuppositions.[27]

What WCS challenged in his day was the hegemony in universities of a supposedly objective paradigm of scientific knowledge. Studying persons subjectively and objectively, for "first approximations" of knowledge, was to him unobjectionable. But studying persons solely as objects commits an "intellectual error" leading to "pseudo-science." Uncompromising objectivity disrupts community and is unjust to the humanity of both knower and known, denying their freedom. Humane knowing values solidarity over particularity, promoting community, and is not manipulative (B 137–38). Would-be scientific students of religion such as Donald Wiebe, however, do not give WCS his definitions of "science" or abandon the ideal of finding universal, objective explanations of religious behavior. They dispute that the royal road to truth is through understanding religious people using categories preferred by devotees, who appeal to esoteric experiences.[28] Their Kantian/Enlightenment methodology ties academic purity to separating cognitive from religio-ethical domains. Instead of "cognitive idealism," they privilege the chemistry of conviction or biology of altruism or whatever current science promises eventually to identify the material factors presumably causing those who declare themselves to be religious to behave as they do.

Not content to exhibit flaws in the prevailing paradigm, WCS offered an alternative under the heading "critical, corporate self-consciousness" (B 123). The passage cited earlier reads:

> In corporate critical self-consciousness, that justice has been done to the matter being studied is testable by the experience of the subject or subjects. Often the former—another observer—is in principle not available, since unlike what obtains in the world of matter, no human situation is truly repeatable. In any case, it is inadequate, partly because all observers are inherently less than the whole . . . and partly because it is intrinsic to human experience that that experience appears differently, and in fact *is* different, from the inside and from without. No statements involving persons is valid, I propose, unless its validity can be verified both by the persons involved and by critical observers not involved. (B 125)
>
> It should be "a law," WCS suggests, "that what a person does is misunderstood if conceived wholly from the outside," or, he adds, "wholly from the inside." Examples of "insider-outsider" groups are men and women and, in North America, blacks and whites (B 135).

Beyond objectivism and subjectivism, according to WCS, critical self-consciousness ideally incorporates the insights of all involved into a communal apprehension of truth. Realizing universal truth entails a "convergent synthesizing" of what is true of the whole, to the point where human beings know the meaning of being members of one global community. True talk should be of "us," not "we-they" or about "you" (B 136–38, 143–44). "The verification test of any statement about women in society [for instance] would be whether both men and women, in so far as they are rational, and a body of investigators, insofar as they are methodologically sophisticated, critical, scientific, could all three endorse it" (B 136). The academic researchers here count as a "third" party, whose membership overlaps with one or both of the others.

The notion of incorporative synthesizing stems from Hegelian accounts of critical historical knowing, which postulate a process of self-projection through historic objectification to actualize a more comprehensive self/subjective agency, aimed eschatologically at achieving liberating self-consciousness, eventually by all human beings.[29] A post-Kantian sense of "critical" regards any "subject" or "object" as an historical construct, not a naturally fixed given. After Kierkegaard, the relevant subject was generally not thought of as a world-historical political groundbreaker, embodying the avant-garde of cultural history, but an alienated individual lost in a flock of sheep and goats, in church or elsewhere. The move to critical self-consciousness, in any case, is not an expression of feeling or intuition. It involves cognitive components shaped by current cultural forms, including for Hegel "science" and "religion." WCS's campaign was never against science as such but against positivism, consumerism, militarism, or materially driven power struggles, as normative frameworks for studies of personal faith and cumulative traditions. He believed that corporate critical self-consciousness "could subsume, in the end, the natural and the life sciences, without infringing their integrity" (B 146).

The classical Augustinian model of self-knowing follows a Neoplatonic ontology of hierarchically ordered modes of being, essentially instantiating eternal forms emanating "down" from a single absolute, "inner," spiritual source. Modern historical models, including that of WCS, upend "the chain of being" and presuppose some kind of cultural evolution. Conclusions about the verification of phenomenologically depicted "facts" of history then turn in part on whether a given scholar presupposes a "top-down" or "bottom-up" model of the "foundations" of knowledge, starting or ending with physics or ethics.[30] WCS's polemic put him in the top-down camp, with religious ethics at the top.

More pragmatic observers note that most arguments circle out from an issue, both "up" and "down," only so far as needed to find common ground among disputants. Realists do not pretend to settle all possible questions that might ever be raised. On personal relations, we generally accept the word of those we trust. In complex situations where the outcome is uncertain, we may rely rather on induction and experiment. What changed perspectives in the twentieth century was not so much the hegemony of science in academe as technology in the working world. Part of the issue, during everyday disagreements, revolves around when personal authority should be decisive, how far technology takes us, and when incontrovertible facts require us to adjust our claims to be in control. The main issue is not science as such, but misplaced confidence in what "science" can do for us.

One virtue of WCS's reliance on contemporary confessors of faith for authoritative expression of a cumulative tradition is that it avoids freezing faith in some bygone era. One major lacuna is his inattention to the fact that few religious communities leave making definitive statements of faith to individuals. Even Quakers, in my experience, rely on hierarchs.[31] In this regard, the interesting question in the study of religion to me is not, for instance, whether the cardinals and others at Vatican II were exhibiting the effects of male menopause, but whether their claim to be guided by the Holy Spirit was valid and why, with hindsight, we might agree with them rather than their reactionary opponents. Often critics removed from practical experience of Abrahamic traditions make paradigmatic the most fundamentalist versions of them, rather than explore such conclaves as Vatican II, ignoring major changes within traditions over time.[32]

In the evolution of knowledge, WCS noted three cosmic transitions. The first resulted in our becoming human beings, the transition "from consciousness to self-consciousness." Then came "the extraordinary moment" marking the birth of science, the transition "from consciousness to critical consciousness." Now we are on the brink of another great moment—vital if we are to avoid extinction—which is the transition to "critical self-consciousness" (B 124). When we are all incorporated into its "end-time" community, we shall achieve one goal of the verification principle, which is that whatever is known should be knowable by all (B 124–25). In this scenario, WCS persuasively redefines "all." Instead of ideally objective outside observers, he wants all academics to reach transformative, intersubjective understanding of what makes all others "some of us." Unacceptable is the misplaced objectivism of naturalistic positivism, which is not only immoral but culturally retarded (B 126, 142–43).

Evidently, not everyone achieves the level of humane knowing. The progression is from ignorance, through random impressions of another culture, through growing "systematic and accurate, yet insensitive and externalist," objective knowledge of facts, to "serious profound humane understanding of the role and meaning of those facts in the lives of the persons involved" (B 127).

WCS's paradigm case argument concerning the Indian temple sketches such levels of awareness, going from travelers' tales to appreciating its architectural wonders to gaining some sense of who the worshippers are. The would-be knower will see this as a sacred space by looking "through sectarian Hindu eyes," realizing that "No building is objectively a temple" (B 127–28). The temple is a symbol that means "one thing for one group of people, something else for another, and perhaps nothing at all for a third group. [This] is a fact without which human history would have been dramatically different from what it has been and is" (B 128). It is not clear what "truth" is shared by the third group.[33]

If we take such pronouncements literally, the temple-going experience is never repeatable for anyone. If we take WCS's description of it symbolically, its meaning is never twice the same for those most involved. Instead of a universally inclusive method of verification, it seems, what corporate critical self-consciousness denotes is a prerequisite for true understanding, which may or may not incorporate critical explanations of phenomena and phenomenologists. By contrast with objective knowledge, humane knowing just might foster world peace (B 129). (Like the Obama Nobel Prize, the story here is more one of aspiration than of proven record.)

The most controversial part of WCS's proposal is the veto power he gives present adherents of a tradition on what counts as currently meaningful faith in keeping with that tradition. An historian's account can only be true if confirmed by practicing Buddhists, for instance, since they are the ones confessedly responding to "the Transcendent" (B 133). In support of this we might cite Robert Slater's conclusion, following dialogues with Burmese abbots, that prevailing Euro-American accounts of Buddhist "pessimism," based on studies of classical Pali texts, missed the optimism of contemporary Buddhists actually living "in the hope of Nibbana."[34] A Wittgensteinian way of stating historians' assertions of fact in such instances might be to declare that "this game is played."[35] Those claiming to understand show that they do so by knowing how to go on using terms correctly in context according to the rules. They know what it means to say that Nirvana is neither immanent nor transcendent, and so on. This is Lindbeck's point in drawing attention to the "grammar" of doctrine and WCS's point in insisting that the reality of God for theists is a presupposition of their whole tradition, not a belief to be proven or disproven.[36]

A more satisfactory account of confessional discourse, in my view, follows from a dialogical understanding of linguistic usage. This does not fixate on literal or symbolic meanings to the exclusion of the other but attends to the whole gamut of discursive juxtapositions of everyday exchanges reverberating with echoes of traditional wisdom, current theory, and whatever else makes up our experience of the universe in our "chronotope." The game cannot be described as only naming things or navigating around the egos of academic experts. Nor is language appealing to "insider" versus outsider perspectives helpful, since any language chosen to describe a situation is prior to the experience in question. Most importantly, actual validation in historical traditions, such as the modern Protestantism discussed by Kelsey, involves references, not abstractly to "the Transcendent," but specifically to biblically based denotations and connotations that ring true or false at particular times of critical self-consciousness for historical communities, as at Vatican II.

A way forward, it seems to me, must ask what is homologous in traditional accounts of being or becoming true in such communities. There is no verification or falsification of faith in general. What are validated or not are actual ways of life variously construed at different times by traditionalist and antitraditionalist subgroups. If we go with Kelsey's map of the territory, we shall note that for WCS, as for Augustine, there is an ontological difference between the "being" of God and human being, yet enough of a connection to warrant faith seeking understanding. Disagreement on this between theists and atheists is a philosophical matter, not a question that can be settled by any scientific procedure. So also is disagreement over how descriptive presuppositions are ingredients of performative utterances.[37] We shall also engage in textual reasoning concerning appeals to the classics of specific movements. This will require historical thinking and literary criticism in relation to concrete issues, such as apartheid in South Africa. We shall rely on the experience of specific communities in critical times, such as the confessing churches in Germany during the Hitler regime, who accorded posthumous authority to Bonhoeffer regarding secularity in the twentieth century, because he more than others voiced what needed to be said there and then. Informing traditions by retrospective stories of the lives of such saints is a major part of any validating process in any tradition lasting more than a few generations.

Dialogical discourse in confessional contexts, as depicted by Bakhtin, includes attending to a "third" voice, variously named God, conscience, the universe, one's peer group, the future, qualified researchers in a later generation, the collective subconscious, or whatever, which is heard by some through the voices of others or one's own alter ego, touching a chord that rings true to followers of a way of life concerning the truth of a situation, both in essence and existentially.[38] What reference to Nirvana underlines, in this connection, is that what is named may be a state of awareness, rather than a person or thing, neither transcendent nor immanent, which is deemed definitive of a process that some experience as genuinely liberating or salvific. What counts as liberating or salvific depends on the community of discoursers in question. In Augustine's Rome, being more otherworldly proved liberating. In

Bonhoeffer's Berlin it did not. In any case, as Augustine pointed out, we develop a sense of happiness or freedom, among mature users of specific languages that carry common wisdom concerning what we are not yet, but may yet enjoy. As some have argued, in living traditions verification or falsification is eschatological.[39]

Augustine's *Confessions* is a classic of confessional discourse. Formally addressed to God, the text is that of a bishop meant to be read by possible aspirants to orthodox faith, who seek reasons for their faith.[40] God does not speak directly, but through Scripture and the bishop's voice who, in turn, relies heavily on Paul's voice. Reasons explored refer to specific problems of evil and confusions concerning creation. Not all conclusions, especially concerning predestination, are endorsed by all who consider this a religious classic. Content is important, but process is more important. Augustine asks more questions than he answers. Centuries later, Tillich called himself an Augustinian without subscribing to Augustine's conception of immutable being. Both exemplify inculturating the Gospel in their day and are part of the history to which WCS refers, when he appeals to "the facts." William Connolly's critique of Augustine on evil, by contrast, is to me an example of a nondialogical reading, because it discounts the reference to an authorial voice other than Augustine's and his readers'.[41] What Augustinianism illustrates is WCS's insight into the *cumulative* nature of tradition. When verifying faith, he pays most attention to traditions with lengthy track records.

If we think of traditions as blends of creeds, codes, and cults, WCS's emphasis on codes may be more germane to our topic than some realize. The falsity of specific statements, such as that Jesus's tomb was empty on the first Easter or that a supernatural agent called Allah is somewhere above the stars, does not falsify Christian or Muslim faith. Religions, like sciences, typically include more cognitive dissonance than theoretical purists admit. That WCS, a professing Christian, has no Christology worth mentioning, for instance, hardly matters if the truth in question is of a way of life. Because Protestants stress justification by grace through faith, differences over their statements of faith have historically fostered schisms. But the biggest killer of faith has arguably been hypocrisy, not heterodox beliefs, regarding values and priorities professed by worshipping communities. If we allow some version of WCS's distinction between faith and belief, therefore, when deciding who is more in touch with reality among disputants, we shall look more for consistency in religious praxis than in dogma. A temptation among Augustinians is to demonize critics. A failure of modern Enlightenment apologists is to address the demonic destructiveness of human communities, often offering nothing more than the mantra that "further research is needed." Both groups need others to keep them honest.

Finally, we weigh live options after thinking them through in everyday languages. Disciplined, neutral monological conclusions from metatheories are not the key. Just because they are neutral, as Bakhtin pointed out, they can become weapons in the service of totalitarian regimes of church or state.[42] Ordinary discourse, such as we find in Gospel parables, carnival folklore, and the modern novels of social critics such as Dostoevsky and Dickens, is key. It incarnates dialogical irony and homespun common sense to render the worlds we share and for which we are answerable. Such discourse is filled with voices from science classes, superstition-filled locker rooms, pop psychology, echoers of the Golden Rule, myths and ideologies, and whatever else is current in a given culture, any of which may or may not be critically examined. In our culture, where few if any are up on all the natural sciences, social sciences, and the humanities, our best route to "truing" ways of life is through ongoing dialogue, with ourselves and others.[43] Our worlds are in our languages and our languages are our philosophies, Bakhtin observed. In Kelsey's communal-experiential corner, when proving doctrine, we do not speak language in general.

In sum, WCS, Hick, and other comparativists in their generation mark an endpoint for studying "religion in general." Too often, in mainline twentieth-century accounts of religious thinking, Protestant belief in some supernatural God-Thing was implicitly paradigmatic for both apologists and their critics, instead of the prioritizing effect on ways of life of different eschatological conceptions of ultimate liberation or salvation. While we may agree with WCS's critics about his inconsistencies and confusions, his challenge to us still is to think self-critically in a global context, learning from the faith of others and doing our best to make sense of what we hear and believe, with as much integrity as he did.

Notes

1. See Wilfred Cantwell Smith, "History in Relation to Both Science and Religion," reprinted in *Modern Culture from a Comparative Perspective*, ed. John W. Burbidge (Albany: State University of New York Press, 1997), pp. 9–17, 12, and 16. Page references from this edition hereafter will be cited in the main text as, for example (B 123).

2. In writing, I shall refer hereafter to "WCS" to differentiate him from Jonathan Z. Smith.

3. See H. Richard Niebuhr, *Christ and Culture* (Harper Torchbook: New York, 1956), p. 238, citing J. S. Mill and F. D. Maurice.

4. For a sympathetic yet critical assessment, see Talal Asad, "Reading a Modern Classic: W. C. Smith's 'The Meaning and End of Religion,'" reprinted in *Religion and Media*, eds. Hent de Vries and Samuel Weber (Stanford, CA: Stanford University Press, 2001), pp. 131–47.

5. The revised edition title of *The Faith of Other Men* (1962) is *Patterns of Faith Around the World* (1998).

6. *Modern Islam in India: A Social Analysis* (London: Victor Gollancz, 1947) retrieves some of the material from the doctoral dissertation failed by Cambridge University examiners.

7. The University of Toronto library has tapes of Macmurray's Toronto addresses delivered in the late 1930s, which WCS attended as a student.

8. Note the subtitle of *Towards a World Theology: Faith and the Comparative History of Religion* (Philadelphia: Westminster Press), 1981. Chapter 1 maintains that we share a common history, including participation in our relation to "the transcendent," pp. 5–6.

9. S. Mark Heim, *Salvations: Truth and Difference in Religion* (Maryknoll, NY: Orbis, 1995), pp. 54, 57.

10. See Norman Kemp Smith, *The Philosophy of David Hume: A Critical Study of Its Origins and Central Doctrines* (London: Macmillan, 1949), pp. 42–43 on Hutcheson's influence on Hume re feelings.

11. The main proponent was Krister Stendahl and exponent was John B. Carman, Smith's successor as Director of the Center. See W. Brede Kristensen, *The Meaning of Religion: Lectures in the Phenomenology of Religion*, trans. John B. Carman (The Hague: Martinus Nijhoff, 1960). Carman reviews Kristensen and van der Leeuw in *Majesty & Meekness: A Comparative Study of Contrast and Harmony in the Concept of God* (Grand Rapids MI: Eerdmans, 1994), pp. 28–36.

12. *Manufacturing Religion: The Discourse on Sui Generis Religion and the Politics of Nostalgia* (New York: Oxford University Press, 1997), pp. 12–14. Note also the reader edited by McCutcheon, *The Insider/Outsider Problem in the Study of Religion* (London: Cassell, 1999), which includes Donald Wiebe's criticism of Smith, "Does Understanding Religion Require Religious Understanding?," chapter 18.

13. See Donald Wiebe, *The Politics of Religious Studies: The Continuing Conflict with Theology in the Academy* (New York: St. Martin's, 1999), and my review in the *Toronto Journal of Theology* 17, no. 2 (2001), pp. 323–24. Wiebe was McCutcheon's thesis director. Wiebe has no problem with teaching theology in faculties of Divinity and is critical of McCutcheon's attempt to give secular ideology the role hitherto enjoyed by "theology" in Religious Studies. See Donald Wiebe, "The Politics of Wishful Thinking? Disentangling the Role of the

Scholar-Scientist from that of the Public Intellectual in the Modern Academic Study of Religion," *Temenos* 41, no. 1 (2005), pp. 7–36.

14. See Peter Slater, "Christ the Transformer of Culture: Augustine and Tillich," in *From Logos to Christos*, eds. Ellen Leonard and Kate Merriman (Waterloo ON: Wilfrid Laurier University Press, 2010). Detailed references to Augustine and Tillich are given there.

15. See *Towards a World Theology*, pp. 62–66.

16. Charles Taylor, *A Secular Age* (Cambridge, MA: Harvard University Press, 2007), portrays a more complex cultural disembedding of the individual from corporate identities fostered by both Catholic and Protestant perspectives on piety and the impact of deism, pp. 66, 146, 211, 280, 465, 541.

17. See William Dray, *Laws and Explanation in History* (New York: Oxford University Press, 1957), pp. 1–21, on the covering law model. On the complexity of concepts and differences of opinion see, for example, Isaiah Berlin, "The Concept of Scientific History," in *Philosophical Analysis and History*, ed. William H. Dray (New York: Harper & Row, 1966), pp. 5–53.

18. See Paul Tillich, "Two Types of Philosophy of Religion," in *Theology of Culture*, ed. Robert C. Kimball (New York: Oxford University Press, 1959), pp. 10–29.

19. George A. Lindbeck, *The Nature of Doctrine: Religion and Theology in a Post-liberal Age* (Philadelphia: Westminster, 1984), p. 34. See also, for example, p. 83.

20. Ibid., p. 21.

21. Smith, *Towards a World Theology*, p. 178.

22. On "the Real" in itself, see John Hick, *An Interpretation of Religion: Human Responses to the Transcendent* (New Haven, CT: Yale University Press, 1989), pp. 246–49. For Hick's comments on WCS see John Hick, ed., *Truth and Dialogue: The Relationship between World Religions* (London: Sheldon, 1975), pp. 140–55.

23. Ian T. Ramsey, *Religious Language: An Empirical Placing of Theological Phrases* (London: SCM, 1957).

24. Robert Lawson Slater, *Paradox and Nirvana: A Study of Religious Ultimates with Special Reference to Burmese Buddhism* (Chicago: University of Chicago Press, 1951), pp. 115–16.

25. Wilfred Cantwell Smith, *What Is Scripture? A Comparative Approach* (Minneapolis: Fortress, 1993), p. 18.

26. Talal Asad, "Reading a Modern Classic," pp. 131–47, 132–33.

27. See David H. Kelsey's analysis in *Proving Doctrine: The Uses of Scripture in Recent Theology* (Harrisburg PA: Trinity Press International, 1999).

28. Donald Wiebe, *The Politics of Religious Studies*, and "On the Transformation of 'Belief' and the Domestication of 'Faith' in the Academic Study of Religion," *Method & Theory in the Study of Religion* 4, nos. 1 and 2 (1992), pp. 47–68.

29. On Hegelian eschatology and WCS see Peter Slater, "On 'Towards a World Theology,'" *Method & Theory in the Study of Religion* 4, nos. 1 and 2 (1992), pp. 115–31.

30. Nancey Murphy, "Post-Modern Apologetics, Or Why Theologians Must Pay Attention to Science," and James E. Loder and W. Jim Neidhart, "Barth, Bohr, and Dialectic," in *Religion and Science: History, Method, Dialogue*, eds. W. Mark Richardson & Wesley Wildman (New York: Routledge, 1996), pp. 105–20 and 271–89. Some post-Kantians subsumed ethics under aesthetics.

31. At the Haverford meeting for worship that I attended in the 1960s, the elders made clear that the Holy Spirit should not move any of us to speak until five minutes after Henry J. Cadbury.

32. On "speaking Scripture" and literalism, note William A. Graham, *Beyond the Written Word: Oral Aspects of Scripture in the History of Religion* (New York: Cambridge University Press, 1987), pp. 162, 167. On material causes of assumptions of transcendence, see, for example, Peter Sloterdijk, *God's Zeal: The Battle of the Three Monotheisms* (Cambridge, UK: Polity Press, 2009).

33. Concerning ambiguities here see Antonio R. Gualtieri, "Objectivity, Subjectivity and Beyond: An Exchange with W. C. Smith," *Method & Theory in the Study of Religion* 4, nos. 1 and 2 (1992), pp. 107–14.

34. Slater, *Paradox and Nirvana*, p. 33.

35. For Wittgensteinian apologetics see D. Z. Phillips, for example *Faith and Philosophical Enquiry* (London: Routledge, 1970).

36. See Smith, *Faith and Belief* (Princeton, NJ: Princeton University Press, 1979), p. 43.

37. For a critical exposition of appeals to performative meaning, see Catherine Bell, *Ritual Theory, Ritual Practice* (New York: Oxford University Press, 1992), pp. 30–46.

38. See the exposition in Peter Slater, "Bakhtin on Hearing God's Voice," *Modern Theology* 23, no. 1 (January 2007), pp. 1–26. Page 13, line 4 from the bottom should read, "God's proposal is of the cross for myself, but of beatitude or loving mercy for others."

39. I. M. Crombie, "Theology and Falsification," in *New Essays in Philosophical Theology*, eds. A. G. N. Flew and A. C. MacIntyre (London: SCM, 1955), p. 118, and John Hick, *Faith and Knowledge* (London: Macmillan, 1957).

40. *Saint Augustine's Confessions*, trans. Henry Chadwick (New York: Oxford University Press, 1991).

41. William E. Connolly, *Identity/Difference: Democratic Notions of Political Paradox* (Minneapolis: University of Minnesota Press, 1991), pp. 64–68, 112, 129, 142, accuses Augustine of solving one problem of evil while initiating another, by demonizing his opponents.

42. His friends who disagreed with Stalin's linguistic theories paid dearly.

43. The image is from carpentry. See John C. Meagher, *The Truing of Christianity* (New York: Doubleday, 1990).

Bibliography

Asad, Talal. "Reading a Modern Classic: W. C. Smith's 'The Meaning and End of Religion.'" Reprinted in *Religion and Media*, edited by Hent de Vries and Samuel Weber, 131–47. Stanford, CA: Stanford University Press, 2001.

Bell, Catherine. *Ritual Theory, Ritual Practice*. New York: Oxford University Press, 1992.

Berlin, Isaiah. "The Concept of Scientific History." In *Philosophical Analysis and History*, edited by William H. Dray, 5–53. New York: Harper & Row, 1966.

Carman, John. *Majesty & Meekness: A Comparative Study of Contrast and Harmony in the Concept of God*. Grand Rapids MI: Eerdmans, 1994.

Connolly, William E. *Identity/Difference: Democratic Notions of Political Paradox*. Minneapolis: University of Minnesota Press, 1991.

Crombie, I. M. "Theology and Falsification." In *New Essays in Philosophical Theology*, edited by A. G. N. Flew and A. C. MacIntyre. London: SCM, 1955.

Dray, William. *Laws and Explanation in History*. New York: Oxford University Press, 1957.

Graham, William A. *Beyond the Written Word: Oral Aspects of Scripture in the History of Religion*. New York: Cambridge University Press, 1987.

Heim, S. Mark. *Salvations: Truth and Difference in Religion*. Maryknoll, NY: Orbis, 1995.

Hick, John. *An Interpretation of Religion: Human Responses to the Transcendent*. New Haven, CT: Yale University Press, 1989.

———, ed. *Truth and Dialogue: The Relationship between World Religions*. London: Sheldon, 1975.

———. *Faith and Knowledge*. London: Macmillan, 1957.

Kelsey, David H. *Proving Doctrine: The Uses of Scripture in Recent Theology*. Harrisburg, PA: Trinity Press International, 1999.

Kristensen, W. Brede. *The Meaning of Religion: Lectures in the Phenomenology of Religion*. Translated by John B. Carman. The Hague: Martinus Nijhoff, 1960.

Lindbeck, George A. *The Nature of Doctrine: Religion and Theology in a Post-Liberal Age*. Philadelphia: Westminster, 1984.

Loder, James E., and W. Jim Neidhart. "Barth, Bohr, and Dialectic." In *Religion and Science: History, Method, Dialogue*, edited by W. Mark Richardson and Wesley Wildman, 271–89. New York: Routledge, 1996.

McCutcheon, Russell. *Manufacturing Religion: The Discourse on Sui Generis Religion and the Politics of Nostalgia*. New York: Oxford University Press, 1997.

———. *The Insider/Outsider Problem in the Study of Religion*. London: Cassell, 1999.

Meagher, John C. *The Truing of Christianity*. New York: Doubleday, 1990.

Murphy, Nancey. "Post-Modern Apologetics, Or Why Theologians Must Pay Attention to Science." In *Religion and Science: History, Method, Dialogue*,

edited by W. Mark Richardson and Wesley Wildman, 105–120. New York: Routledge, 1996.
Niebuhr, H. Richard. *Christ and Culture.* Harper Torchbook: New York, 1956.
Ramsey, Ian T. *Religious Language: An Empirical Placing of Theological Phrases.* London: SCM, 1957.
Saint Augustine's Confessions. Translated by Henry Chadwick. New York: Oxford University Press, 1991.
Slater, Peter. "Review of *The Continuing Conflict with Theology in the Academy.*" *Toronto Journal of Theology* 17, no. 2 (2001), pp. 323–24.
———. "Christ the Transformer of Culture: Augustine and Tillich." In *From Logos to Christos*, edited by Ellen Leonard & Kate Merriman. Waterloo ON: Wilfrid Laurier University Press, 2010.
———. "On *Towards a World Theology.*" *Method & Theory in the Study of Religion* 4, nos. 1 and 2 (1992), pp. 115–31.
———. "Bakhtin on Hearing God's Voice." *Modern Theology* 23, no. 1 (January 2007), pp. 1–26.
Slater, Robert Lawson. *Paradox and Nirvana: A Study of Religious Ultimates with Special Reference to Burmese Buddhism.* Chicago: University of Chicago Press, 1951.
Sloterdijk, Peter. *God's Zeal: The Battle of the Three Monotheisms.* Cambridge: Polity Press, 2009.
Smith, Norman Kemp. *The Philosophy of David Hume: A Critical Study of Its Origins and Central Doctrines.* London: Macmillan, 1949.
Smith, Wilfred Cantwell. "History in Relation to Both Science and Religion." reprinted in *Modern Culture from a Comparative Perspective*, edited by John W. Burbidge, 9–17. Albany: State University of New York Press, 1997.
———. *Modern Islam in India: A Social Analysis.* London: Victor Gollancz, 1947.
———. *Towards a World Theology: Faith and the Comparative History of Religion.* Philadelphia: Westminster Press, 1981.
———. *What Is Scripture? A Comparative Approach.* Minneapolis: Fortress, 1993.
———. *Faith and Belief.* Princeton NJ: Princeton University Press, 1979.
Taylor, Charles. *A Secular Age.* Cambridge, MA: Harvard University Press, 2007.
Tillich, Paul. "Two Types of Philosophy of Religion." In *Theology of Culture*, edited by Robert C. Kimball, 10–29. New York: Oxford University Press, 1959.
Wiebe, Donald. *The Politics of Religious Studies: The Continuing Conflict with Theology in the Academy.* New York: St. Martin's, 1999.
———. "The Politics of Wishful Thinking? Disentangling the Role of the Scholar-Scientist from That of the Public Intellectual in the Modern Academic Study of Religion." *Temenos* 41, no. 1 (2005), pp. 7–36.
———. "On the Transformation of 'Belief' and the Domestication of 'Faith' in the Academic Study of Religion." *Method & Theory in the Study of Religion* 4, nos. 1 and 2 (1992), pp. 47–68.

Study of Religion as Study of Religious Persons

K. R. Sundararajan

Personally, my interest in the study of "other religions" has been sparked by my encounters with persons of "other faiths" at a deep and interpersonal level. This happened to me after I came to the United States in 1970 to stay at the Center for the Study of Religions at Harvard University. Though I had contacts with Muslims, Christians, and Sikhs when I was in India as a student and then as a member of the faculty at Punjabi University, Patiala, these contacts did not affect me significantly on a personal level. The prejudices and sense of ethnic superiority that I had inherited from the society in which I grew up still dominated my dealings with others, whether fellow Hindus or members of other religious communities. I owe to the legacy of Professor Wilfred Cantwell Smith the fundamental changes in my perception of others and a willingness to open myself to be affected "existentially" and to be transformed by others. The study of religion as the study of religious persons and their quality of faith, as Professor Smith emphasized in his writings, has been largely responsible for these changes. In what follows, I will illustrate how Smith's perspective radically altered my understanding of persons of other faiths, as well my own self-understanding as a Hindu, and has deeply shaped my teaching of comparative religion.

I began to develop a greater appreciation and interest in the study of Islam after I came in contact in 1973 with Dr. Mushirul Haq, a colleague in the Department of Religious Studies at Punjabi University. Dr. Haq, in his person, combined scholarship with openness and friendliness in social interactions. This was certainly different from the vision of Muslims my upbringing brought to me, despite the fact that I had a few Muslim friends when I was in high school. After meeting Dr. Haq, my vision of Muslims changed considerably, and increasingly I came to see him as a "model Muslim" with whom I could interact with ease and pursue dialogue on religious matters. The "secularist strand" that Dr. Haq combined with deep scholarship in Islam also shaped my academic study of Islam. He was vice chancellor of Kashmir University when I met him again at a conference in Srinagar, and sadly I learned later that he was a victim of terrorist violence in Kashmir, having been abducted and then murdered a few days later. To me, Dr. Haq represented the best of Islam, and thereafter I could not study or teach Islam or any other religion without looking for and highlighting their best. Thus, my contact with Dr. Haq, besides turning my indifference, denigration, and even mild hostility to Islam into positive and respectful appreciation of Islam, also motivated me to look for the best among all religions that I teach about in my courses in comparative religion. This "person-based" approach to the study of religion, which is indeed one of the legacies of Professor Smith, continues to shape my academic life.

The point that when we are studying other religions we are in fact learning about living persons also shaped my interest in the study of religions of China. In addition to formal studies, my interest has also been strengthened by the fact that I have several "living personal connections" to China, with my wife and in-laws, who are from Taiwan, and with several others, young and old, whom I met at conferences in China. These contacts with "living persons" invigorated my interest in China. To appreciate this one must understand the context of general Indian indifference to China and the Chinese that I had inherited, and of personal hostility as the result of a conflict between China and India in the early 1970s, in which my eldest brother, an officer in the Indian Air Force, was dropping supplies in war zones. Knowing a few Chinese "personally" changed my indifference and hostility to a deep sense of respect and appreciation for Chinese traditions and values. What I have learned from Professor Smith strengthened these "personal conversions" in my academic life and transformed my approach to those whom I had seen as the "other," "the alien," and "the strange."

The focus on persons in the study of religion is one of the major themes in Smith's writings. For him, this focus is very important in the study of comparative religion and in interreligious encounters, because it encourages one to approach these endeavors with respect and seriousness. In "Comparative Religion: Whither—and Why?," Smith writes:

> The first altogether fundamental step has been the gradual recognition of what was always true in principle, but was not always grasped: the study of religion is the study of persons. Of all branches of human inquiry, hardly any deals with an area as personal as this. Faith is a quality of men's lives. . . . For religions do not exist up in the sky somewhere elaborated, finished, and static. They exist in men's hearts.[1]

The emphasis on faith follows his focus on persons. Equating faith with "religiousness," Smith writes:

> The primary focus of religiousness is persons, not things. And the study of religious history is secondarily the study of things, of phenomena, not in themselves but in their relation to persons—to particular persons and groups; so that the relation is always historical, specific, contingent.[2]

The emphasis on religious persons instead of religious dogma also shapes his response to the questions of religious truth—"Can Religions Be True or False?" Responding to this question, he writes,

> Religious truth is utterly crucial, [it] is the paramount and inescapable issue, before which all other religious matters, however mighty, must bow. It is final. The great question, however, is, where does it lie—and the immediate question is, does it lie in the religions. I am suggesting that it does not, (that it lies elsewhere; namely, in persons).[3]

"Religious truth is a question of persons,"[4] he goes on to say, and the truth or falsity of religions could only be addressed in terms of the "personal participation" of the members of the religious community, on the extent and quality of participation of individual persons.

> Christianity, I would suggest, is not true absolutely, impersonally, statically; rather it can become true, if and as you or I appropriate it to ourselves and interiorize it, in so far as we

live it out from day to day. It becomes true as we take it off the shelf and personalize it, in dynamic actual existence.[5]

My Christianity may be more true this morning than it was yesterday afternoon. It may collapse altogether in some crisis tomorrow morning. . . . One man's Christianity may be (must be) more false than another's. Your Christianity may be truer than the Christianity of your next-door neighbor. I know two Christians of whom the religion of one is more true than the religion of the other.[6]

In terms of understanding the "religiousness" or the faith quality of "another," one has to learn to look at the world through that person's eyes, says Smith.

To understand Buddhists, we must not look at something called Buddhism but at the world; so far as possible through Buddhist eyes. For this, we must among other matters learn to use the total system of Buddhist doctrine or worldview as Buddhists use it; as a pattern for ordering the data of observation—not as among the data to be ordered.[7]

Worldview is a conceptual framework of the individual within which the universe is framed: the universe and man; life; oneself; one's hopes and failures, frustrations and joys; one's marriage; one's child's lameness; all that one sees and knows. It has to be grasped as it has been: not part of what a person knows but the vision by and within which he or she knows (knows, or guesses, or is aware of not knowing). It does not *mean* something; it confers *meaning*.[8]

Thus, the worldview reflects the faith quality of human beings, rendering coherence, providing meaning and purpose to their lives. Referring to Islam to illustrate this point, Smith writes:

Islam is not one of the items in the pattern of a devout Muslim's life, but is itself the pattern into which the various items in his life cohere—into meaningfulness. If he loses faith, maybe nothing in the world will change; the various items in his life may remain as they were—except that they no longer cohere into a pattern for him, are no longer integrated and rendered significant.[9]

Thus, what from the modern Western point of view would be considered "secular" in contrast to religious becomes an integral part of this total coherence. Smith remarks:

> Many modern Westerners have such an ideational framework, one that includes a dichotomy between the religious and secular, as part of its pattern. . . . Conceptual outlooks of this kind are exceedingly deep, often, and therefore firm; and such people have extreme difficulty in understanding, say, traditional Asian patterns that are Islamic, or Hindu, or whatever, not in the sense of having an Islamic or Hindu "religious factor" within a larger social complex like the West's, but in the sense having an Islamic or Hindu overarching pattern within which the secular fits, as a subordinate part.[10]

The religious encounter with "other persons" in an interreligious dialogue, Smith points out, enables one not only to understand and appreciate the religiousness of other persons, but also enlarges "one's vision of truth without losing loyalty to one's own."[11] This personal enrichment could also happen in a different manner. No one individual fully understands the meaning of his or her tradition, writes Smith.

> It can happen that in coming to understand the meaning that an alien symbol has had for an alien community, you may discover therein a meaning—of life, of the universe, on man's destiny, or whatever—that was in your own heritage all along but that previously you personally had not seen.[12]

By understanding "the other," one personally establishes a link with the other person's tradition and faith, which could eventually lead even to the weakening and dissolution of religious boundaries.

> However incipiently, the boundaries segregating off religious communities radically and finally from each other are beginning, just a little, to weaken or to dissolve, so that being a Hindu and being a Buddhist, or being a Christian and not being a Christian, are not so starkly alternatives as once they seemed.[13]

Several years ago when I read John Moffitt's *Journey to Gorakhpur*, I had been troubled by his statement in the very first paragraph, "I am a Christian, but I can no longer say I am not a Hindu or a Buddhist." I had been brought up with the notion that if you are Hindu you are not a Christian. I was indeed puzzled when I studied the Chinese tradition and realized that a Chinese person could be Confucian, Daoist, Buddhist, and a Christian if he or she chooses to be. By shifting the focus from dogma to person, I could understand the weakening and dissolution of boundaries. This is one of the things that happened to me when I came to know Dr. Haq. I realized that he was not very different from me in several ways; for instance, he was as secular as I was. Though that does not mean that I would become a Muslim, as becoming a Muslim is still not a "palatable option" to a Brahmin Hindu, still through him the boundaries and barriers I had built in my understanding of Islam seem to have weakened. I am sure that Professor Smith would not go to the extent of John Moffitt regarding loyalty to "one's own" religion. Perhaps the statement, "The participant is concerned with God; the observer has been concerned with religion"[14] would be his way of not endorsing the statement of John Moffitt! In this regard I remember when some of the "non-Christians" from the Center went with him to one of the Christian services, he told us to remain in our seats when worshippers lined up to receive the sacraments.

Professor Smith once asked me in a private conversation, how I would state my religious identity had I been living in the fifteenth or sixteenth century in South India. My first impulse was to respond by saying, "I am Hindu," but then I realized that such labels are recent. Perhaps a description of myself as a *Vaisnava* would have been more adequate, because such distinct identities developed at a time of conflict and confrontation. Interestingly enough, at the Center when I was a Fellow from 1970 and 1973, I had to assume a "Hindu label" and also bear the heavy burden of being a "model Hindu!" Coming from a time when I had not even seen a television set in India and did not have access to many electronic gadgets, my first visit to the Lechmere store in Cambridge inspired awe and wonder, and this department store indeed became a place of my pilgrimage. Taking this "pilgrimage" perhaps two to three times a month, I began to buy electronic gadgets with whatever limited finances I could spare from my monthly fellowship money. I remember one day a fellow member at the Center remarking that he was surprised at my craze for electronic gadgets; he was wondering how a Hindu could be so interested in material possessions. I was in his eyes not acting like an ideal Hindu, who ought to be detached and be above the level of Western materialism. Thus, paradoxically, at a time when Professor Smith was director of the Center, I was usually labeled a Hindu, and many expected me to be model Hindu!

The legacies of Professor Smith have influenced my teaching. Actually my teaching career started when I joined the theology faculty at St. Bonaventure University in 1976. Though I had worked as a lecturer in Hindu Studies for several years before at Punjabi University, it did not involve much teaching. In my courses in the area of world religions, I have always emphasized the fact that religious labels, such as Hindu, Buddhist, or Jain, are in the first place, not indigenous and self-chosen by the practicing community, but are given to them by outsiders, and "isms" have a tendency to mislead us in the direction of looking for "defining essences" that could be clearly formulated, covering or masking the very fact that religious traditions are marked by rich internal plurality and diversity. As Professor Smith points out, the concept of "religion" is very inadequate and constraining.

> Hinduism refers not to an entity; it is the name that the West has given to a prodigiously variegated series of facts. It is a notion in men's minds—and a notion that cannot but be inadequate. To use this term at all is inescapably a gross oversimplification. There is an inherent contradiction between history and this order of idea.[15]

All "religions" have history. But describing the religious traditions in terms of "isms" denies that history. "Essences do not have history," says Professor Smith. "Yet it is an observable and important fact that what have been called religions do, in history, change."[16]

"To define Hinduism is to deny the Hindu his right to the freedom and integrity of his faith. What he may do tomorrow no man can say today."[17]

Such a focus on history, for Professor Smith, leads to his rejection of what he describes as "nature and origin" theory, which holds that "the earliest form of religion or of a particular religion is somehow the true form, with all subsequent development an aberration."[18]

> To equate Buddhism starkly with the Buddha's teachings or the first decades of the Sangha's life is to dismiss with scant justice the rich elaboration of the Mahayana tradition in China

and Japan. This is virtually to posit something called religion and then to assert that it has no history; to leave unexplained and unnoticed almost the whole religious history of man.[19]

This tendency to compare and justify one's (right) understanding of a tradition is often displayed by many modern Hindu scholars, and the approach of Professor Smith on this issue has shaped my understanding of religious traditions as well as my teaching of courses in world religions. In terms of teaching I always stress the fact that among the rich diversity of schools within each tradition, it is often difficult to find something that is "common," an "essence" of which the diversity and variety could be seen as various "manifestations." For instance, looking for a "Hindu essence" among the richly divergent elements of the Hindu tradition may prove to be futile.

> The common element theory has just not seriously faced the very problem with which, in a less informed day, it was put forth to deal: the inebriating variety of man's religious life not only in general but within each one of the great traditions.[20] In the first place, there is no *a priori* reason, perhaps no historical evidence, for believing that all instances of "Hinduism," for example, or "Taoism" or "Buddhism" must have something in common. It is both logically and historically possible that two quite different things can both be Hindu. Two very different things indeed, or a hundred different things, have all been Buddhist. Secondly, even if there were a least common denominator, it does violence to such religious faith as men have historically had to discount as unessential and irrelevant whatever is particular or special or unique in any case.[21]

Reflecting the legacy of Professor Smith, I tend to stress in my teaching that the "historicity" of religious traditions is as much an essential aspect in the study of these traditions as are the foundational sources, persons, or scriptural writings. Here, one cannot ignore the rich diversification or divergence that has marked the history of all religious traditions and consider them as simple aberrations.

I have used as one of the textbooks for the undergraduate course on comparative religion Professor Smith's *The Faith of Other Men*. Professor Smith writes in the introduction:

> My aspiration is not to get you to understand, for instance, Buddhism; but to help you understand Buddhists. And this means basically, trying to help you to see the world as a Buddhist sees it. Another way of expressing the same point is to say that I do not propose to talk about other men's customs and beliefs, but about other men's faith.[22]

For him, the task of comparative religion should be a disciplined scholarly study at three levels: discovering the outward facts, learning the religious meaning, and drawing generalizations.[23] To accomplish this task, he takes one aspect of each of the religious traditions that he deals with in his book, and shows the worldview that follows from it for the "insider," and also how "outsiders" could understand and make sense of it.

> If inner faith rather than outward system is to be our concern, then how are we deal with it? The method that I have adopted is this, and I am hopeful that you may find it rewarding: I will choose one characteristic item from the system of each major group, an item that may serve in a small way to represent the faith of that community, and I will explore with you the meaning that item may have for those to whom it serves as an expression of their faith. The items are of varying sorts—an image, a phrase, a ceremony; in each case we will examine it as a symbol.[24]

Smith goes on to say, "Our aim in these essays, then, will be, basically, to arrive at a more vivid awareness of the religious quality of the lives of these persons, who are nowadays our neighbors."[25]

I will focus for our present purposes Professor Smith's chapter on the Hindus, to indicate how the methodology he proposed had been worked out, and how successfully. He acknowledges that the task of finding an item which could present the reader the flavor of "Hindu faith" is indeed difficult.

> One has begun to understand the religious life of India only when one has recognized that on principle nothing can be typically Hindu. The sprawling variety is deliberate and serious. There is no system to which something could be central. And Hindus have felt there should not be. A persistent affirmation

in India has been that there are as many facets of the truth as there are persons to perceive it.[26]

By focusing on an Upanishadic phrase that includes three words, *tat, tvam, asi* ("that—you are—to be"), Professor Smith acknowledges that he is possibly leaving out "the orientations of devout and fervent Bhakti worshippers, or the serenity of the detached activist, or the ritual of the humble villager."[27] "By considering any aspect of the Hindu complex, we should be considering some Hindus and omitting many, many others."[28] The understanding of this key phrase enables one to gain a profound insight and appreciation of Hindu faith, at least one facet of it. It is a phrase that arose because "some perceptive and outstanding religious person wrestled with problems of life and thought, and finally came up with a report of how he saw the universe."[29] For Hindus, the phrase has given "insight into transcendence and into human destiny."[30] This truth is a mystery, Professor Smith says, which as one handles it, opens up before one "facet after facet of previously unsuspected wisdom, and at the same time new depths of previously unsuspected, and as yet unplumbed uncertainty—a continuing sense that there is still more and more to be explored."[31] He himself shares a sense of mystery, he points out, when he, as a Christian, attempts to understand it and in that process perhaps "misunderstands" it. Such misunderstandings are always possible whenever anyone attempts to interpret a religious faith other than one's own.

"We can all understand this more forcefully if we reflect on the attempts of outsiders to understand our faith. How many Hindus or Muslims or Jews understand what we Christians mean when we say that in Christ we find God revealed, and that in him we find the power to live and to love? How many Jews feel that Christians, for all our study and contact, understand the Jewish faith? Interreligious understanding is a new field of endeavor, still at a tentative and explorative stage."[32]

Though one might feel that Professor Smith's treatment of *Tattvamasi* is not sufficiently descriptive to show its meaning in different Vedanta schools, I feel that its value lies in the fact that his treatment stresses the fact that the religious insights are not any longer the exclusive possessions of a religious community, a point highlighted by him also in his *The Meaning and End of Religion*. His treatment assumes a situation of active interreligious involvement and interreligious dialogue. In this context, his exploration and implications of *tattvamasi* in four areas of human life—the intellectual, the aesthetic, the moral, and historical development and creativity—are significant. The chapter concludes in what I consider "the Smithian fashion" by raising the question, "What does it mean to me?"

It is this "personalizing orientation" of Professor Smith in the study of religion that I consider his major legacy. It has helped me to approach theological and religious issues in a "humane" way. It has enabled me to read theological treatises as expressions of the writer's faith and not as abstract metaphysical works. The statement of Professor Smith, "The participant is concerned with God; and the observer has been concerned with religion,"[33] has largely shaped my approach to interreligious dialogue where I try to look for the "opening to transcendence" even in the doctrinal formulations and ritual observances of "others" that initially struck me as alien and strange. With the legacy of Professor Smith's stress on "history," I am able to understand the "legitimacy" of new religious movements and developments and appreciate the enormous diversity within the Hindu tradition. Finally, thanks to the historical legacy of Professor Smith, I am also able to label myself as a Hindu, a *Vaishnava* in terms of academic training and scholarship, without feeling guilty about the "modernity" that surrounds my person and my life.

Notes

1. Wilfred Cantwell Smith, *Religious Diversity: Essays*, ed. Willard G. Oxtoby (New York: Harper & Row, 1976), p. 142.
2. Wilfred Cantwell Smith, *Towards a World Theology: Faith and the Comparative History of Religion* (Philadelphia: Westminster Press, 1981), p. 87.
3. Wilfred Cantwell Smith, *Questions of Religious Truth* (New York: Scribner, 1967), p. 67.
4. Ibid., p. 79.
5. Ibid., p. 68.
6. Ibid., p. 69.
7. Smith, *Towards a World Theology*, p. 82.
8. Ibid.
9. Ibid., p. 83.
10. Ibid.
11. Ibid., p. 89.
12. Ibid., p. 90.
13. Ibid., pp. 90–91.
14. Smith, *The Meaning and End of Religion*, p. 119.
15. Ibid., p. 130.
16. Ibid.

17. Ibid., p. 131.
18. Ibid., p. 134.
19. Ibid.
20. Ibid., p. 135.
21. Ibid., pp. 134–35.
22. Wilfred Cantwell Smith, *The Faith of Other Men* (New York: Harper & Row, 1963 [1972]), p. 17.
23. Ibid., p. 15.
24. Ibid., pp. 17–18.
25. Ibid., p. 18.
26. Ibid., p. 25.
27. Ibid., p. 26.
28. Ibid., p. 25.
29. Ibid., p. 29.
30. Ibid., p. 30.
31. Ibid.
32. Ibid., pp. 31–32.
33. Smith, *The Meaning and End of Religion*, p. 119.

Bibliography

Smith, Wilfred Cantwell. *Religious Diversity: Essays*, edited by Willard G. Oxtoby. New York: Harper & Row, 1976.
———. *Towards a World Theology: Faith and the Comparative History of Religion.* Philadelphia: Westminster Press, 1981.
———. *Questions of Religious Truth.* New York: Scribner, 1967.
———. *The Faith of Other Men.* New York: Harper & Row, 1963.

The Moral Imagination of Wilfred Cantwell Smith

Donald K. Swearer

Although his reputation for sometimes being contentious was not mentioned in a February 2000 obituary, which lauded him as "one of the past century's most influential contributors to interfaith dialogue and the comparative study of religion,"[1] few historians of religion in America are as well-known and controversial as Wilfred Cantwell Smith.

When I began my teaching career at Oberlin College in the mid-1960s, Wilfred Cantwell Smith and Mircea Eliade bookended religious studies for me. Although their approaches to religion were in many respects a picture in contrasts—history of religions versus history of religion, historical diversity, faith, and transcendence versus hermeneutics and patterns—both brought to the field a moral commitment that expressed their "ultimate concern."[2] In inaugurating the journal *History of Religions*, for instance, Eliade made a strong case for the comparative study of religions as playing a vital "cultural role," "not only because an understanding of exotic and archaic religions will significantly assist in a cultural dialogue with the representatives of such religions. It is more especially because by attempting to understand the existential situations expressed by the documents he is studying, the historian of religions will inevitably attain a *deeper knowledge of . . . [what it means to be human].* It is on the basis of such a knowledge that a new humanism, on a worldwide scale, could develop."[3]

No doubt Smith would quibble with the meaning of "*representatives of such religions*" and "humanism," but he would be very sympathetic to

Eliade's language of "existential situations" and a "deeper knowledge of what it means to be human," for Smith viewed religion in terms of the matrix of the existential encounter among persons, and as an essential quality of what it means to be human.

As a critic, Smith attacked contemporary philosophical discussions of religious language for failing to reckon with its religious and historical quality within a comparative context, for failing to treat religious statements as essentially human and personal, and for lack of sensitivity to the profound, elusive, and complex quality of human life.[4] In like manner, he took on historians of religion cum phenomenologists for addressing religious objects and patterns but not the persons related to them[5]—even though, as we shall see, Smith did use the terminology of "patterns." Smith's criticisms continued to be refined and elaborated in his many publications subsequent to the appearance of his seminal monograph, *The Meaning and End of Religion*, published in 1962.

Smith has been controversial, in part, because he chose to be contentious, and he was contentious because he thought that many professionals in the field treat religion as a system, an "ism," a simplistic and sterile, overly conceptualized, static entity that has little to do with the personal and historical reality that we label "religion." In other words, those of us who teach religions do not really teach "religion." Rather, we teach a text, a methodology, the sociology of religion, the philosophy of religion, and so on—pursuits that are far removed from the mystery and manure of real-life persons trying to make sense of a world that is often boring and meaningless, and at the same time seemingly in danger of falling apart at the seams. Smith's controversial "personalism" upheld the view that religious truth does not lie in religious systems, but in persons.

This is my own personal, normative assessment of Smith's contribution, through a constructive—rather than a critical—interpretation of Smith's 1981 monograph, *Towards a World Theology*, which captured my attention more than twenty-five years ago.[6] I was gratified to see that Kenneth Cracknell's 2001 anthology of Smith's work, *Wilfred Cantwell Smith: A Reader*, confirmed the significance of *Towards a World Theology* among the many works in the Smith oeuvre. In Cracknell's view, *Towards a World Theology* offers an overview and recapitulation of Smith's main concerns. He includes five selections from this work in four of his anthology's seven divisions: Smith as comparativist, critic, theologian, and prophet. Cracknell and many others highlight the categories of *faith* and *transcendence* as two major themes in Smith's thought. While I do not disagree with this emphasis, I find the categories of *person*, *community*, and *imagination* equally if not more significant.

In *Towards a World Theology*, Smith tilts at the windmills of the academic study of religion on an even grander scale than in his earlier writings. Have we not really subjected our teaching—if not our understanding—of religion to the epistemology of the natural sciences, he asks, which locates the truth in objects, which claims that the truth can be manipulated, tested, repeated, verified empirically, and so on? What kind of truth is that? Is it religious truth? Surely not, he suggests. Religious truth, truth in the most profound sense, truth that emerges from those intersecting moments of our mundanity and transmundanity, cannot be so quantified. Truth in this sense is fundamentally personal. It involves a knower—not simply the human context in which a person knows—and an object that is known. Knowing the truth, then, is not a question of subjective versus objective, internal states of mind versus external objects, but an organically whole "act of truth." It is, in Smith's terms, a "critical, rational, inductive, self-consciousness by which a community of persons is aware of any given particular human condition or action as a condition or action of itself as a community . . . and is aware of it as it is experienced and understood simultaneously both subjectively [personally, existentially] and objectively [externally, critically, analytically]."[7]

To know the moon from the standpoint of humane studies, Smith argues, would include exploring knowledge of the role of the moon in human life and in the history of human culture, including poetry and religion and love, as well as the natural sciences, technology, and space travel. To understand the Meenakshi Temple in Madurai, South India, would not only involve dates, sizes, and composition, but how it feels to be a worshiper within it, its significance in the lives of the shopkeepers in its environs, and its role in the life of the city.[8] Knowing the truth in this sense is an art requiring a series of human qualities, including "faith." In practical terms, it involves a community of both practitioners and scholars.

To know another, contends Smith, we must be able to stand in that human situation, realizing that there is no person on earth we can fully understand, and yet, no person that we cannot understand at least somewhat. Humane knowledge is integrative of the *person* and the *community*, in contrast to objective knowledge, which presumes separation and leads to fragmentation. Objective knowledge stresses method and implies that what is known is both dominant and dominated. By way of contrast, humane learning involves being open to a greater-than-oneself, which Smith calls "transcendence"; it is a process of becoming, not simply one of knowing.

In *Towards a World Theology* Smith is not saying that those who teach religion should not be rational or rigorous or any of those qualities we associate with being objective and descriptive rather than normative and subjective. He is saying, however, that such a posture jeopardizes not only the kind of learning that ought to take place in the academy, but the very nature of religious truth itself. Religious truth for Smith is multivalent and multiplex, a four-dimensional crossroads where we extend our critical self-understanding into the breadth of the human community, the depth of our personal self-understanding, and the extended reach of our transcendence—an insight both timely and timeless, historical and transcendent.

Smith is not asking academics who teach religion to be persons of faith, although his own understanding depends very much on the fact that he is a person of faith; nor is he asking those of us who teach religion to "do" religion. But he is, by his own terms, asking us to teach not only religious traditions (or "cumulative tradition," as he characterizes it), but "faith," with all that implies both for the pedagogy and epistemology of this enterprise. We might say that Smith calls on us to teach religion with sufficient background and training in the history, languages, and cultures of a religious tradition, so that any living being at any existential moment is understood to mirror a world at once particular and universal, who is thus a unique individual who is part of a much larger diachronic and synchronic framework and whose personal story is seen as part of a cosmic story, both human and divine.

Smith calls on professionals in the field of religion to become a part of that story, to enter *imaginatively* into what it means to be a particular Buddhist, Hindu, Muslim, or Jew, rather than teaching the "isms" or the "ologies." His point might be seen in dialectical terms, in that he asks us to move between the particular and the generic. This is at the very foundation, I believe, of what Smith means by a "world theology," or perhaps it would be more apt to say the dynamic, interactive process that gives shape to a world theology. He is convinced that we can teach "faith," "salvation," and "sacraments" from a generic perspective, that the challenge of teaching "sacraments" within the context of world religion is really no different than teaching it within a particular tradition.

Let me illustrate what I understand to be Smith's point here by referring to his discussion of Buddhists (N.B., not Budd*hism*) in his 1965 book, *The Faith of Other Men*, originally delivered as radio talks over the national network of the Canadian Broadcasting Corporation and revised and republished in 1998 under the title *Patterns of Faith Around the World*.[9] In this slim volume, Smith organizes his discussion of each community of religious persons around a single symbol, "in the hope that through it we may gain an insight into the religious life of those for whom it is meaningful" (p. 49). For Buddhists, he chose *Shinbyu*, the Burmese novitiate ordination ceremony.

He begins the chapter with a description of the physical space in which the ceremony takes place—a temple in a village setting sufficiently demarcated to symbolize its sanctity, set apart but near enough to be relevant and involved with everyday problems. "Between the recognized norm and the actuality of everyday life, between the abiding and the transient, the sacred and the profane, the relation is close, yet the two are not identical" (p. 49).

Smith situates the *Shinbyu* comparatively within the framework of a rite of passage: "In the broad sweep it compares to 'joining the church' or First Communion or Confirmation in the Christian pattern, *Bar Mitzvah* in the Jewish, and to related ceremonies through the world" (p. 50). He then turns to a description of the ritual as a reenactment of the "Going Forth" or "Great Renunciation" of Siddhartha Gautama, the *bodhisattva*, the future Buddha, that he characterizes as a "spiritual quest to seek out a remedy for humanity's ills" (p. 51). Like the comparable rites of passage to which Smith refers, a village *Shinbyu* is a major gala event for the families whose male children are being ordained, and for the entire village.

After describing the *Shinbyu* ceremony within the particular social and physical space in which it takes place, and the normative narrative that the ritual reenacts, Smith moves to a generic interpretation: "[B]eyond the forms there is . . . an intimation of a transcending, limitless truth. This infinite becomes in part available to us within the finite, through these finite channels that a society inherits and cherishes, and uses to express its faith and to nourish it. Can we learn something of that faith, and appreciate in part that inner meaning, by exploring the significance of its outwards forms?" (p. 52)

For Smith, the truth to which a religious symbol points cannot be fully apprehended, either by those outside a tradition or by those inside it. Whereas, for Smith, the *Shinbyu* as religious symbol points to a transcendent "greater than," equally important is the fact that it is situated in a multivalent matrix of diachronic and synchronic meanings that challenge facile generalization. His personalist interpretation of the ritual involves what he refers to as "poetic truth," the Going Forth myth that symbolizes a more universal psychological and spiritual truth. He concludes: "Interpretation, then, must be suggestive rather than conclusive" (p. 53). This cautionary note does not undermine interpretation, but engenders a degree of hermeneutical humility in the interpretative act.

In reading *Towards a World Theology*, one is reminded of the priority Smith assigns to "faith" as a category of understanding religion, of his insistence that religious truth is personal, and of the connection between the two. Faith for him is much like Martin Buber's "Between," that sense of essential connectedness that underlies all apparent me-and-thems, us-and-theys, which transforms the objective "I-It" attitude toward the world into an "I-Thou" attitude, an "orientation of the whole personality," an "organizing principle by which the person is open to the infinite and is enabled to see all that is finite in relationship to that infinite."[10]

A theology of religion or a world theology builds from this premise—not a premise in a logical deduction, but a premise on which we understand all religious persons to base their lives. In reading *Towards a World Theology*, I began to understand more clearly what he means about converting noun-terms for religion—the "ities" and "isms"—into adjectives and adverbs, what it means to be "Muslimly" or to act "Christianly." In "faith," in the most basic sense of what it means to be a human being, I am the other and the other is me. Theology in a living, real sense is not Christian or Muslim or Jewish, but a "self-theology" which at one and the same time excludes no one.[11]

What does such a claim mean? A Christian or a Buddhist or a Muslim is not only identified with a particular religious tradition, but with a world human history or story. On this point Smith becomes a visionary, not of a vision of a world religion, but of a world community predicated on faith. This also means that when Smith, as a faithful person within the Christian community, talks about a theology of comparative religion with special reference to Muslim, Hindu, Jewish, and Buddhist communities, he is not trying to represent Islam as a religious system, or to "do" Hindu or Jewish theology in general. He is, odd as it may sound, doing his best to be adjectively Hindu, Jewish, and Buddhist, by representing a particular Muslim, a Hindu person, an actual Thai Buddhist living in Bangkok in 2010. That is, as a person of faith, he is trying not only by his reason but also his *empathetic imagination* to look at the world as *a* Buddhist or *a* Jew might, rather than as *the* Buddhist or *the* Jew.

I have brought Smith's perspective to my own teaching. Several of the readings in the Buddhist-Christian encounters course I taught recently reflect his emphasis on the religious person. One example is Kosuke Koyama's *Water Buffalo Theology*, a personal theological reflection first published in 1974 and reissued in 1999. Koyama confesses that after three years as a missionary in Chiang Mai, Thailand, his interest shifted from Buddh*ism* to Buddhist people, with the discovery that what really matters is not a set of doctrines called Buddhism, but *people* who are trying to live according to the Buddha's teachings:[12] "Buddhism does not and cannot engage in dialogue with Christianity. Buddhists can. Christianity neither eats nor sleeps. Christians do. Buddhism does not sweat under the hot Bangkok sun. Buddhists do. Islam does not recite the Qur'an. Muslims do. . . . The reality of these traditions lies in living persons."[13]

From a person-centered perspective, *Towards a World Theology* is at one and the same time Smith's own particular theology, an expression of his faith or "I-Thou" posture toward the world, but, embryonically at least, it is also a theology of religion. A Buddhist or a Muslim might, indeed, quibble with his understanding and interpretation of his or her tradition, but these disagreements will be no more and no less than disagreements that might arise among those who stand within one historical religious community. These disagreements will be fruitful and insightful, if illumined by faith in Smith's sense, and not mere intellectual confrontation. While Smith's interpretation of a notion such as "transcendence" might sound too Christian or theistic for a Theravada Buddhist, for example, interreligious encounter in Smith's sense would welcome such disagreement, for without it the dialectic between the particular and the generic might be obfuscated or even lost.

Some—perhaps many—might be uncomfortable with Smith's approach, in part because his style can be that of a crochety moralist, going so far as to label the use of "objective" knowledge in humane studies as "immoral." Beyond his sometimes tough moralism, Smith's approach to religion and religious studies may provoke discomfort because, while historical and inductive, it also embraces paradox and celebrates the elusiveness of what it means to be authentically human. From this perspective, I am tempted to say that the value of *Towards a World Theology* lies less in its theology—of which it has very little in any conventional sense—and more in the challenge it offers to the way we as students and teachers approach religious studies.

What would it mean if we were to teach religion "faithfully," in Smith's sense? In the first instance, it would mean that courses in a particular religious tradition or aspect of that tradition should take account of its "cumulative" nature. To be sure, one course in religion or a particular religious tradition must set reasonable limits on what it can cover and accomplish. Regardless of its focus, however, any single course that does not reflect the richness and diversity constituting its broader context runs the risks of reductionism and distortion. The New Testament, for example, should certainly be studied from historical and literary-critical perspectives, but, as Smith argues,[14] it should also be understood as sacred scripture that has influenced lives and shaped perceptions throughout a two-thousand-year history. From this perspective, a New Testament course in historical or literary criticism might be important in the development of exegetical skills, but it fails as a study of sacred scripture in the sense suggested by Smith if it neglects the nature and role of the New Testament in the lives of Christians and Christian communities. Syllogistically, I propose that for Smith "Bible" is to "scripture" as "belief" is to "faith."

A Smithian "holistic" approach to the study and teaching of religion calls for a cognizance of the relationship of a particular subject matter to the total life of a religious community in its historical and contemporaneous dimensions. Within the context of a "world theology," a particular course dealing with theology, scripture, sacraments, ethics, and so on, would have a generic dimension built into it. For example, the New Testament course which has as part of its structure an exploration of the transformative power of scripture within the lives of individuals and communities, could explore this perspective in terms of the Bhagavad Gita in relationship to Hinduism or the Qur'ān in relationship to Islam. "The Qur'ān is significant not primarily because of what historically went into it but because of what historically has come out of it," opines Smith. "The attempt to understand the Qur'ān is to understand how it has fired the imagination, and inspired the poetry, and formulated the inhibitions, and guided the ecstasies, and teased the intellects, and ordered the family relations and the legal chicaneries, and nurtured the piety, of hundreds of millions of people in widely . . . divergent centuries."[15]

Smith's position has profound implications not only for the substance of what we teach, but for the way in which we go about teaching it. Teaching religion, he contends, requires interpretation, imagination, insight, perceptivity, human sympathy, and humility. It should not be engaged as an exercise in conveying a series of "facts" duly observed and recorded, or as simply the logic of belief devoid of poetry and paradox.

In my view, the role of *imagination* in Smith's writings has been undervalued, despite the frequent occurrence of the term in many of his books and articles. For Smith, imagination has both epistemic and moral connotations. Epistemologically, coupling imagination with faith enhances the apprehension of transcendence, but also the understanding of persons and religious communities. To my knowledge, Smith did not write poetry, and his English prose can be quite tortured and Germanic, but his understanding of the theological underpinnings of faith and transcendence, person and community, is attuned to the nuances of symbol, metaphor, and poetry.

The *moral* dimension of imagination finds expression in empathic understanding and sympathy, terminology used by Smith. "Is it too fanciful," Smith asks, "to hold that our one-worldedness is bringing all humanity together in such a way that every one of us is being caught up in the processes of all?"[16]

It is his deep moral sense, I believe, that undergirds and inspires Smith as a constructive critic and prophet visionary not only of religious studies as a discipline, and of the academy, but of culture. To highlight this claim I close with a passage that exemplifies the vision that Wilfred Cantwell Smith communicated as teacher and scholar, and as director of the Center for the Study of World Religions at Harvard Divinity School from 1964 to 1973. It is a vision even more cogent, compelling, and relevant today than it was when Smith penned it more than a decade ago:

> [H]uman development has reached a point where we must construct some kind of world order, or we perish. And . . . this world order must have intellectual and moral dimensions, as well as economic and political. . . .
>
> Some of you will perhaps say that surely we can get on with the business of political structures, of economic planning, of technical advance, of strategic defense, without raising "extraneous" issues of religious faith or cultural convictions: issues that may be interesting in themselves, but are irrelevant to secular concerns. This division of life into two spheres, religious and secular, is a characteristically Western pattern. We tend to assume that everyone else will share it . . . that

the problem of building a new world order is that of imposing Western civilization on the world. . . .

[Fortunately] there has been some recognition, though belated and partial, that the nineteenth-century solution of Western domination by force must be abandoned . . . [and along with it] the arrogance of cultural superiority. . . .

The new world that is waiting to be born is a world of cultural pluralism, of diverse faith. . . . Let no one imagine that building the new world community will be easy. . . . Is this possible? . . . I do not know, [but it is] the fundamental challenge facing humanity today; whether we shall rise to it or not remains to be seen. My own faith is that it can be achieved. . . .

[The] movement, pioneering, historically crucial, with vast new issues at stake, involving the highest ideals of humankind through history on the one hand, and the most delicate, realistic, and practical international problems on the other . . . is stirring. Those who are reaching for the stars these days in a literal sense are, surely, launched on an exciting endeavor; but a metaphorical reaching for the stars that is involved in this quest for world community is more exciting, more significant, more rewarding.[17]

These remarks were given as part of the Center for the Study of World Religion's 50th Anniversary Symposium held on April 16, 2010.

Notes

1. "Wilfred Cantwell Smith, July 21, 1916–February 7, 2000"; www.ageofsignificance.org/people/wcsmith/index.html.

2. The terminology "ultimate concern" is identified, in particular, with Paul Tillich, who taught at Harvard Divinity School (1955–1962) and the University of Chicago (1962–1965).

3. Mircea Eliade, "History of Religions and a New Humanism," *History of Religions* 1, no. 1 (Summer 1961), pp. 2–3. Italics and words in brackets are mine.

4. Wilfred Cantwell Smith, *Belief and History* (Charlottesville: University of Virginia Press, 1977), pp. 5–7.

5. Wilfred Cantwell Smith, *Faith and Belief* (Princeton, NJ: Princeton University Press, 1979), p. 7.

6. I have adapted elements of previous comments on *Towards a World Theology* into this essay; see Donald K. Swearer, "How Do We Teach Religion?" *Theology Today* 40, no. 3 (October 1983), pp. 319–25.

7. Wilfred Cantwell Smith, *Towards a World Theology: Faith and the Comparative History of Religion* (Philadelphia: Westminster Press, 1981), p. 60.

8. Ibid., pp. 65, 66.

9. Wilfred Cantwell Smith, *Patterns of Faith Around the World* (Oxford, UK: OneWorld Publications, 1998). Page references for following quotations are to this edition.

10. Smith, *Towards a World Theology*, pp. 110–11.

11. Ibid., p. 124.

12. Kosuke Koyama, *Water Buffalo Theology*, 25th anniversary ed. (Maryknoll, New York: Orbis Books, 1999), p. 93.

13. Ibid., p. xiv.

14. Wilfred Cantwell Smith, "The Study of Religion and the Study of the Bible," *Journal of the American Academy of Religion* 29, no. 2 (June 1971), pp. 131–40.

15. Ibid., pp. 134, 133.

16. Smith, *Patterns of Faith Around the World*, p. 109.

17. Excerpted and adapted from *Patterns of Faith Around the World*, part one, conclusion, pp. 110–20.

Bibliography

Eliade, Mircea. "History of Religions and a New Humanism." *History of Religions* 1, no. 1 (Summer 1961), pp. 2–3.

Koyama, Kosuke. *Water Buffalo Theology*, 25th anniversary ed. Maryknoll, New York: Orbis Books, 1999.

Smith, Wilfred Cantwell. *Belief and History*. Charlottesville: University of Virginia Press, 1977.

———. *Faith and Belief*. Princeton, NJ: Princeton University Press, 1979.

———. *Towards a World Theology: Faith and the Comparative History of Religion*. Philadelphia: Westminster Press, 1981.

———. *Patterns of Faith Around the World*. Oxford, UK: OneWorld Publications, 1998.

———. "The Study of Religion and the Study of the Bible." *Journal of the American Academy of Religion* 29, no. 2 (June 1971), pp. 131–40.

Swearer, Donald K. "How Do We Teach Religion?" *Theology Today* 40, no. 3 (October 1983), pp. 319–25.

Wilfred Cantwell Smith: A Bibliography

Books—Authored

Believing: An Historical Perspective (Oxford, UK: Oneworld, 1998), vi. 136 pp.
Faith and Belief: The Difference between Them (Oxford, UK: Oneworld Publications, 1998), ix. 347 pp.
Patterns of Faith Around the World (Oxford, UK: Oneworld, 1998). 154 pp.
What Is Scripture? A Comparative Approach (Minneapolis, MN: Fortress Press, 1993). 381 pp.
Scripture: Issues as Seen by a Comparative Religionist (Claremont, CA: Claremont Graduate School, 1985). 22 pp.
On Understanding Islam: Selected Studies (The Hague: Mouton, 1981), xiii. 351 pp.
Towards a World Theology: Faith and the Comparative History of Religion (London: Macmillan, and Philadelphia: Westminster, 1981), vi. 206 pp.
Faith and Belief (Princeton, NJ: Princeton University Press, 1979), ix. 347 pp.
Belief and History (Charlottesville: University Press of Virginia, 1977), vi. 136 pp.
Questions of Religious Truth (New York: Charles Scribner's Sons, and London: V. Gollancz, 1967). 127 pp.
Modernisation of a Traditional Society (Bombay: Asia Publishing House, 1965). 61 pp.
The Meaning and End of Religion: A New Approach to the Religious Traditions of Mankind (New York: Macmillan, 1963), v. 340 pp.
The Faith of Other Men (Toronto: Canadian Broadcasting Corporation, 1962). 60 pp.

Islam in Modern History (Princeton, NJ: Princeton University Press, 1957). 317 pp.

Pakistan as an Islamic State: Preliminary Draft (Lahore: Shaikh Muhammad Ashraf, 1951). 114 pp.

The Azhar Journal: Survey & Critique. PhD Dissertation, Princeton University, Department of Oriental Languages and Literature, 1948. 155 leaves.

The Muslim League, 1942–1945 (Lahore: Minerva Book Shop, 1945). 57 pp.

Modern Islām in India: A Social Analysis (Lahore: Minerva Book Shop, 1943), vi. 399 pp.

Books—Edited

Wilfred Cantwell Smith: A Reader, ed. Kenneth Cracknell (Oxford, UK: Oneworld, 2001), xiv. 258 pp.

Modern Culture from a Comparative Perspective, ed. John W. Burbridge (Albany: State University of New York Press, 1997), xii. 174 pp.

Religious Diversity: Essays, ed. Willard G. Oxtoby (New York: Harper & Row, 1976), xxiv. 198 pp.

Books—Chapters

1. "Islamic Resurgence." *Consciousness and Reality: Studies in Memory of Toshihiko Izutsu*, eds. Sayyid Jalāl al-Dīn Āshtiyānī et al. (Leiden: E. J. Brill, 2000), pp. 3–16.
2. "Religious Pluralism in Its Relation to Theology and Philosophy—and of These Two to Each Other." *The Three Loves: Philosophy, Theology, and World Religions: Essays in Honour of Joseph C. McLelland*, eds. Robert C. Culley and William Klempa (Atlanta: Scholars Press, 1994), pp. 173–84.
3. "Can Believers Share the Qur'an and the Bible as Word of God?" *On Sharing Religious Experience: Possibilities of Interfaith Mutuality*, eds. Jerald D. Gort, Hendrik M. Vroom, et al. (Grand Rapids, MI: Wm. B. Eerdmans Publishing Co., 1992), pp. 55–63.
4. "Retrospective Thoughts on *The Meaning and End of Religion*." *Religion in History: The Word, the Idea, the Reality = La religion dans l'histoire: le mot, l'idée, la réalité*, eds. Michel Despland and Gérard Vallée (Waterloo, ON: Published for the Canadian Corporation Studies in Religion/Corporation canadienne des sciences religieuses by Wilfred Laurier University Press, 1992), pp. 13–21.
5. "A Note on the Qur'ān from a Comparativist Perspective." *Islamic Studies Presented to Charles J. Adams*, eds. Wael B. Hallaq and Donald P. Little (Leiden: E. J. Brill, 1991), 183–92.
6. "The Introductory Course, the Most Important Course." *Teaching the Introductory Course in Religious Studies: A Sourcebook*, ed. Mark Juergensmeyer (Atlanta: Scholars Press, 1991), pp. 177–84.

7. "Scripture as Form and Concept: Their Emergence for the Western World." *Rethinking Scripture: Essays from a Comparative Perspective*, ed. Miriam Levering (Albany: State University of New York Press, 1989), pp. 29–57.
8. "The Study of Religion and the Study of Bible." *Rethinking Scripture: Essays from a Comparative Perspective*, ed. Miriam Levering (Albany: State University of New York Press, 1989), pp. 18–28.
9. "Idolatry: In Comparative Perspective." *The Myth of Christian Uniqueness*, Faith Meets Faith Series (Maryknoll, NY: Orbis Books, 1987), pp. 53–68.
10. "Theology and the World's Religious History." *Toward a Universal Theology of Religion* (Maryknoll, NY: Orbis Books, 1987), pp. 51–72.
11. "Introduction." *India and the West, the Problem of Understanding: Selected Essays*, ed. Jaswant Lal Mehta (Chico, CA: Scholars Press, 1985), pp. xiii–xvii.
12. "Responsibility." *Modernity and Responsibility: Essays for George Grant*, ed. Eugene Combs (Toronto: University of Toronto Press, 1983), pp. 74–84.
13. "Traditions in Contact and Change: Towards a History of Religion in the Singular." *Traditions in Contact and Change: Proceedings of the XIVth Congress of the International Association for the History of Religions*, eds. Peter Slater and Donald Wiebe, with Maurice Boutin and Harold Coward (Waterloo, ON: Wilfred Laurier University Press, 1983), pp. 1–23.
14. "Islamic Studies and the History of Religions." *Essays in Islamic and Comparative Studies: Papers Presented to the 1979 Meeting of the American Academy of Religion*, ed. Ismaʿīl Rājī al Fārūqī (n.p.: International Institute of Islamic Thought, 1982), pp. 2–7.
15. "An Attempt at Summation." *Christ's Lordship and Pluralism*, eds. Gerald H. Anderson and Thomas F. Stransky (Maryknoll, NY: Orbis, 1981), pp. 196–203.
16. "Faith as Tasdīq." *Islamic Philosophical Theology*, ed. Parviz Morewedge (Albany, NY: State University of New York Press, n.d. [sc. 1981]), pp. 96–119.
17. "Understanding Islam." *Funk & Wagnalls New Encyclopaedia 1981 Yearbook* (n.p. [sc. New York]: Funk & Wagnalls, 1981), pp. 22–35.
18. "The Christian in a Religiously Plural World." *Christianity and Other Religions: Selected Readings*, eds. John Hick and Brian Hebblethwaite (London: Collins [Fount Paperbacks], 1980), pp. 87–107.
19. "Divisiveness and Unity." *Food/Energy and the Major Faiths*, ed. Joseph Gremillion (Maryknoll, NY: Orbis, 1978), pp. 71–85.
20. "An Historian of Faith Reflects on What We Are Doing Here." *Christian Faith in a Religiously Plural World*, eds. Donald G. Dawe and John B. Carman (Maryknoll, NY: Orbis, 1978), pp. 139–48.
21. "Arkān." *Essays on Islamic Civilization Presented to Niyazi Berkes*, ed. David P. Little (Leiden: E. J. Brill, 1976), pp. 303–16. Translated into Turkish (1977).

22. "Methodology and the Study of Religion: Some Misgivings." *Methodological Issues in Religious Studies*, ed. Robert D. Baird (Chico, CA: New Horizons Press, 1975), pp. 1–25. Discussion: pp. 25–30.
23. (With Jacob Neusner and Hans H. Penner). "Is the Comparative Study of Religion Possible? Panel Discussion." *Methodological Issues in Religious Studies*, ed. Robert D. Baird (Chico, CA: New Horizons Press, 1975), pp. 95–109, with "Rejoinder," pp. 123–24.
24. "Objectivity and the Humane Sciences: A New Proposal." *Transactions of the Royal Society of Canada* (Ottawa: Royal Society of Canada, 1975), Series 4, 12 (1974), pp. 81–102. Reprinted: in abridged form in *Religious Studies* (ed. Willard G. Oxtoby [New York and London: Harper & Row, 1976], pp. 158–80); *Symposium on the Frontiers and Limitations of Knowledge/Colloque sur les frontières et limites du savoir*, eds. Claude Fortier et al. (Ottawa: Royal Society of Canada, 1975), pp. 81–102.
25. "University Studies of Religion in a Global Context." *Study of Religion in Indian Universities: A Report of the Consultation held in Bangalore in September, 1967* (Bangalore: Bangalore Press, n.d. [1970]), pp. 74–87.
26. "The End Is Near." [Annotated translation from Urdū of Ṣiddiq Ḥasan Khān, *Iqtirāb al-Sā'ah*] *Muslim Self-Statement in India and Pakistan 1857–1968*, eds. Aziz Ahmad and G. E. von Grunebaum (Wiesbaden: Otto Harrassowitz, 1970), pp. 85–89. Published anonymously.
27. "Secularity and the History of Religion." *The Spirit and Power of Christian Secularity*, ed. Albert Schlitzer (Notre Dame: University of Notre Dame Press, 1969), pp. 33–58. Discussion: pp. 59–70.
28. "The Crystallization of Religious Communities in Mughul India." *Yād-Nāme-ye-Irāini* [sic]*-ye Minorsky*, eds. Mojtaba Minovi and Iraj Afshar. Ganjine-ye Taḥqiqāt-e Irāni, no. 57; Publications of Tehran University, no. 1,241 (Tehran: Intishārāt Dāneshgāh, 1969), pp. 197–220.
29. "'Traditional Religions and Modern Culture.'" *Proceedings of the XIth International Congress of the International Association for the History of Religions*, I, The Impact of Modern Culture on Traditional Religions (Leiden: E. J. Brill, 1968), pp. 55–72. Reprinted in slightly abridged form in *Religious Diversity*, ed. Willard G. Oxtoby (New York: Harper & Row, 1976), pp. 59–76.
30. "The Mission of the Church and the Future of Missions." *The Church in the Modern World: Essays in Honour of James Sutherland Thomson*, eds. George Johnston and Wolfgang Roth (Toronto: The Ryerson Press, 1967), pp. 154–70.
31. "Non-Western Studies: The Religious Approach." *A Report on an Invitational Conference on the Study of Religion in the State University. Held October 23–25, 1964 at Indiana University Medical Center* (New Haven, CT: The Society for Religion in Higher Education, 1965), pp. 50–62. Comments and discussion: pp. 62–67.
32. "The Concept of Shari'a among Some Mutakallimun." *Arabic and Islamic Studies in Honor of Hamilton A. R. Gibb*, ed. George Makdisi (Leiden: E. J. Brill, 1965), pp. 581–602.

33. "The 'Ulamā' in Indian Politics." *Politics and Society in India*, ed. C. H. Philips (London: George Allen & Unwin Ltd., 1963), pp. 39–51.
34. "The Historical Development in Islam of the Concept of Islam as an Historical Development." *Historians of the Middle East*, eds. Bernard Lewis and P. M. Holt. Historical Writing on the Peoples of Asia, 4 (London: Oxford University Press, 1962), pp. 484–502.
35. "The Comparative Study of Religion in General and the Study of Islam as a Religion in Particular." *Colloque sur la sociologie musulmane: Actes, 11–14 septembre 1961*, Correspondance d'Orient, 5 (Brussels: Publications du Centre pour l'étude des problèmes du monde musulman contemporain, 1962), pp. 217–31.
36. "Modern Muslim Historical Writing in English." *Historians of India, Pakistan and Ceylon*, ed. C. H. Philips. Historical Writing on the Peoples of Asia, 1 (London: Oxford University Press, 1961), pp. 319–31.
37. "Comparative Religion: Whither—and Why?" *The History of Religions: Essays in Methodology*, eds. Mircea Eliade and Joseph M. Kitagawa (Chicago: University of Chicago Press, 1959), pp. 31–58. Reprinted in slightly abridged form in *Religious Diversity*, ed. Willard G. Oxtoby (New York and London: Harper & Row, 1976), pp. 138–57. Translated into Urdu (1962), Japanese (1962), and German (1963).
38. "The Christian and the Religions of Asia." *Changing Asia: Report of the Twenty-Eighth Annual Couchiching Conference: A Joint Project of the Canadian Institute on Public Affairs and the Canadian Broadcasting Corporation* (Toronto: Canadian Institute on Public Affairs, 1959), pp. 9–16. Reprinted in abridged form, The Beacon (London) 39 (1962): 337–40; *Occasional Papers*, Department of Missionary Studies, International Missionary Council (World Council of Churches), London, 5 (Apr. 1960); as "Christianity's Third Great Challenge." *The Christian Century* 77:17 (27 Apr. 1960): 505–8.
39. "Some Similarities and Differences between Christianity and Islam: An Essay in Comparative Religion." *The World of Islam: Studies in Honour of Philip K. Hitti*, eds. James Kritzeck and R. Bayly Winder (London: Macmillan, and New York: St. Martin's Press, 1959), pp. 47–59. Translated into Urdu (1964).
40. "The Intellectuals in the Modern Development of the Islamic World." *Social Forces in the Middle East*, ed. Nettleton Fisher (Ithaca, NY: Cornell University Press, 1955), pp. 190–204.
41. "Islam Confronted by Western Secularism: Revolutionary Reaction." *Islam in the Modern World: A Series of Addresses Presented at the Fifth Annual Conference on Middle East Affairs, Sponsored by the Middle East Institute*, ed. Dorothea Seelye Franck (Washington, DC: Middle East Institute, 1951), pp. 19–30. Translated into Arabic (1953).
42. "The Comparative Study of Religion: Reflections on the Possibility and Purpose of a Religious Science." *McGill University, Faculty of Divinity, Inaugural Lectures* (Montreal: McGill University, 1950), pp. 39–60.

43. "The Muslim World." *One Family*, vol. II (Toronto: Missionary Society of the Church of England in Canada, 1947–48), pp. 27–32.

Encyclopedia Entries

1. "Religion as Symbolism." Introduction to Propaedia, part 8, "Religion." *Encyclopaedia Britannica*, 15th ed. (Chicago: Encyclopaedia Britannica, 1974), pp. 498–500.
2. "Koran (Qur'ān)." *Encyclopaedia Britannica* (Chicago: Encyclopaedia Britannica, 1964).
3. "Druze." *Encyclopædia Britannica* (Chicago: Encyclopaedia Britannica, 1963).
4. "Iblis." *Encyclopædia Britannica* (Chicago: Encyclopaedia Britannica, 1962).
5. "India, Religion and Philosophy: Islam." *Encyclopedia Americana* (Danbury, CT: Grolier, 1960). Reprinted: *India, Pakistan, Ceylon*, ed. W. Norman Brown. Rev. ed. (Philadelphia: University of Philadelphia Press, and London: Oxford University Press, 1964), pp. 104–7.
6. "Aga Khan III." *Encyclopaedia Americana* (New York: Americana Corporation, 1958).
7. "Amir Ali, Sayyid." *Encyclopaedia of Islam*, new ed. (Leiden: E. J. Brill, 1956). Translated into French (1956).
8. "Ahmadiyyah." *Encyclopaedia of Islam*, new ed. (Leiden: E. J. Brill, 1956). Translated into French (1956).
9. "Propaganda (Muslim)." *Twentieth Century Encyclopaedia of Religious Knowledge*, vol. II (Grand Rapids, MI: Baker, 1955), pp. 767–68.
10. "Pakistan." *Collier's Encyclopaedia* (New York: P. F. Collier & Son, 1953).

Articles

1. "Vedānta and the Modern Age." *Religious Studies and Theology* 13/14:1 (Apr. 1995): 12–20.
2. "The Academic Study of Religion: The Challenge of the World Parliaments of Religion." *Religious Studies and Theology* 13/14:1 (Apr. 1995): 5–11.
3. "Reconsidérer l'Écriture à la lumière de la théologie et de l'étude de la religion." *Revue de théologie et de philosophie* 124:4 (1992): 369–88.
4. "The 'Authority' of Scripture." *Touchstone* 10:3 (Sept. 1992): 3–7.
5. "Fundamentalism in the Modern World." *India International Centre Quarterly* 17:1 (Spring 1990): 33–43.
6. "Response to Robert E. Florida." *Buddhist-Christian Studies* 10 (1990): 263–73.
7. "Thoughts on Transcendence." *Zeitschrift für Religions- und Geistesgeschichte* 42:1 (1990): 32–49.
8. "Mission, Dialogue and God's Will for Us." *International Review of Mission* 77:307 (Jul. 1988): 360–74.

9. "Images of Eternity: Concepts of God in Five Religious Traditions." *Theology* 91:742 (Jul. 1988): 365–68.
10. "Theology and the Academy Study of Religion." *Iliff Review* 44:3 (Fall 1987): 9–18.
11. "Muslim-Christian Relations: Questions of a Comparative Religionist." *Institute of Muslim Minority Affairs* 8 (Jan. 1987): 18–21.
12. "The Modern West in the History of Religion." (American Academy of Religion, Annual Meeting 1983: The Presidential Address) *Journal of the American Academy of Religion* 52:1 (Mar. 1984): 3–18.
13. "On Mistranslated Book Titles." *Religious Studies* 20:1 (Mar. 1984): 27–42.
14. "History in Relation to both Science and Religion." *Scottish Journal of Religious Studies* 2:1 (1981): 3–10.
15. "Belief: A Reply to a Response." *Numen* 27:2 (1980): 247–55.
16. "The True Meaning of Scripture: An Empirical Historian's Non-Reductionist Interpretation of the Qu'ran." *International Journal of Middle East Studies* 11:4 (Jul. 1980): 487–505.
17. "Aziz Ahmad, 1913–78." *Proceedings of the Royal Society of Canada* 18 (1980): 44–46.
18. "Thinking about Persons." *Humanitas* 15 (1979): 147–52.
19. "Tauḥid and the Integration of Personality." *Studies in Islam: Quarterly Journal of the Indian Institute of Islamic Studies*, New Delhi, 16 (1979): 127–28. Discussion: pp. 128–29.
20. "Interpreting Religious Interrelations: An Historian's View of Christian and Muslim." *SR: Studies in Religion/Sciences religieuses* 6 (1976–77): 515–26. Reprinted: *Christianity and Islam: The Struggling Dialogue*, ed. Richard W. Rousseau (Scranton, PA: Ridge Row Press, 1985), pp. 1–13.
21. "Iqbal the Progressive." *Oriental College Magazine* 53 (1977): 177–93.
22. "Faith and Belief (Some Considerations from the Islamic Instance)." *Al-Hikmat: A Research Journal of the Department of Philosophy*, University of the Punjab, Lahore, 6 (1975 [sc. 1976]): 1–20.
23. "Faith and Belief (Some Considerations from the Christian Instance)." *Al-Hikmat: A Research Journal of the Department of Philosophy*, University of the Punjab, Lahore, 6 (1975 [sc. 1976]): 21–43.
24. "World Religions, in 'What's in Store for '74? Looking Ahead in Various Areas of Contemporary Life.'" *The Christian Century* 91:1 (1974): 16.
25. "'The Finger that Points to the Moon': Reply to Per Kvaerne." *Temenos*, Helsinki, 9 (1973): 169–72.
26. "On 'Dialogue and Faith': A Rejoinder." *Religion* 3 (1973): 106–14.
27. "Programme Notes for a Mitigated Cacophony." *The Journal of Religion* 53 (1973): 377–81.
28. "A Human View of Truth." *SR: Studies in Religion/Sciences religieuses* I (1971): 6–24. Reprinted: *Truth and Dialogue in World Religions: Conflicting Truth-Claims*, ed. John Hick (Philadelphia: Westminster Press, 1974), pp.

20–44; with a new addendum: "Conflicting Truth-Claims: A Rejoinder." *Truth and Dialogue in World Religions: Conflicting Truth-Claims* (Philadelphia: Westminster Press, 1974), pp. 156–62.

29. "The Study of Religion and the Study of the Bible." *Journal of the American Academy of Religion* 39:2 (1971): 131–40. Reprinted: with minor alterations in *Religious Diversity*, ed. Willard G. Oxtoby (New York: Harper & Row, 1976), pp. 41–56.

30. "Participation: The Changing Christian Role in Other Cultures." *Occasional Bulletin*, Missionary Research Library, New York, 20:4 (1969): 1–13. Reprinted: *Religion and Society*, Bangalore, 17:1 (1970): 56–74; in abridged form in *Evangelization*, eds. Gerald H. Anderson and Thomas F. Stransky (New York: Paulist Press, and Grand Rapids: Eerdmans, 1975) pp. 218–29; *Religious Diversity*, ed. Willard G. Oxtoby (New York and London: Harper & Row, 1976) pp. 117–37.

31. "Religious Atheism? Early Buddhist and Recent American." *Milla wa-Milla*, Melbourne, 6 (1966): 5–30. Reprinted: *Comparative Religion: The Charles Strong Trust Lectures 1961–70*, ed. John Bowman (Leiden: E. J. Brill, 1972), pp. 53–81.

32. "Secularism: The Problem Posed." *Seminar*, New Delhi, 67 (1965): 10–12.

33. "The Islamic Near East: Intellectual Role of Librarianship." *Library Quarterly* 35:4 (Oct. 1965): 283–94. Discussion: pp. 294–97. Reprinted: *Area Studies and the Library*, eds. Tsuen-Hsuim Tsien and Howard W. Winger (Chicago: University of Chicago Press, 1966), pp. 81–92. Discussion: pp. 92–95.

34. "Mankind's Religiously Divided History Approaches Self–Consciousness." *Harvard Divinity Bulletin* 29:1 (1964): 1–17. Reprinted in slightly abridged form in *Religious Diversity*, ed. Willard G. Oxtoby (New York: Harper & Row, 1976), pp. 96–114. Translated into German (1967).

35. "The YMCA and the Present." *Bulletin*, National Council of Young Men's Christian Associations of Canada, Toronto, 34:4 (Jun. 1960): 3–5.

36. "Law and Ijtihad in Islam: Some Considerations on Their Relation to Each Other and to Ultimate and Immediate Problems." *Dawn* (Karachi, 5 Jan. 1958). Reprinted: *Pakistan Quarterly*, Karachi, 8 (1958): 29–31, 63; *International Islamic Colloquium Papers: December 29, 1957–January 8, 1958* (Lahore: Panjab University Press, 1960), pp. 111–14. Translated into Urdu (1958), Arabic (1960).

37. "Independence Day in Indonesia." *The McGill News*, Montreal (Winter 1957): 23–24.

38. "Islam in the Modern World." *Current History* 32 (1957): 321–25. Reprinted: *Enterprise*, Karachi (4 Jan. 1958); *Morning News*, Karachi (12 Apr. 1959).

39. "The Christian and the Near East Crisis." *The British Weekly* (London) 138, no. 3,658 (20 Dec. 1956): 5. Reprinted: *The Presbyterian Record*, Toronto, 82:1 (Jan. 1957): 16–17.

40. "The Place of Oriental Studies in a Western University." *Diogenes* 16 (1956): 104–11. Translated into French (1956), German (1957), and Spanish (1958).
41. "The Importance of Muhammad." *The Canadian Forum* 34 (Sept. 1954): 135–36.
42. "The Institute of Islamic Studies [McGill University]." *The Islamic Literature*, Lahore, 5 (1953): 173–76.
43. "Modern Turkey—Islamic Reformation?" *Islamic Culture*, Hyderabad, 25:1 (1952): 155–86. Reprinted in abridged form, with comments: *Die Welt des Islams* 3 (1954): 269–73. Translated into Turkish (1953).
44. "The Muslims and the West." *Foreign Policy Bulletin*, New York, 31:2 (Oct. 1951): 5–7.
45. "Hyderabad: Muslim Tragedy." *Middle East Journal* 4:1 (Jan. 1950): 27–51.
46. "Lower-Class Uprisings in the Mughal Empire." *Islamic Culture*, Hyderabad, 20 (1946): 21–40.
47. "Objective Tests in History." *Education*, Lucknow, 24:2 (1945): 53–60. Reprinted: *The Punjab Educational Journal*, Lahore, 29 (1944): 309–13, 336–45.
48. "Achievement Tests in History." *Education*, Lucknow, 24:1 (1945): 57–62.
49. "The Mughal Empire and the Middle Class: A Hypothesis." *Islamic Culture*, Hyderabad, 18 (1944): 349–63.

Book Reviews

1. Review of Ninian Smart, *Beyond Ideology: Religion and the Future of Western Civilization* (1981), in *The Journal of Religion* 64:1 (Jan. 1984): 136–38.
2. Review of Reynold A. Nicholson, *Studies in Islamic Mysticism* (1978), in *Religious Studies* 17:2 (Jun. 1981): 281–82.
3. Review of Murray Ross, *The University: The Anatomy of Academe* (1976), in *Dalhousie Review* 57 (1977–78): 540–49.
4. Review of M. M. Thomas, *Man and the Universe of Faiths* (1975), in *Ecumenical Review* 29:4 (Oct. 1977): 429–30.
5. Review of Erich Heck, *Der Begriff Religio bei Thomas von Aquin: seine Bedeutung für unser heutiges Verständnis von Religion* (1971), in *Speculum* 49:2 (Apr. 1974): 342–43.
6. "Programme Notes for a Mitigated Cacophony." Review of R. C. Zaehner, *Concordant Discord: The Interdependence of Faiths. Being the Gifford Lectures on Natural Religion Delivered at St. Andrews in 1967–1969* (1970), in *The Journal of Religion* 53:3 (Jul. 1973): 377–81.
7. Review of Louis Gardet, *Dieu et la destinée de l'homme; les grands problèmes de la théologie musulmane; essai de théologie comparée* (1967), in *Journal of the American Oriental Society* 92:2 (Apr.–Jun. 1972): 377–81.
8. Review of Kenneth Cragg, *Christianity in World Perspective* (1968), in *Journal of the American Academy* 37:3 (Sep. 1969): 305–6.

9. Review of Ved Prakash Luthera, *The Concept of the Secular State* (1964), in *International Journal* 21:2 (Spring 1966): 272–74.
10. Review of Edward B. Harper, *Religion in South Asia* (1964), in *The Journal of Asian Studies* 25:2 (Feb. 1966): 354–55.
11. Review of *Studies in Islam* (Quarterly Journal of Indian Institute of Islamic Studies, New Delhi, 1:1 [Jan. 1964]), in *Journal of the American Oriental Society* 84:4 (Oct.–Dec. 1964): 419–20.
12. Review of Donald Eugene Smith, *India as a Secular State* (1963), in *International Journal* 19:1 (Winter 1963/64): 105–6.
13. Review of Leonard Binder, *Religion and Politics in Pakistan* (1961), in *Journal of the American Oriental Society* 83:1 (Jan.–Mar. 1963): 136–38.
14. Review of Clifford Geertz, *The Religion of Java* (1960), in *Economic Development and Cultural Change* 11:2, Part 1 (Jan. 1963): 203–6.
15. Review of Constance E. Padwick, *Muslim Devotions: A Study of Prayer-Manuals in Common Use* (1961), in *Bulletin of the School of Oriental and African Studies*, University of London, 25:1/3 (1962): 351–53.
16. Review of Arthur Jeffery, *Islam: Muḥammad and His Religion* (1958), in *Journal of the American Oriental Society* 80:2 (Apr.–Jun. 1960): 146–47.
17. Review of Erwin I. J. Rosenthal, *Political Thought in Medieval Islam: An Introductory Outline* (1958), in *The Canadian Journal of Economics and Political Science/Revue canadienne d'économique et de science politique* 25:4 (Nov. 1959): 530–31.
18. Review of C. A. O. van Nieuwenhuijze, *Aspects of Islam in Post-Colonial Indonesia: Five Essays* (1958) and Harry J. Benda, *The Crescent and the Rising Sun: Indonesia Islam under the Japanese Occupation 1942–45* (1958), in *Annals of the American Academy of Political and Social Science*, Partnership for Progress: International Technical Co-Operation, 323 (May 1959): 211–12.
19. Review of Kenneth W. Morgan, *Islam—the Straight Path: Islam Interpreted by Muslims* (1958), in *Journal of the American Oriental Society* 78:4 (Oct.–Dec. 1958): 309–11.
20. Review of Richard N. Frye, *Islam and the West: Proceedings of the Harvard Summer School Conference on the Middle East, July 25–27, 1955* (1957), in *Middle East Journal* 11:4 (Autumn 1957): 437–38.
21. Review of Kenneth Cragg, *The Call of the Minaret* (1956), in *The Journal of Religion* 37:3 (Jul. 1957): 201–2.
22. Review of John Norman Hollister, *The Shi'a of India* (1953), in *Pacific Affairs* 28:3 (Sep. 1955): 287–88.
23. Review of George Kirk, *Survey of International Affairs, 1939–46: The Middle East in the War* (1952), in *International Journal* 9:3 (Summer 1954): 230–32.
24. Review of Stanley Jackson, *The Aga Khan: Prince, Prophet and Sportsman* (1952), in *Middle East Journal* 8:2 (Spring 1954): 217.
25. Review of Fazlur Rahman, *New Education in the Making of Pakistan: Its Ideology and Basic Problems* (1953), in *Pacific Affairs* 27:1 (Mar. 1954): 82–84.

26. Review of Hazrat Mirza Bashir-ud-Din Mahmud Ahmad (Khalifatul Masih II), *Introduction to the Study of the Holy Quran* (1949), in *Journal of Bible and Religion* 20:1 (Jan. 1952): 58–59.
27. Review of Joachim Wach, *Types of Religious Experience, Christian and Non-Christian* (1951), in *The Journal of Religion* 33:4 (Oct. 1953): 303–4.
28. Review of Begum Liaquat Ali Khan, *Pakistan: The Heart of Asia* (1951), in *Pacific Affairs* 24:2 (Jun. 1951): 216–17.
29. Review of Richard Symonds, *The Making of Pakistan* (1950), in *Middle East Journal* 5:2 (Spring 1951): 254–55.
30. Review of Earl Edgar Elder, *A Commentary on the Creed of Islam: Saʻd al-Dīn al-Taftāzāni on the Creed of Najm al-Dīn al-Nasafī* (1950), in *Journal of Bible and Religion* 18:4 (Oct. 1950): 265–67.
31. Review of C. H. Philips, *India* (1949), in *Middle East Journal* 4:3 (Jul. 1950): 363.

Pamphlets

1. *The Role of Asian Studies in the American University*. The plenary address of the New York State Conference for Asian Studies, Colgate University, October 10–12, 1975 (Hamilton, New York: Colgate University, 1976).
2. *Orientalism and Truth: A Public Lecture in Honor of T. Cuyler Young, Horatio Whitridge Garrett Professor of Persian Language and History, Chairman of the Department of Oriental Studies* (Princeton, NJ: Program in Near East Studies, Princeton University, 1969). 16 pp.
3. *The Muslim World*. Current Affairs for the Canadian Forces series, X, 4 (Ottawa: Bureau of Current Affairs, Department of National Defense, 1956). 26 pp. Translated into French (1956).

Publications in Translation

ARABIC

1. (*Islam in Modern History*, 1957, authorized translation) *Al-Islām fī al-taʼrīkh al-ḥadīth*, trans. with a foreword by M. Kāmil Ḥusayne (Bayrūt: al-Muʼassasah al-ʻArabiyah li-al-baḥth wa-al-nashr, 1975).
2. (*Islam in Modern History*, 1957, pirated edition, abridged) *Al-Islām fī al-taʼrīkh al-ḥadīth*, Kutub siyāsiyah, 163 (Cairo: n.d. [1960]).
3. (*Islam in Modern History*, 1957, partial translation) "Al-Islām wa al-taṭ awwur" and "Al-Islām fī al-taʼrīkh al-ḥadīth." *Dirāsāt Islāmiyah*, ed. Niqūlā Ziyādah (Bayrūt: Dār al-Andalus, 1960), pp. 295–402.
4. ("Islam Confronted by Western Secularism: Revolutionary Reaction, 1951") "Al-Islām yuwājih alʻilmāniyah al-gharbiyah," trans. Isḥāq Mūsá al-Ḥusayni

with notes by 'Ali 'Abd al-Wāḥid Wāfi, Philip K. Hitti, et al. *Al-Islām fi naẓar al-Gharb* (Bayrūt: Dār Bayrūt, 1953), pp. 38–59.

French

1. (*Islam in Modern History*, 1957) *L'islam dans le monde moderne*, preface and trans. A. Guimbretière (Paris: Payot, 1962).
2. (*The Muslim World*, 1956) *Le monde musulman* [brochure]. Séries Actualités, revue destinée aux forces canadiennes, X, 4 (Ottawa: Bureau des actualités, Ministère de la défense nationale, 1956). 26 pp.
3. ("Amir Ali, Sayyid," 1956) "Amir Ali, Sayyid," *Encyclopédie de l'islam*, new edition (Leiden and Paris: E. J. Brill, 1956).
4. ("Ahmadiyyah," 1956) "Ahmadiyyah." *Encyclopédie de l'islam*, new ed. (Leiden: E. J. Brill, 1956).
5. ("The Place of Oriental Studies in a Western University," 1956) "Le role de l'université dans un monde à civilisations multiples," trans. Nicole Laming. *Diogène*, Paris, 16 (1956): 3–13.

German

1. "Menschlicher Glaube—Das gemeinsame Zentrum aller religiösen Traditionen," trans. by A. Grünschloss. *Horizontüberschreitung: die pluralistische Theologie der Religionen*, ed. Reinhold Bernhardt (Gütersloh: Gerd Mohn, 1991), 156–74.
2. ("Mankind's Religiously Divided History Approaches Self-Consciousness," 1964) "Das erwachende Selbstbewusstsein von der geschichtlichen Vielfalt der Religionen," trans. by von Hans-Joachim Klimkeit. *Religion und Religionen: Festschrift für Gustav Mensching zu seinem 65. Geburtstag*, ed. Rudolf Thomas (Bonn: Ludwig Rohrscheid Verlag, 1967) pp. 190–208.
3. ("Comparative Religion: Whither—and Why?" 1959) "Vergleichende Religionswissenschaft: wohin—warum?" trans. Elizabeth Schmitz-Mayr-Harting. *Grundfragen der Religionswissenschaft: Acht Studien*, eds. Mircea Eliade and Joseph M. Kitagawa (Salzburg: Otto Müller Verlag, 1963) pp. 75–105, 239–56.
4. (*Islam in Modern History*, 1957) *Der Islam in der Gegenwart*, trans. Hermann Stiehl (Frankfurt: Fischer Bücherei, 1963).
5. ("The Place of Oriental Studies in a Western University," 1956) "Die Orientwissenschaft an einer Universität des Westerns." *Diogènes*, Köln-Marienburg, 16 (1957): 522–30.

Indonesian

1. (*Islam in Modern History*, 1957) *Islam dalam sedjarah modern*, trans. Abusalamah. 2 vols. (Djakarta: Bhratara, 1962–64).

Japanese

1. (*Islam in Modern History*, 1957) *Gendai ni okeru Isurāmu*, trans. Nakamura Kōjirō yaku (Tokyo: Kinokuniyashoten, 1974).
2. (*Questions of Religious Truth*, 1967) *Shūkyō no shinri*, trans. Kasai Minoru (Tokyo: Riso Sha, 1971).
3. "Shoshūkyō no kyōryoku wa kanōka—Jinrui kyōdōtai e rekishiteki shimeikan o" ["Is Inter-religious Co-operation Possible? The Problem of World Community in Historical Perspective"]. *Yomiuri Shimbun*, Tokyo (9 Jan. 1966): 11. Published only in Japanese.
4. ("Comparative Religion: Whither—and Why?" 1959) "Korekara no hikakushūkyōgaku no arikata," trans. Kishimoto Hideo. *Shūkyōgaku nyumon*, eds. M. Eliade and J. M. Kitagawa (Tokyo: Tōkyō daigaku-shuppankai, 1962), pp. 47–87. Reprinted: 1966.

Persian

1. (*Islam in Modern History*, 1957) *Islām dar jahān-i imrūz*, trans. Husayn 'Ali Hiravī (Tihrān: Intishārāt-i Dānishgāh-i Tihrān, 1977).

Spanish

1. ("The Place of Oriental Studies in a Western University," 1956) "La Función de la universidad en el complejo cultural de nuestro mundo." *Diógenes*, Buenos Aires, 3 (1958): 3–12.

Swedish

1. (*The Faith of Other Men*, 1963) *Människor av annan tro*, trans. Axel Ljungberg and Alf Ahlberg (Stockholm: Natur och Kultur, 1965).
2. (*Islam in Modern History*, 1957) *Islam i modern tid*, trans. Ulla Carlsted. Foreword H. S. Nyberg (Stockholm: Natur och Kultur, 1961).

Turkish

1. ("Arkān," 1976) "*Erkân*," trans. Mehmet Dağ. *İslâm Ilimleri Enstitüsü Dergisi*, Ankara, 3 (1977): 301–14.
2. ("Modern Turkey—Islamic Reformation?" 1952) "Modern Türkiye dini bir reforma mï gidiyor?" *İlâhiyat Fakültesi Dergisi*, Ankara, 2 (1953): 7–20.

Urdu

1. (*Islam in Modern History*, 1957, partial translation) *Islām daur-i hāzir men: muntakhab mazāmīn*, trans. Mushīrulḥaqq (Na'ī Dihlī: Maktabah-yi Jāmi'ah, 1984).

2. ("Some Similarities and Differences between Christianity and Islam," 1959) "Islām awr Masiḥiyat—Kuchh farq, kuchh yaksāniyān: Ek taqābuli muṭ āliʿah'-i mazāhib." *Dunyā-e Islām*, tarjamah'-i Sayyid Hāshimi Fardābādī (Lahore: Maqbūl Akayḍami, 1964): 73–94.
3. ("Comparative Religion: Whither—and Why?" 1959) "Mazhab kā taqābuli muṭāliʿah: Kiyūṇ awr kis ṭaraḥ," mutarjamah'-i jināb Sayyid Mubārizu-d-Din Ṣāḥib Rafʿat awr Ḍākṭar Abū Naṣr Muḥammad Ṣāḥib Khālidi, *Burhān*, Delhi, 49 (1962)," 197–216, 262–81, 348–55.
4. (*Islam in Modern History*, 1957, partial paraphrase) "Pākistān ki Islāmi riyāsat, parofaysar Ismith ki naẓar men," paraphrase by ʿAbdu-r-Raḥmān ʿAbd, *Chirāgh-i-Rāh* (Naẓariyah'i Pākistān nambar), Karachi, 12:12 (Dec. 1960): 277–90. "Istidrāk," (Khurshid Aḥmad): 290–94. "Muzākirah: Pākistān awr Islāmi naẓariyah—Ḍākṭar Wilfarayḍ Kaynṭwal Ismith" ["Discussion: Pakistan and Islamic Theory"], pp. 363–66. Response to, and elaboration of, pp. 277–94; published only in Urdu.
5. (*Islam in Modern History*, 1957, partial translation) "Islām in māḍarn hisṭ ari: Ek bāb kā tarjamah," Mutarjim: Ziyā'u-l-Ḥasan Fārūqi, *Burhān*, Delhi, 14 (1958): 285–300, 349–64; 15 (1959): 45–58.
6. "Ek Sawāl" ["A Question"]. *Aligarh Maygazin*, Aligarh (1955): 81–83. Published only in Urdu.

Contributors

Ellen Bradshaw Aitken (in memory) was Dean of the Faculty of Religious Studies at McGill from 2007 to 2014. She passed away in June 2014. She had been a member of that faculty since 2004, teaching in the area of early Christian history and literature. Prior to arriving at McGill, she was on the faculty of the Divinity School at Harvard University. She held degrees from Harvard and the University of the South, with training in folklore and mythology, the classics, and religious studies. Her last research project, funded by SSHRC, investigated the relationship between Greco-Roman hero cults and ancient Christianity. She was ordained in the Episcopal (Anglican) Church in 1986 and had been recognized widely as a leader in both the scholarly and ecclesial communities. She also received two awards for teaching excellence.

Purushottama Bilimoria is Professor of Philosophy and Comparative Studies at Deakin University and a research fellow at the University of Melbourne, Australia. He is also a Shivdasani Fellow at the Oxford Centre for Hindu Studies. He has published widely on Indian philosophy, diaspora studies, bioethics, and personal law in India. Dr. Bilimoria is editor-in-chief of *Sophia, Journal of Philosophy of Religion, Metaphysical Theology and Ethics* (Springer).

John B. Carman is Parkman Professor of Divinity and Professor of Comparative Religion, Emeritus, at Harvard Divinity School, where he taught from 1963 to 2000 and where from 1973 to 1989 he was Director of the Center for the Study of World Religions. His main scholarly interests have been in Dutch phenomenology of religion, comparative ethics, the relation of Christian theology to the academic study of religion, Hindu devotional religion (*bhakti*) and its relation to Christianity, and village Christian churches in South India. He is now retired in South Portland, Maine, making occasional visits back to Cambridge, Massachusetts, and to India, Thailand, and Japan.

Thomas B. Coburn is President Emeritus of Naropa University. Previously he taught for twenty-nine years at St. Lawrence University, where he was the Charles A. Dana Professor of Religious Studies and served as Dean of Academic Affairs and Vice President of the university. Trained as a historian of religion and a student of Wilfred Cantwell Smith, he has published broadly on the Goddess traditions of India, comparative topics, and, most recently, contemplative education.

Harvey Cox is Hollis Research Professor of Divinity at Harvard, where he began teaching in 1965, both at the Divinity School and in the Faculty of Arts and Sciences. An American Baptist minister, he was the Protestant chaplain at Temple University and the director of religious activities at Oberlin College; an ecumenical fraternal worker in Berlin; and a professor at Andover Newton Theological School. His research and teaching interests focus on the interaction of religion, culture, and politics. Among the issues he explores are urbanization, theological developments in world Christianity, Jewish-Christian relations, and current spiritual movements in the global setting (particularly Pentecostalism). He has been a visiting professor at Brandeis University, Seminario Bautista de Mexico, the Naropa Institute, and the University of Michigan. He is a prolific author. His most recent book is *The Future of Faith* (HarperCollins, 2009). His *Secular City*, published in 1965, became an international bestseller and was selected by the University of Marburg as one of the most influential books of Protestant theology in the twentieth century. His other books include *When Jesus Came to Harvard: Making Moral Decisions Today*; *The Feast of Fools*; *The Seduction of the Spirit*; *Religion in the Secular City*; *The Silencing of Leonardo Boff: Liberation Theology and the Future of World Christianity*; *Many Mansions: A Christian's Encounters with Other Faiths*; *Fire from Heaven: The Rise of Pentecostal Spirituality*; *The Reshaping of Religion in the Twenty-First Century*; and *Common Prayers: Faith, Family, and a Christian's Journey through the Jewish Year*.

Diana Eck studied at Harvard with Wilfred Cantwell Smith and is now Professor of Comparative Religion and Indian Studies at Harvard University, as well as a Master of Lowell House and the Director of the Pluralism Project at Harvard. Among other works, she is the author of *Banaras, City of Light*; *Darsan: Seeing the Divine Image in India*; *Encountering God: A Spiritual Journey from Bozeman to Banaras*; *A New Religious America: How a Christian Country Became the World's Most Religiously Diverse Nation*; and most recently, *India: A Sacred Geography*. She is in the Department of South Asian Studies, on the Committee on the Study of Religion, and is a member of the Faculty of Divinity.

William A. Graham was appointed Dean of Harvard Divinity School and joined its faculty in 2002. He has been a member of the Harvard Faculty of Arts and Sciences since 1973. He has served as director of the Center for Middle Eastern Studies, Master of Currier House, and Chair of the Department of Near Eastern Languages and Civilizations, the Committee on the Study of Religion, and the Core Curriculum Subcommittee on Foreign Cultures at Harvard. He is also former chair of the Council on Graduate Studies in Religion (U.S. and Canada). His scholarly work has focused on early Islamic religious history and textual traditions and problems in the history of world religion. In October 2000 he received the quinquennial Award for Excellence in Research in Islamic History and Culture from the Research Centre for Islamic History, Art and Culture, the research institute of the Organisation of the Islamic Conference. He has held John Simon Guggenheim and Alexander von Humboldt research fellowships and is a fellow of the American Academy of Arts and Sciences. His book *Divine Word and Prophetic Word in Early Islam* was awarded the American Council of Learned Societies History of Religions Prize in 1978. He is coeditor of *Islamfiche: Readings from Islamic Primary Sources* (1982–87), and he is also the author of numerous articles and reviews. He is a summa graduate of the University of North Carolina at Chapel Hill and holds honorary doctorates from UNC and Lehigh University.

John Stratton Hawley specializes in the devotional traditions of North India and has taught at Barnard and Columbia since 1986. Hawley has written several books that focus on the worship of Krishna and his consort Radha; his other books explore themes in Hindu poetry and hagiography and in modern Hindu religion. Dr. Hawley's most recent project, a book called *India's Real Religion: The Idea of the Bhakti Movement*, is devoted to deconstructing and reconstructing one of the principal ways in which Indians have told their religious history. Its focus is *bhakti*: the religion of song, of radical engagement, and of the heart. Dr. Hawley has served as Director of Columbia University's South Asian Institute and has received multiple awards from the National Endowment for the Humanities, the Smithsonian, and the American Institute of Indian Studies.

Jonathan R. Herman is an associate professor at Georgia State University and affiliate faculty member with the Center for Asian Studies at GSU. He is also an officer in the Society for the Study of Chinese Religion, and a member of the Committee on the Public Understanding of Religion with the American Academy of Religion. Dr. Herman's areas of interest include Taoism, Confucianism, Buddhism, comparative mysticism, theory and method in the study of religion, and religion and popular culture.

Amir Hussain is Professor of Theological Studies at Loyola Marymount University, the Jesuit university in Los Angeles. His most recent publication is the edited textbook *World Religions: Western Traditions* (Toronto: Oxford University Press, 2011). He is also the editor of the *Journal of the American Academy of Religion*.

Sheila McDonough is Professor Emeritus and was a longtime member of Concordia's Department of Religion in Montreal. The first woman Islamic scholar in Canada, she received an honorary doctorate at the spring convocation of Queen's University in 2002. As an undergraduate at McGill, Dr. McDonough came under the influence of religious historian Wilfred Cantwell Smith, and became the first female graduate student at McGill's Institute of Islamic Studies. She taught for three years at Kinnaird College for Women in Lahore, Pakistan, to gain experience in the Muslim world, and that experience shaped her academic interests and her interest in promoting the understanding of Islam.

Robert A. Segal is the Century Chair in Religious Studies at the University of Aberdeen, where he has taught since 2006. He is the author or editor of, among other works, *The Poimandres as Myth* (1986); *Religion and the Social Sciences* (1989); *Joseph Campbell: An Introduction* (rev. ed. 1990); *Explaining and Interpreting Religion* (1992); *The Gnostic Jung* (1992); *The Myth and Ritual Theory* (1998); *Jung on Mythology* (1998);

Theorizing about Myth (1999); *Myth: A Very Short Introduction* (2004); and *The Blackwell Companion to the Study of Religion* (2006).

Peter Slater is Professor Emeritus and was a member of the Faculty of Divinity, Trinity College, Toronto. He graduated from McGill (1954), Cambridge (1957), and Harvard (1964) universities in philosophy, theology, and religion. He was a founding editor of the *Toronto Journal of Theology*; author of *The Dynamics of Religion* (1979); coeditor of *Traditions in Contact and Change* (IAHR Congress papers, 1980) and *Augustine: From Rhetor to Theologian* (1992); compiler of *Religion and Culture in Canada/Religion et Culture au Canada* (1977); and sometimes chair of the departments of religion at Haverford College, PA, and Carleton University, Ottawa.

K. R. Sundararajan is currently Professor of Theology at St. Bonaventure University in western New York. He received his PhD degree from the University of Madras (1967) and was at the Center for the Study of World Religions, Harvard University, as a postdoctoral fellow (1970–73). He was a lecturer in Hindu Studies at Punjabi University in Patiala from 1967 to 1975. He joined the faculty of the Department of Theology at St. Bonaventure University in 1975. He was one of the participants in the multireligious dialogue sponsored by the World Council of Churches in 1974 and has attended a variety of other conferences and seminars throughout the U.S., Canada, Europe, Africa, and India. He is widely published, with numerous articles in academic journals in the U.S., U.K., and India, and with contributed chapters to a number of books. He has edited the second volume of *Hindu Spirituality: Post Classical and Modern* in the World Spirituality series. His publications are in the following areas: Hinduism; theistic Vedanta and Vaishnavism; comparative studies—Hindu and Christian; Indian and Chinese religions; and interreligious dialogue. He served as a senior academic advisor to the Hindu Encyclopedia Project for several years.

Donald K. Swearer served as the director of the Center for the Study of World Religions and Distinguished Visiting Professor of Buddhism at Harvard Divinity School from 2004 to 2010. He joined HDS after teaching at Swarthmore College from 1970 to 2004, and Oberlin College from 1965 to 1970.

Arvind Sharma is the Birks Professor of Comparative Religion in the Faculty of Religious Studies at McGill University in Montreal. He has published and edited numerous books on a variety of topics, ranging from *Women in World Religions* to *Problematizing Religious Freedom*, with particular focus on Hindu thought, human rights, interreligious dialogue, and Advaita Vedanta. Dr. Sharma has been instrumental in organizing three global congresses on world's religions after September 11, which took place in Montreal in 2006, 2011, and 2016. A Universal Declaration of Human Rights by the World's Religions was formally released on September 15, 2016, at the end of the last conference.

Index

Abrahamic traditions, 2–3, 48, 55, 107, 195
American Academy of Religion (AAR), 56, 118, 132n2
anthropology of religion, 28, 48, 105, 112, 175, 187, 189, 194, 198
Asad, Talal, 101; critique of Smith, 102–6, 110–12, 191
Asani, Ali, 123, 132n18
Augustine, Saint, 50, 197–98

Buddhism: history of, 14–15; influence on contemplative studies, 71; study of, 211–12; study of Buddhists, 178, 208, 213, 220, 223; as world religion, 10–11, 27, 129, 188

Cambridge University: approach to history, 185; Nehru at, 150; Smith's work at, 1–2, 86, 88, 110, 137, 141, 153, 184, 200n6; socialist ideals at, 148–49, 164
Christianity, 127; as Abrahamic tradition, 2–3, 10, 53; Christian scholars, 11, 22, 29–30, 51, 106–7, 139, 166, 198, 208; Christian social gospel, 147–150, 157, 169n6; as dominating worldview, 89; history of, 13, 24, 50, 80, 128, 153, 189; influence of contemplative studies, 71; and modernity, 6; and pluralism, 6–8, 57, 130, 152, 158, 209, 210; Sermon on the Mount, 7; study of, 28–29, 40, 149, 181n8, 221; study of Christians, 4, 11, 141, 149, 214, 222, 223–24; as world religion, 11, 27. *See also* theology
Center for the Study of World Religions: approach of, 26–28, 40, 92, 101, 186; architect of, 43; colloquia, 22, 28, 30; contradictions of, 107; seminars at, 26, 28; Slater as director of, 38; Smith as director of, 2, 9, 39, 43, 101, 107–8, 225; students of, 108, 205, 210
colonialism, 15, 85–88, 95, 138–39, 149–50

249

comparative religion: as methodology, 15, 56, 73, 106, 118, 174, 178, 213, 217; Smith and, 6, 24, 37, 44, 110, 112, 119, 132n9, 163, 183, 185, 206, 218, 222; in universities, 31, 38–39, 41–42, 149, 212

Confucianism, 10, 24, 210; Smith and, 111, 126

contemplative studies, 9, 65; goal of, 69–71; influence of Buddhism on, 68, 70–71; influence of Smith on, 67; as liberal arts, 71; at Naropa University, 67

corporate critical self-consciousness, 12, 90–91, 183, 193–96

Dalai Lama, 30, 67, 70

Dalhousie University, 30, 37, 39, 97n32; Department of Religious Studies, 2, 38

dialogue approach, 4–5, 73, 199; critique of, 173–74, 178, 180; interfaith, 119, 126–27, 189, 209, 214–17; Smith on, 12, 24–25, 109, 128. *See also* insider-outsider approach

Durkheim, Émile, 176, 180

East and West binary, 2–3, 43, 85, 91, 94, 120–21, 124–25, 130, 177–78, 180, 225

Eliade, Mircea, 2, 10; and comparative studies, 24, 215, 217; and phenomenology, 11, 186; on the study of religion, 176–77, 179–80, 190, 218

Enlightenment: and religion, 48, 55, 60, 108, 124, 127, 185, 192, 198

faith (concept), 73–74, 78–79, 81–83, 93, 173, 186, 191, 197, 213, 219, 220, 222; critique of, 106–7, 180, 181n14; Smith's definition of, 12, 28, 57, 179, 207–8, 224; vs. belief, 28, 50–53, 77–80, 83, 102–4, 106–7, 181n8, 198

Ferahian, Salwa, 92

Freud, Sigmund, 78, 176

Forman Christian College, 2, 23, 37, 110, 149

Gandhi, Mahatma, 7, 72, 155

Gibb, H.A.R., 1, 86, 88, 149, 163, 184

God, 7; and faith, 80, 82; in monotheism, 28, 48; and personalist religion, 50, 82, 128–29, 141, 210; and politics, 152–54, 156–58, 164; in religious studies, 29, 49, 52, 57, 104–5, 126, 179, 183, 186, 189, 196–97; in religious traditions, 52–53, 56, 58–59, 121, 125, 160, 198–99, 214

Harvard University, 4, 77, 81, 90, 100, 108, 140, 143, 185; Committee on the Study of Religion, 2, 30, 38, 132n1; Divinity School, 21, 29, 39, 66, 123; Smith's contribution to religious studies at, 10, 25, 37–39; Smith's departure from, 30, 117; Smith's move to, 2, 27, 30; Study of Religion (department), 30, 32. *See also* Center for the Study of World Religions

Hegel, Georg Wilhelm Friedrich, 48, 100, 110, 194

Hick, John (philosopher), 11, 13, 142, 199

Hinduism, 22, 49, 56, 62n19, 129, 158; beliefs, 52–53, 57, 59; Bhagavad Gita, 32, 224; *dharma*, 26–27; history of, 14; Mīmāṃsā, 53, 55–59; Shaivism, 187; *shraddha*, 26, 28, 32; Smith's study of, 24, 40, 42, 88, 94, 107, 195, 205, 214,

220; Vaishnavism, 187, 210, 215; Vedanta, 42, 49, 214; Vedas, the, 26, 28, 52–53, 55–58, 62n19; as umbrella term, 11, 14–15, 59, 129, 180, 188, 211–4; Upanishads, 24, 59, 214; as world religion, 10, 27; as worldview, 42, 180, 208
Hume, David, 185–86, 188

Iqbal, Muhammad (poet): critique of Marxism, 161; influence on Smith, 154–55, 167; ideas on religion, 151–52, 155–56; and morality, 160–61; and Nehru, 156; Smith's critique of, 157–59, 161
Islam: controversy and, 122–25; diasporic, 139; history of, 14, 55; Khilafat movement, 155, 160; Qu'ran, 28, 57, 117–31, 136, 160–61, 223–24; religion of, 2–4, 42, 120, 167–68, 167; as worldview, 188, 208–9, 154, 209; as world religion, 10, 53
Islamic studies, 30, 55, 123, 136, 206; evolution of, 137–38; future developments in, 139; as study of Muslims, 95, 129, 137, 141, 208, 223; Smith and, 3, 23, 44, 59, 87, 88, 92–93, 110, 119, 149, 153, 222
Independence and Partition, 2, 88, 110, 161–63, 187; effect on Smith, 163–64; violence of, 163
India, 41–44; Hindu-Muslim tensions in, 1, 150, 163; Henry Martyn Institute, 120; Lucknow, 151; Punjabi University in, 41, 205, 211; Smith in, 2, 41, 86, 120, 137, 149, 156–59, 187; study of, 22, 24, 55, 88, 219
insider-outsider approach, 9, 12, 14–15, 25, 51, 55, 91, 109, 120, 130, 183, 193–94, 196. *See* corporate critical self-consciousness

Institute of Islamic Studies, 26, 40, 92–93, 108, 143; founding of, 2, 38, 86, 137, 167

Judaism, 12, 71, 124, 28, 139, 158, 187, 221; study of Jewish people, 5, 30, 214; as world religion, 2–3, 10, 53

Kant, Immanuel, 48, 100, 185, 188, 189, 192, 194, 202n30
King, Martin Luther, Jr., 13, 72
Kristeva, Julia, 77–82

Lahore, 2, 23, 86, 88, 110, 140, 147–68
Lindbeck, George (theologian), 188–90, 196
Loyola Marymount University, 139

McCutcheon, Russell (sociologist), 119, 132n1, 186–87, 200n13,
McGill University, 37–38, 40, 43, 93, 100–1, 143, 163, 185; Faculty of Religious Studies, 1; symposium at, 1, 37. *See also* Institute of Islamic Studies
McMaster University, 56, 149
Middle East, 14, 85, 112, 125

Nehru, Jawaharlal, 149–52, 155–56, 159, 161–62; influence on Smith, 150, 152
Niebuhr, H. Richard, 82–83, 183

orientalism, 3, 25–26, 85–95; Smith's critique of, 88–89, 91–94, 138
Oxtoby, Willard, 5–6, 136, 140

Pakistan, 23, 44, 144, 161–68, 187; National Islamic University, 120
Parliament of the World's Religions, 101

personalist approach, 13, 40, 73, 95, 103, 128–29, 130, 137–38, 141, 153, 173–75, 183, 205–15, 218–23; critique of, 107, 174–75; development of, 3–5; and theology, 29; vs. objectivism, 51, 69, 73, 90, 94, 187, 191–92
Princeton University, 2, 140, 163
Protestantism, 106–7, 185, 187–88, 192, 197–99, 201n16

Ramadan, Tariq, 30
religion: dynamism of, 6, 11–12, 22–23, 27, 29, 31, 128, 130, 220; folk religion, 9; fundamentalism, 124–25, 191, 195; globalization and, 6–7, 22, 24, 30, 91–92, 178, 185, 193; henotheism, 51–52, 58; history of, 23–25, 38, 47, 77, 128, 148, 152, 207, 211–12, 217; modernity and, 5, 21, 88, 91, 93, 106–7, 154, 159, 209; morality and, 50, 78, 126, 159; plurality, 5–6, 22, 24, 48, 121–23, 126, 210; primal religions, 10, 48; as a reactionary force, 150–54, 157–59, 167; rituals, 25, 52–53, 58–59, 103, 143, 175, 181n8, 214, 221; women and, 4
religion, Smith's critique of, 9–12, 27, 93, 102–3, 173
religious studies, approaches to: collaborative, 26, 28–29, 40–41, 67; deconstruction, 51, 59–60; diagnosis, 174, 177–80; empiricism, 51, 73, 91, 94, 154, 185–86, 219; essentialism, 23, 100, 103, 141, 184, 191, 211–12; evolution of, 3–4, 13–15, 22, 25, 27, 39–40, 117, 126, 131, 153, 175–76; functionalism, 175, 178–79; phenomenology, 11, 51, 186, 189, 192, 194, 196, 218; philosophy of, 47, 49, 218; postcolonialism, 26, 85, 138, 144; postmodernism, 51, 73, 100, 119; psychology, 78, 176; as social science, 40, 49, 118, 178–80, 183–84; teaching, 67–68, 118–19, 219, 223–24; reflexivity, 22, 25, 73, 90, 128
Rushdie, Salman, 144; *The Satanic Verses*, 122–25, 132n18

Said, Edward, 3, 25, 85–87, 89, 91–95, 97n32, 136, 138–39, 140; critique of, 86–87. *See* orientalism
Saiyidain, K.G., 156–57, 161–63
Santayana, George (philosopher), 79, 81–83
Schimmel, Annemarie, 132n18, 136
scripture: and religion, 10, 198; in religious studies, 27, 59, 126, 192, 224; Smith on, 11, 26, 28–29, 53–57, 191
secularism, 6, 130, 187; argument for, 177–78; critique of, 78, 177, 188, 200n13; and religious studies, 10, 22, 30, 60, 118, 137, 180, 206; Smith on, 182n19, 209, 225–26; as western construct, 48, 60, 188, 208; as worldview, 25–27
September 11, 2001, 3, 124–25, 131, 141
Sikhism, 10, 23–24, 30, 149, 152, 158, 163, 205
Smith, Huston, 10
Smith, legacy of Wilfred Cantwell: on academic institutions, 38; on the study of religion, 1, 3, 6, 9, 12–13, 47, 93, 102, 119, 127, 130, 215; on students, 22, 37, 66–67, 131, 137, 142–43, 205–6, 215
Smith, Muriel, 30–31, 39, 44, 111, 135–36, 140–44, 151
Smith, Wilfred Cantwell: advocacy, 31, 93, 147, 194–95; as "architect," 38; colleagues, 30, 31, 39, 184; devotion to speech, 106; early life,

147–49; fastidiousness, 32–33, 37, 72, 99, 184; as humanist, 9, 25, 32, 55, 90, 105, 111–12, 129, 140, 142, 192, 220; Indian Education Commission work, 41–42; on intellectualism, 51–52, 112–13; on interdisciplinarity, 139; interest in Islam, 3, 23, 59, 88, 140–41; and language, 126, 191; Marxism, 1, 88, 110–11, 141, 148–53, 157–61, 164–66, 185, 187; as mentor, 32, 143; as missionary, 109; as "orientalist," 86; and morality, 29, 90, 166, 188, 191, 223, 225; personal religious beliefs, 31, 44n1, 49, 51–52, 106, 126, 147–48, 185, 187, 198, 210, 214, 222; as "public intellectual," 119, 126; on the role of universities, 42, 89, 192; shift away from idealism, 154–55, 157, 163–68; as teacher, 38, 40, 66, 93, 225. *See also* Center for the Study of World Religions; Institute of Islamic Studies

Smith, writings of: *Belief and Faith*, 28, 30; *Belief and History*, 181n8; "Comparative Religion: Wither—and Why?," 2, 207; "The Comparative Study of Religion," 125; *The Faith of Other Men/ Patterns of Faith Around the World*, 31, 108, 129, 212, 221; *Faith and Belief*, 26, 28, 30; *History of Religions*, 2; *Islam in Modern History*, 93, 141, 169n41; "Is the Qur'an the Word of God?," 119–20, 122, 125, 130; "Mankind's Religiously Divided History Approaches Self-Consciousness," 21, 25, 90, 111; *Modern Islam in India*, 88, 95, 141, 150, 152; *The Meaning and End of Religion*, 4, 27, 43, 66, 101–2, 107, 128, 141–42, 214, 218; "Objectivity and the Humane Sciences: A Proposal," 184; *Pakistan as an Islamic State*, 164, 168; *Questions of Religious Truth*, 120, 129, 207; "The Modern West in the History of Religion," 27; "Thinking about Persons," 94; *Towards a World Theology*, 7, 128–30, 139, 218, 222–23; "Traditional Religions and Modern Cultures," 88, 93; *What Is Scripture?*, 28, 53

Sophia (journal), 47

South Asia, 2, 26, 28, 137–38, 164; violence in, 161–63

technology, 69, 80, 122, 131, 157, 194, 219

theology: as an academic discipline, 30, 38, 49, 78, 118, 137; Christian, 6, 29, 49; critiques of, 49, 118; and faith, 50, 81; and philosophy, 83, 190; Smith and, 50, 52, 119–22, 149, 160, 192, 223; world theology, 5, 220, 222, 224

Tillich, Paul (philosopher), 178, 184, 186–87, 189–90, 192, 198

transcendence (concept), 26, 99: criticisms of, 186, 190, 197; in religion traditions, 9, 54–55, 58–60, 154, 167–68; Smith's definition of, 31, 56, 65–66, 129, 165–66, 220, 223; for the study of religion, 12, 47–49, 94, 104–5, 183–84, 215, 217, 225; vs. immanence, 154, 168

United Church of Canada, 31, 44n1, 148

University of Toronto, 1, 136–37, 147, 200n7; Center for Religious Studies, 142; Trinity College, 2

Wiebe, Donald, 187, 192, 200n12–13

Wittgenstein, Ludwig, 55, 74, 81, 188–92, 196

world religions (concept), 14; Smith's critique of, 4, 23; Smith on, 10, 107–9, 129, 220, 222; in universities, 38, 66, 101, 131, 211–12. *See also* Center for the World Religions

Yale University, 82, 119, 120, 136